Indigenous Peoples and Forests

*Cultural, Historical and Political Ecology
in Central Africa*

by

Mitsuo Ichikawa

Indigenous Peoples and Forests

*Cultural, Historical and Political Ecology
in Central Africa*

by

Mitsuo Ichikawa

Kyoto University Press

TRANS
PACIFIC
PRESS

Published in 2024 jointly by:

Kyoto University Press
69 Yoshida Konoe-cho
Sakyo-ku, Kyoto 606-8315, Japan
Telephone: +81-75-761-6182
Fax: +81-75-761-6190
Email: sales@kyoto-up.or.jp
Web: http://www.kyoto-up.or.jp

Trans Pacific Press Co., Ltd.
PO Box 8547
#19682
Boston, MA, 02114, United States
Telephone: +1-6178610545
Email: info@transpacificpress.com
Web: http://www.transpacificpress.com

© Mitsuo Ichikawa 2024.
Edited by Karl Smith, Melbourne, Australia
Layout designed and set by Ryo Kuroda, Tsukuba-city, Ibaraki, Japan
Book cover designed by hamdanas

Library of Congress Cataloging-in-Publication Data

Names: Ichikawa, Mitsuo, author.
Title: Indigenous peoples and forests : cultural, historical and political
    ecology in central Africa / by Mitsuo Ichikawa.
Description: Boston : Trans Pacific Press, 2024. | Includes bibliographical
    references and index. | Summary: "African tropical rainforests are in
    rapid decline, and their conservation is an urgent priority. However,
    forest conservation efforts have typically neglected the rights of
    people like pygmies, who have long and strong connections to the forests
    on which they depend. The forests that they have long inhabited have
    been designated as protected areas, the people have been forcibly
    removed, and their customary livelihood activities are now illegal. This
    book addresses the negative impacts of conservation policies on the
    Pygmy people of the central African rainforests with respect to their
    lifestyle and culture. Based on half a century of field research, this
    book presents a clear picture of the relationship between indigenous
    peoples and forests, and explores the use of non-timber forest resources
    - "using forests without cutting them down" - as an integrated solution
    to the two major issues surrounding forests today: forest conservation
    and improving indigenous peoples' well-being through the use of forest
    resources"-- Provided by publisher.
Identifiers: LCCN 2024000335 (print) | LCCN 2024000336 (ebook) | ISBN
    9781920850302 (hardback) | ISBN 9781920850289 (paperback) | ISBN
    9781920850296 (epub)
Subjects: LCSH: Human ecology--Africa, Central. | Rain forest
    ecology--Africa, Central. | Forest management--Africa, Central. | Forest
    policy--Africa, Central. | Pygmies--Social life and customs--21st
    century. | Traditional ecological knowledge--Africa, Central.
Classification: LCC GF730 .I245 2024 (print) | LCC GF730 (ebook) | DDC
    304.20896067--dc23
LC record available at https://lccn.loc.gov/2024000335
LC ebook record available at https://lccn.loc.gov/2024000336

Table of Contents

List of Figures vi

List of Photos vi

List of Tables vii

Acknowledgements viii

Introduction 1

1 Conservation of Tropical Rainforests and Indigenous Peoples 15

2 Where Humans Coexist with Forests 57

3 Bushmeat and the New Forest Law in Central Africa 97

4 Toward a Sustainable Use of Non-Timber Forest Products 129

5 Hunter-Gatherers Way of Life in Modern Society 173

References 207

Index 225

List of Figures

0.1: Distribution of "Pygmy" hunter-gatherer groups in central Africa 9

2.1: Distribution of the Mbuti territories and camps in the Teturi area 78
2.2: Distribution of old village sites in the southern part of the Ituri Forest 78

3.1: Life stage and number of animal species avoided among the Mbuti 109

4.1: Project Design 140
4.2: Zoning of project area, southeastern Cameroon 143
4.3: Price change (CFA/*combo* in dry weight) of *peke*
 (*Irvingia gabonensis*) in different transactions 158

5.1: Changes in commodity price, minimum wage and
 real wage from 1975 to 1983 196
5.2: Change in relative prices between products and services 197

List of Photos

0.1: Timber carrying truck (rainy season) 2
0.2: Newly opened logging road 3
0.3: Logging operation near a Baka village in remote forest 4

1.1: Logging base near Kisangani 22
1.2: The Congo River near Kisangani 24
1.3: Forest near Lomami river 25
1.4: Fishing camp on the bank of Ruki river 26
1.5: Bushmeat sold at local market 33
1.6: Edible caterpillars sold at a local market 34
1.7: Logging base in southeastern Cameroon 47

2.1: Satellite image of the southeastern part of the Ituri Forest 65
2.2: Gold miners dug up the former river course and stripped the bark of
 giant trees to create flumes for gold sorting 66
2.3: A Mbuti forest camp 67
2.4: Forest as cornucopia of food plants 68
2.5: Plants used for material culture 69
2.6: Plants used for arrow poison 70
2.7: Honey collecting 70
2.8: Non-timber forest products sold at local market 73
2.9: Forest viewed as a "womb" 94
2.10: "Children of the forest" 94

3.1: Using a child to distribute the meat 105

3.2: Examples of *kuweri* animals 108

3.3: Mbuti hunter polishing a spear 112

3.4: A young elephant killed with a spear 112

3.5: A Blue duiker in the net 114

3.6: Brush-tailed porcupine 114

3.7: Meat trader visiting a Mbuti forest camp 114

3.8: Red duiker weighing 15–25 kg 122

3.9: Blue duiker weighing 4–6 kg 122

4.1: Construction of research station 144

4.2: Research station in Gribe 144

4.3: Cacao garden 147

4.4: Slash-and-burn field with mixed crops 147

4.5: Old secondary forest near Gribe village 148

4.6: Fruit of *Irvingia gabonensis* 152

4.7: Fruit drops survey 152

4.8: Baka girl cracking *Irvingia* fruit 153

4.9: Roasted nuts used as oily condiment 153

4.10: Drying *peke* and *tondo* in village 160

4.11: *Peke*, *tondo* and *gobo* sold at Yokadouma market 160

4.12: Group photo after the workshop in Gribe 168

5.1: Mbuti boys wearing trendy pants 192

5.2: Girls wearing favorite cloths 192

5.3: People selling products at a local market, but there were
few Mbuti people 194

List of Tables

2.1: The density of annual yams and light environment 82

2.2: Comparison of reproduction and growth between *mbau*
(*Gilbertiodendron dewevrei*) and *eko* (*Julbernardia seretii*) 89

3.1: Composition of the catches by protection class 123

3.2: Maximum sustainable catch (MSC) and actual catch before and after
construction of the logging roads 127

4.1: Amounts of NTFPs sold by the Baka and Kounabembe 156

Acknowledgements

The year 2024 marks 50 years since I first visited Zaire (now the Democratic Republic of Congo). I first conducted research on the Mbuti hunter-gatherers in the Ituri Forest from 1974 to 1975. After five years spent in Japan and Kenya, I returned to Ituri for further research in 1980. Almost every year since then I have visited one of the three major hunter-gatherer groups in central Africa, the Mbuti, the Aka in the Republic of Congo and the Baka in eastern Cameroon, and have learned much from them about their relationships with the forests. I published a book in 2021 summarizing my recent research on the relationship between the central African forests and the hunter-gatherers, particularly the Mbuti and Baka, in the contemporary economic and political contexts. This book is an English version of that book with some revisions.

I am indebted to so many people during the last 50 years from the initial research to the compilation of this book. Without the generosity of the Mbuti people in Ituri and the Baka people in eastern Cameroon, who welcomed me warmly and taught me much about the forests, I would not have been able to conduct this research. I also thank the *Institut de Recherche Scientifique (IRS)* of the Democratic Republic of Congo, the *Ministère de la Recherche Scientifique et l 'Innovation, (MINRESI)* and the *Institut de Recherches Agricole pour le Développement (IRAD)* of Cameroon which granted me research permits and/or joint research fellowships.

In conducting this research, I benefited from the support and cooperation of my predecessors, colleagues, and former students. Late Professor Junichiro Itani, late Dr. Reizo Harako and late Dr. Tadashi Tanno had provided valuable advice since my first research in Ituri. I shared nice experiences as well as hardships with Dr. Hideaki Terashima and Dr. Masato Sawada, during our research in Ituri. Dr. Hirokazu Yasuoka, Dr Shiho Hattori, Dr Masaaki Hirai and other young researchers with whom I worked in Cameroon provided a lot of information and stimulating inspiration for research.

Most of the research was funded by the Ministry of Education, Culture, Sports, Science and Technology, Japan. For collecting literature for this publication, Kakenhi (Grant No. 20K12370) was used.

I am grateful to Mr. Tetsuya Suzuki and Ms. Shoko Nagano of Kyoto University Press and Ms. Yuko Uematsu of Trans Pacific Press for their consistent cooperation and assistance in publishing this book.

This publication was supported by JSPS KAKENHI Grant Number JP23HP5086.

Introduction

1. Changes in the forest world

In November 1996, we were heading to Yokadouma, the district center in the East Region of Cameroon, in a four-wheel drive car. After two hours travelling on the tarmac road from Yaounde, the capital city of Cameroon, we crossed the Nyong river. The tarmac ended on the far side of the river, with unpaved rattling road leading us the rest of the way to Yokadouma. The rainy season had ended earlier than usual that year, and the laterite road surface was already dry when we travelled. The car kicked up the red dust. While mindful of oncoming vehicles, we overtook a number of large trucks full of beer cases and miscellaneous goods. Coming in the other direction were large trucks with 3–5 logs with a diameter of nearly one meter, slowly growling and passing by. Immediately after passing a truck, nothing was visible because of the dust. After a while, the dust subsided, but soon another truck appeared, and we were wrapped in dust again. By the time we got to Yokadouma, we had passed dozens of trucks carrying logs and timber.

The logs and timber on the trucks were cut in the tropical forests of the Eastern Region. There are usually one or two trees with diameters exceeding 1m per hectare of the forest in this region. If a hundred trucks pass the road from Yokadouma, each with three logs on the average, 150 to 300 hectares of forest are estimated to be logged every day, at least in the logging season. Around the main national road connecting the district center with the state capital, freshly opened logging roads extended into the depths of the forest. If logging progresses at this pace, a large part of the forests in southeastern Cameroon, that are connected to the great Congo Basin forests and have grown up over many centuries, are likely to disappear in the near future.

Along the road, wild animals caught in the forest were casually hung on sticks and sold. This was so-called "bushmeat," which included the limbs of duikers (forest antelopes), porcupines and monkeys. The main customers are truck drivers who pass through the road. We visited the market at Bertoua (capital of the East Region) and found there a corner selling a variety of wild animal meat. In addition to various duiker species and bush pigs, various other animals such as monkeys,

Photo[1] **0.1** Timber carrying truck (rainy season)

porcupines, pangolins, tortoises and lizards were lined up on the shelves. Most of the meat sold there was smoked and blackened, but some was sold raw. All of them were caught in the forests of the East Region. I was overwhelmed by the amount and variety of the animals on display. I came to understand the people's strong preference for bushmeat and became uneasy about the future of wild animals in this region.

In the 1990s, international NGOs such as the World Wildlife Fund (WWF) and the Wildlife Conservation Society (WCS) actively conducted wildlife surveys, then worked with the Cameroon government's Ministry of Forestry and Wildlife (*Ministère des Forêts et de la Faune*, MINFOF) to formulate nature conservation plans based on the results of these surveys. Soon after, nature reserves (national parks) were established in the area, and poaching by local people was strictly controlled. The offices of the MINFOF and WWF in Yokadouma held collections of confiscated steel traps, old firearms, and other types of "illegal" hunting equipment. In the local villages, we heard of Baka hunter-gatherers who had been arrested as poachers by the forest guards.

---

1   All the photographs in this book are taken by the author and most of them are stored in the Digital Image Archives (DiPLAS) at the National Museum of Ethnology in Osaka.

Introduction

Photo 0.2 Newly opened logging road

Bushmeat was the main source of protein for the inhabitants of the region and a valuable source of income for the hunter-gatherers who had no other source of cash income. The region was also a major source of bushmeat for the urban population of Cameroon, but trade in bushmeat has become increasingly restricted. In recent years, the threat of infectious diseases transmitted from wild animals has led to stricter controls on hunting and trading of wild animals. It was not difficult to imagine the plight of the people who depended on meat from the forest for their food (protein source) and cash income.

As we proceeded further south from Yokadouma to Moloundou, on the border with the Republic of Congo, the forests on both sides crept closer and closer. However, it is only a kind of partitioning screen that hides the devastation of the forest that spreads behind it. Large parts of the forest in the area had already been included in the logging plan, and logging operations had begun. Here and there, villages appeared on both sides on the roadside, covered in red dust raised from the road by trucks. Many of the villages consisted of square, mud walled and palm-leaf thatched farmers' dwellings, but next to them there were settlements of dome-shaped huts, inhabited by hunter-gatherers, the Baka people. They had come out of the forest in search of the meager wages and crops they could earn from helping the farmers in the fields. Their small

Indigenous Peoples and Forests

Photo 0.3 Logging operation near a Baka village in remote forest

dome-shaped dwellings, thatched with plant leaves, blend harmoniously with the surrounding landscape when in the forest. But they were out of place on the roadside, covered with dust and looking very rough. When I recollected how they had guided me every time I visited the forest and had taught me about the animals and plants in the forest, I felt indescribable. I wondered what they thought of this life on the roadside, when they were so lively and confident in the forest.

In the forests of Cameroon, three phenomena were occurring in parallel. The first was massive deforestation promoted in the name of "development," and the second was the (nature conservation) movement to protect the forests from development. These were closely related to the global economic and political situation, as we will see in later chapters. Third, was how this development changed the lives of the local people, especially the indigenous forest hunter-gatherers, who have long been heavily dependent on the forests. They were suffering from the hardship of being caught between these two movements for "development" and "conservation." While forests in which they have lived for many centuries are being destroyed by logging, they are also being shut out of the remaining forests in the name of nature conservation. The focus of this book is on the relationship between the forest people, indigenous hunter-gatherers who are in this predicament, and the forest world that

Introduction

has traditionally supported their life and nurtured their unique forest-based culture.

2. Indigenous forest peoples in central Africa

I have been conducting anthropological research and area studies in Africa for nearly half a century since the mid-1970s. I have been particularly fascinated by the lives and societies of the forest people, commonly called "Pygmies," who have been at the center of my research interest.[2]

The existence of people of short stature living in the interior of African continent has long been a topic of discussion. In the tomb of the Egyptian Pharaoh from about 2500 BCE, there was a report of a commander who entered a great forest to the west of the Mountains of the Moon and discovered there a people of the forest, a tiny people who sang and danced to their god. The Pharaoh ordered the commander to bring one of these Dancers of God back with him (Turnbull, 1961). Some 2,000 years later, in Aristotle's work, *History of Animals*, there is a description of them as living "in the lake district at the source of the Nile." Furthermore, Homer's epic poem, *The Iliad*, mentions them in a distorted form as "Pygmies fighting a flock of cranes." A wall painting from Pompeii captioned "Pygmies hunting a hippopotamus" can be seen at the National Archaeological Museum of Naples, Italy. However, recent studies (Kitanishi, 2014a, 2014b) indicate that the people appearing in these ancient records were not necessarily ancestors of the Pygmy population who became known in modern times.

It was not until the latter half of the 19th century, when exploration of the interior of Africa was underway, that the Pygmies came back into the limelight. Du Chaillu (1872), a French-American, visited a camp of short people called Obongo in the area that is now Gabon, and later claimed that they were the Pygmies known in the ancient world. Also,

---

2   The word Pygmy is derived from the Greek unit of measurement from elbow to hand (*pgmayeoi*) (Kitanishi, 2011). It was an exaggeration of their short stature, but at some point, this became a general term for short people living in central Africa and elsewhere. In anthropology, it is used to refer to human groups with an average male height of 150 centimeters or less. French anthropologists sometimes refer to African groups as Negrille to distinguish them from the Asian group Negrito. Negrille means small Negro.

when a German explorer Schweinfurth travelled to southern Sudan (Schweinfurth, 1874), he encountered the short statured Akka people in the village of the Mombutto (Manbetsu) chief in southern Sudan. Thinking that they were the Pygmies known from ancient times, he accompanied one of them on his journey (unfortunately, the man died during the journey). In these ways, the Pygmies were widely introduced to the Western world. Various studies have been conducted since the "discovery" of the Pygmy people, and their lives, distribution, and the names by which they were known in different areas were reported in the 20th century (see Chapter 5 in this book).

They mainly live in the forest regions of central Africa, in particular, the Congo Basin, and are called by different names in each region. The group in the Great Rift Valley, which runs north-south across the African continent, i.e., in what is now the eastern part of the Democratic Republic of Congo, Uganda, Burundi, and Rwanda, is called Batwa. The Ituri Forest, located to the northwest of the Batwa, is inhabited by the groups called Mbuti and Efe. In the Equateur Province of the Democratic Republic of Congo, there are Batswa or Batua, and to the west, on the right bank of the Ubangi River, there are Aka people (also called Bayaka or Babendjele). Further to the west, in the southeastern part of Cameroon, and in the forests on the western edge of the Congo Basin, there is a group called the Baka. There are no accurate population statistics for these people, but all of these groups together number at most several hundred thousand people. In terms of population size, they are small minority groups of the region, representing only 0.1 percent of the total African population.

Until recently, these peoples were dispersed in small groups of several dozen, living in the forest, and mainly subsisted by hunting and gathering. These groups share similar external characteristics such as short stature, relatively light skin color, and broad noses. Recent genetic studies suggest that the Mbuti of the eastern Congo Basin and the Baka of the western Congo Basin diverged genetically as much as 20,000 years ago (Verdu and Destro-Bisol, 2012). Despite the passage of so many years, these forest peoples still have many things in common, such as a hunter-gatherer livelihood and material culture dependent on the forest, polyphonic song and dance performances and the religion (belief in the forest spirits) that supports these performances, and a similar intonation

Introduction

of speech styles despite belonging to different language groups. The similarities in the culture among these groups are striking. Whether these similarities are due to a common origin, cultural adaptation to the similar environment of the rainforests (i.e., convergence), or cultural transmission through the Congo River system remains to be clarified.

Some researchers insist that it is inappropriate to refer to these groups collectively as Pygmies because they are distributed over a considerable distance and speak different languages. There is also a movement to avoid the name Pygmy itself, as it has a discriminatory meaning that exaggerates their short stature. However, as mentioned above, despite their wide distribution and genetic distance, these groups have very similar cultures and lifestyles, and face common challenges such as discrimination by neighboring ethnic groups, environmental destruction, and development in the modern world. In addition, as the indigenous peoples' movement has become active, they have begun to network with similar groups, which were previously dispersed into smaller groups, to address the common issues surrounding them. Under these circumstances, they came to use the name Pygmies themselves as a generic term for "indigenous peoples living in the central African forests." For this reason, the name Pygmy will be used in this book as necessary.

Recently, international attention has been focused on these minority groups. Especially since the *Decade of the World's Indigenous People* (1994–2004), *Second International Decade of the World's Indigenous People* (2005–2014) and the *Declaration on the Rights of Indigenous Peoples* (adopted in 2007) that followed, they have been the focus of increasing attention. With the support of international human rights NGOs and other organizations, the indigenous peoples themselves have become increasingly aware of their status as indigenous peoples, and their dispersed groups have become more networked. In addition, they have drawn attention as "forest people" who have been coexisting with the forest environment in the context of the rapidly growing movement to protect the tropical rainforests. As will be discussed in Chapter 1, they are now required to be given special consideration in development and conservation projects by national and international organizations to ensure that they are not harmed by the projects. These changes will sooner or later bring about major changes in their lives.

Indigenous Peoples and Forests

3. Forest conservation and indigenous peoples

The Congo Basin Forest, located in the heart of Africa, is home to the world's second largest tropical rainforest block after the Amazon, covering an area of approximately 150 to 200 million hectares. The forest is currently receiving global attention for a variety of reasons. First, it is valued as a source of timber, including the African ebony and the tall trees of the Meliaceae family, known as African mahogany. Countries in the region have been deriving a significant portion of their exports (and national revenue) from the timber. Second, the region is a treasure trove of biodiversity. The warm and humid tropical rainforest environment provides ideal conditions for many species. There are approximately 10,000 species of tropical plants in the Congo Basin, of which 30 percent are unique to the region. Endangered mammals such as forest elephants, chimpanzees, bonobos, and lowland and mountain gorillas, okapis and leopards inhabit the forests. Moreover, 400 other species of mammals, 1,000 species of birds and 700 species of fish are also found here (WWF n.d.). To conserve this biodiversity, international conservation organizations have established 11 "landscape areas" in the region to protect nature and to sustainably use forest resources (OFAC, 2008). Third are the "environmental services" provided by forests. In addition to "provisioning services" such as the production of a variety of useful materials, forests also provide "regulating services" such as the maintenance of the earth's atmosphere, moisture and soil conservation. In particular, tropical rainforests, which store 250 to 300 tons of carbon per hectare (Debroux, et al., 2007), are drawing global attention as a huge "carbon sequester" to prevent global warming. For these reasons, it is argued that the protection of the Congo Basin rainforest is a challenge that must be addressed on a global scale.

However, there are approximately 75 million people in the region (WWF, n.d.), who depend on the forests. These people use the plants and animals of the forests in a variety of ways, as food, fuel, medicine, tool materials, building materials, ornaments, and for various ritual purposes. There are "indigenous" peoples with their own unique cultures in the remote forest areas that have been left behind by development and still retain a rich biodiversity. Many of the rainforests in central Africa, which are a treasure trove of biodiversity, overlap with the areas inhabited by indigenous peoples such as the Pygmy people described in this book.

Introduction

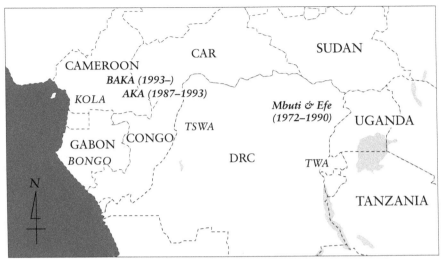

Fig. 0.1 Distribution of "Pygmy" hunter-gatherer groups in central Africa. (Numbers in brackets refer to the years of the study by the Kyoto University researchers.)

The question, therefore, is how to reconcile the global concern for forest conservation with the livelihoods and cultures of local people, especially indigenous forest peoples.

4. Forest issues viewed from indigenous peoples' perspectives

4.1 Three approaches of ecological anthropology

To reconcile the global issue of rainforest conservation with the livelihoods and cultures of its inhabitants, it is first necessary to understand the relationship between forests and humans in the region. How, then, can we understand the relationship between nature and humans in the central African Forests? I would like to approach this problem from a position as close as possible to the local people, that is, from the eyes of the "indigenous forest people." However, the relationship between nature and humans in a region have developed in the context of the historical background it has followed, and the political and economic conditions of the wider society that envelops it. To understand the relationship between humans and nature with such constraints, we

Indigenous Peoples and Forests

think it is effective to approach the issue from the "three approaches of ecology," cultural ecology, historical ecology, and political ecology.

First, cultural ecology is an inquiry into the synchronic aspects of the nature-human relationship in the region, including all the material and spiritual, direct and indirect, relationships between humans and nature. So-called "cultural ecology" was proposed by Julian Steward (1955), a leading figure in American anthropology in the middle of the 20th century and is concerned with the adaptive relationships found between the natural environment, technology, economy, and social organization. The scope of "cultural ecology" here, however, is not limited to such adaptive relationships among nature, economy, and society. It covers not only the technological and economic relationship with the natural environment, but also the totality of the relationship between humans and nature, including the representational culture found in religion and rituals. It aims to reveal how strongly and in various ways human life and culture depend on the forest. This is an area that has been lacking in former, conventional ethnological studies of hunter-gatherer societies in central Africa (e.g., Schebesta, 1938–50; Turnbull, 1965), which have focused on language, religion, and social organization, without paying much attention to the natural environment. It is also an area that, worldwide, had not been adequately studied in anthropological research until a few decades ago. Today, with the growing interest in environmental issues of forests, the use and perceptions of natural environment by indigenous peoples, such as hunter-gatherers and slash-and-burn agriculturalists, are coming to be seen as examples of "guardians of forests" or "models of sustainable users of forests," but until the 1970s there were not many researchers interested in such issues.

Second, historical ecology attempts to review the local natural environment from an eco-historical perspective. The forest landscapes we see today, even those that appear to remain in pristine condition, are often the result of hundreds or even thousands of years of interaction between nature and humans. Historical ecology is the study of the historical changes in such interactions between humans and nature, specifically, the reading of human footprints imprinted in nature. Such work forces a reexamination of "nature isolated from human influence" and takes a position similar to that known as "environmental revisionism" (Ichikawa, 1998; Headland, 1997). Forest peoples not only recognize and use the diverse resources provided by the forest, but also contribute to its maintenance and reproduction. By revealing this, we can envision a world in which forests and people co-exist, supporting each other.

The third falls under the category of "political ecology." Although the meaning of the term differs slightly depending on the academic field, such as geography or anthropology, it generally describes and analyzes the ecology of human-nature relations at the local micro level in the contexts of the political and economic frameworks of broader society, such as ethnic relations, national systems, and the international political and economic conditions of the world, particularly in relation to the power relations within them. Local human-forest systems of coexistence do not exist in isolation from the outside world. Even the remote African forest world is now more or less in contact with the national and international economic and political system. The conservation movement and the deforestation that triggered it are closely linked to the global economic, political, and informational trends. If we try to build a "world where forests and people coexist," insulated from such conditions in the broader society, we may end up creating a "living human museum," as the governments of the countries concerned and development theorists criticize. A living human being and their environment are not museum specimens but transformed by the interaction between external relationships and internal dynamics. I would like to situate the dynamics of forests and humans in central Africa within the wider world context, and to backlight world movements from the perspective of forest people. In other words, I would like to critically examine global trends from the eyes of the indigenous forest people.

As described above, the way to understand the relationship between forests and people is through cultural ecology that shows how human culture depends on the nature of forests, historical ecology that shows how human settlements and livelihood activities are related through time to the dynamics of forest ecosystems, and a political ecology perspective that shows how these are related to the macro political and economic situation. In this book, I will intertwine these three approaches to depict the relationship between forests and humans, and on this basis I will then examine the contemporary movements concerning forest conservation in central Africa.

4.2. Structure of the book

In Chapter 1, "Conservation of Tropical Rainforests and Indigenous Peoples," I review World Bank projects for forest reform in the Democratic Republic of Congo (hereafter DRC) as an expert of the Inspection Panel of the World Bank and identify problems with the projects. I show how World Bank-supported projects threatened the livelihoods and culture of the indigenous forest peoples, and how disconnected the situation on the ground is from what project planners stated in documents prepared in Washington and Kinshasa. However, I stress that the Inspection Panel's review activities criticizing the World Bank's projects will not suffice to improve the situation, which will in fact require interaction between these activities and various stakeholders, including nature conservationists and human rights NGOs that support indigenous peoples. I point out the importance of sustainable use of non-timber forest resources as an alternative to large-scale logging and to integrate forest conservation with indigenous forest peoples' livelihoods and cultures. In addition, as a background to the World Bank's projects and the activities of the Inspection Panel, I describe the recent international movements concerning tropical rainforests and the people, such as those related to global warming and its effects as pointed out in *The Economics of Climate Change* (Stern, 2006) and REDD+ (Reducing Emissions from Deforestation and Forest Degradation), and the UN Declaration on the Rights of Indigenous Peoples (2007), and discuss these issues in relation to the indigenous forest peoples in central Africa.

In Chapter 2, "Where Humans Coexist with Forests," I review the research I conducted on the relationship between forests and indigenous peoples in the Congo Basin. After considering the nature of environmental problems in contemporary society and their social and economic backgrounds, I show, on the one hand, how hunter-gatherers, the "indigenous people of the forest," perceive and use the forest from the viewpoint of cultural ecology and point out that they need "the forest in its entirety," rather than specific resources, to maintain their lives and culture. On the other hand, I show that their habitation and livelihood activities also contributed to the maintenance of the forest as a living environment, highlighting the interdependent relationship between the people and the forest environment. I also review related studies from the perspective of historical ecology and identify the positive human

Introduction

impacts on the forests in various parts of Africa, especially in the central African forests where traces of human activities are found even in seemingly intact forests. Based on these findings, I critically examine the modern idea of nature conservation and its protection schemes, which have typically viewed humans and nature in opposition and excluded human activities from protected areas.

Chapter 3, "Bushmeat and the New Forest Law in Central Africa," addresses the issue of wild game meat (bushmeat), which is one of the most important non-timber forest resources on which local people depend and for which both conservation and sustainable utilization have become urgent issues. The use of bushmeat has recently been severely restricted, not only for wildlife protection (biodiversity conservation), but also as a source of new infectious diseases such as Ebola, SARS and COVID-19. This chapter demonstrates the nutritional and cultural significance of wild animal meat among the forest peoples of the Congo Basin, and points out how hunting regulations, tightened by the recently revised forest law, ignore these realities, thus threatening the livelihoods of the forest peoples. At the same time, I demonstrate that the recent trade in bushmeat has led to excessive hunting pressure on animal populations and discuss the possibility of sustainable hunting by the local peoples and the measures necessary to achieve this.

In Chapter 4, "Toward a Sustainable Use of Non-Timber Forest Products," I describe a project aimed at "integrating forest conservation with the welfare of the local peoples," which has been my major concern in recent decades. This project was an overseas cooperation project called the *Science and Technology Research Partnership for Sustainable Development* (SATREPS). It was a five-year project that began in 2011, and I oversaw the forestry unit of this project. I present the major findings from this project, mainly based on the work of young participating researchers. First, I point out that the current extraction level of major non-timber forest products, except bushmeat, is under-utilized compared with the ecological potential of the resources, and that they remain a promising source of cash income. The sustainability of hunting for subsistence has been threatened by the expansion of commercial meat trade in recent years. To avoid overhunting, I point to the necessity of monitoring and adjusting the number of animals hunted by the local people themselves, using a simple indicator of the changes in the species composition of the catch, developed by Yasuoka (2006a), one of our team members. While the commercialization of forest products has provided the local people with a new economic opportunity for cash income, it has widened the economic gap between the indigenous hunter-gatherers and the agricultural people. I point out that such ethnic disparity and inequality are caused by the "immediate return orientation" of the hunter-gatherers and the "control of the trade" by the agriculturalists, and that such unequal relationships have been reinforced throughout the historical relationship between the two groups.

Chapter 5, "Hunter-Gatherers Way of Life in Modern Society," the final chapter, discusses the "immediate return orientation" or "present orientation" of the hunter-gatherers. I outline how such a "way of life" is characteristic of the "immediate return system" (Woodburn, 1982) of hunter-gatherers, in which the cycle from labor input to outcome is repeated in a short period of time. I then examine old travelogues, historical literature from the 17th century onward, and show that central African hunter-gatherers had contact with the global trading network through trade in ivory and other forest products, but they avoided direct contact with the outside society. Even after Western colonization, they were not fully incorporated into the colonial administrative structure but specialized as hunter-gatherers (i.e., providers of forest products), unlike the agriculturalists who controlled the trade of these products. These factors have maintained and reinforced their "present orientation" and the unequal relationship with the agriculturalists. Then, in response to the view that such an attitude toward life is an obstacle to "development," I point out its positive aspects in the modern society. For example, in the DRC (former Zaire) in the 1970s and 1980s, the "way of life" of the (Mbuti) hunter-gatherers provided a buffering effect for the chaotic national economy and over-exploitation of forest resources. The case of the exchange of the Mbuti hunter-gatherers in these difficult years provides us with an opportunity for reconsidering the economic system of our own society. At the same time, however, I discuss the dangers that such a "way of life" is utilized by the dominant ethnic groups in times of peace, and ultimately leads to their marginalization and widening inequalities by allowing the unequal exchange system between them to continue.

Chapter 1

Conservation of Tropical Rainforests and Indigenous Peoples

Chapter 1

Photo on the previous page: Local people waiting for the arrival of inspection panel

1.1. Request from the World Bank Inspection Panel

In April 2006, I received an e-mail from the World Bank Inspection Panel (hereafter referred to as "Inspection Panel"). I was asked to provide my telephone number so that they could contact me directly. I had never been involved with the World Bank before and had no recollection of receiving such a call, but I felt as if I could not leave it alone. I wrote back with my phone number and a time when I could be reached. Since there was a 13-hour time difference between Washington, D.C., where the World Bank is located, and Japan, I specified an early morning (Japan Standard Time) the next day. I received a phone call the next morning from Prof. Edith Brown-Weiss, the chairperson of the Inspection Panel. The subject of the call was as follows.

In the DRC, which had been in a state of civil war since the late 1990s, the World Bank began various aid programs following a peace agreement in 2002. One of these was a forestry-related institutional reform project, which began in 2005. However, a group of indigenous peoples living in Congo's forest areas requested the Inspection Panel to examine the project because of the negative impacts it would have on them. They said that various problems are arising because this forest reform project aims to promote large-scale logging in the rainforests where they live, and because there was no consensus building nor consultation with the local people at the start of the project (World Bank, 2006a).

The role of the Inspection Panel is to monitor the Bank's aid operations to ensure that they are not in violation of the Bank's Operational Directives and Operational Policy. Upon receiving this request, the Inspection Panel sent a mission to DRC to conduct a preliminary investigation. As a result, the Inspection Panel confirmed that the indigenous peoples' concerns about the project were valid and reported that further investigation was needed (Inspection Panel, 2006). The report was approved by the Bank's Board of Directors, and a full-scale investigation was initiated to review the project. In order to conduct a full-scale investigation in DRC, it was decided that experts were needed to review the project, and my name came up as the expert on the indigenous peoples who filed this request.

I had not been involved in this type of work before. Instead, I have been interested in research such as "evolution of human society" and "ethnoscience," which are not of much use in our practical lives. However,

Chapter 1

for more than 30 years I have been concerned about the plight of the people with whom I have been involved and their vision for the future. Especially in the 1990s, when the destruction of tropical rainforests accelerated in many parts of central Africa, I became concerned about the future livelihood and culture of the forest people, and the rich forests that nurtured their culture. I went to the Japanese Embassy in Kinshasa, the capital of the country, with a plan to conduct a survey and provide assistance to preserve both the rainforest and the welfare of the people living there. However, due to political unrest in the region at the time, the embassy did not take the matter seriously. I decided to accept the request from the Inspection Panel because I thought it would be a good opportunity to connect my past research and interests to issues in the contemporary world.

1.2. Investigation activities

The Inspection Panel's review work on the Bank's project was comprised of (1) a review of Bank documents and Congolese government documents related to the project (e.g., forest law, various government decrees and ordinances, project plans, etc.), and (2) interviews with World Bank officials implementing the project, Congolese government officials receiving assistance, forest logging companies, private company contracted to implement the project, and various non-governmental organizations working on the issues of forests and indigenous peoples. Particularly, the purpose of (2) is to ascertain whether there is any discrepancy between what is written in the plans and reports of the World Bank and the Congolese government (what is claimed in Washington and Kinshasa), and what is actually happening on the ground in the region. This is why the core inspection activities were "fact finding," or "discovery and confirmation of facts."

Shortly after receiving a phone call in April from the Inspection Panel, I was invited to the World Bank headquarters in Washington in late May. The purpose was to interview Bank staff involved in the project. In fact, I had to prepare for the interviews, and hoped that my visit to Washington would have been scheduled a little later. But in early June, the Inspection Panel was scheduled to conduct a field investigation in the DRC. The DRC was scheduled to hold presidential elections soon, and the Inspection Panel was planning to conduct the field investigation before the expected turmoil in the election process. However, the situation in Congo was already extremely unstable in the run-up to the presidential election, and the field investigation was eventually postponed until after the election.

As soon as I returned home from my first visit to Washington, I received a series of files related to the project. I also searched the Internet to gather related materials myself. The materials included World Bank reports, minutes of meetings on the project, reports from various NGOs involved in the project, Congo's new forest law (*Code Forestier*, 2002) and various related laws, decrees, and ordinances, as well as the new constitution that had been enacted that year. Printing out these documents accumulated about two large cardboard boxes in a short period of time. Many of them were written in French, and it took me a lot of time to understand their contents. The most important documents were translated into English by interns at the World Bank, which was a big help.

The review activities of the inspection panel, in which I was involved, can be broadly described as "applied research." Until I started to work with the Inspection Panel, I had been involved in research that was read by only a few people around the world, or at most several dozen people even if a group of people with some interest is taken into account. I suppose that is generally how it is with "professional" research. However, this review work required me to look through a number of cross-disciplinary materials outside my field of expertise, including the Forest Law and various other laws, constitutions, project plans and reports, and minutes of meetings. As I intensively read the materials I gathered, I gradually came to understand the project's contents, the objectives and background intended by its proponents, the appeals of indigenous peoples who were concerned about the project, and the movements of international NGOs (some working for the World Bank Project, and others supporting the indigenous peoples). While one of the important pillars of the World Bank's institutional reform support project was the "capacity development" of the government officials and local people involved in the project, I myself became committed to my own "capacity development" through this activity.

Chapter 1

1.3. Field Investigation in DRC

The on-site investigation scheduled for June 2006 was postponed for eight months due to the unstable political situation in the DRC. It took place in February the following year, after the presidential elections were held in December 2006 and their results came out. The postponement gave me time to look through the relevant materials, so by the time we started the on-site investigation, I had a better understanding of the current situation in DRC and of the aid projects and their problems. The field investigation was conducted by a team of six members, two from the Inspection Panel, the chairperson, Professor Edith Brown-Weiss, and the next chairperson, Dr. Werner Kiene, along with Dr. Peter Lalas from the secretariat and Mr. Serge Seluwan, responsible for the logistics. Dr. Ralph Schmidt and I joined as experts of forestry and anthropology (on indigenous peoples), respectively. We started the investigation in the DRC at the beginning of February 2007.

On 1 February 2007, we arrived in the capital Kinshasa, and started the investigation the following morning. In Kinshasa, we spent a week interviewing World Bank officials working there, DRC government project officers, consultants and experts entrusted with actual works, representatives of NGOs and other civil society organizations, and others. We then flew to Kisangani, the capital of Oriental Province, by plane operated by the UN forces, and conducted interviews with local people, logging companies and others. From Kisangani, we attempted by UN military helicopter to visit a village of indigenous people, called Batswa (who were named Jofe by the Belgian missionary, Gustaaf Hulstaert, in his report of 1986), near Ikela. While the Batswa people were awaiting a visit by the Inspection Panel, this contact was not successful, as I will explain later. We also flew to Bafwasende, a village at the western end of the Ituri Forest, to interview Mbuti men and women who had come there. We then returned to Kinshasa and then flew to Mbandaka in Equateur Province to interview the Batswa (or Batua) people living in the area. From Mbandaka, we went up the Ruki river, a tributary of the Congo River, in a large outboard-powered wooden dugout boat, to visit a Batswa village near Ingende. In total, the trip lasted about three weeks. Apart from a reconnaissance flight to Ikela, where the Jofe people were said to be waiting for us, a helicopter visit to Bafwasende and a canoe visit to Ingende, most of the investigation comprised interviews with officials of the World Bank and the DRC government, consultants contracted by the World Bank, and the indigenous people living on the outskirts of the cities and NGO organizations that support them.

Although the interviews were conducted with the local indigenous people, they usually consisted of statements and demands prepared in advance by representatives of the indigenous people who were waiting for our visit, and the question-and-answer sessions were not sufficient. Moreover, the content of what was read out was what we had expected beforehand, such as condemnation of logging activities and requests for support for their welfare and education. While this was undoubtedly the reality of the situation and their wishes, I could not help but feel that there must be a 'real voice' that could convey facts that could not be expressed in a formal written text. So, when we were returning to our lodgings after completing our interview with a logging company on the outskirts of Kisangani, I decided to stop at a village on the way and try to conduct informal interviews. I started with small talk and tried to get a frank opinion about the logging business, the economic opportunities it offers and the social responsibility (*Cahier des Charges*, discussed below) that logging companies promised to undertake when signing a contract.

According to the inhabitants of that village, the logging company had made little progress with the social responsibility project of building a school and a clinic. The wages of the villagers employed for these projects were so low that no one wanted to do them. When villagers became frustrated about the slowdown in the work of construction, the logging companies would secretly hand over bribes to the village chief. This, they said, usually subsides the immediate frustration. I wondered if other villagers put up with it. I wanted to ask more about this, but another member of the mission interrupted me, so I had to stop the interview. However, having come all the way to the area, it was not enough just to listen to the pre-prepared, formal statements. I felt frustrated and wondered if this was not 'fact-finding'. I strongly felt that if we really wanted to do fact-finding, we should spend several months with a small group of people in the community and endeavor to share what they really feel, rather than opinions spouted by outside activists.

During our visit to Kisangani, I was to visit a village called Samanda, which is inhabited by the indigenous Batswa people (known in the

Chapter 1

Photo 1.1 Logging base near Kisangani

literature as Jofe). However, nobody knew where Samanda was located. A check at the office of the UN force stationed in Kisangani revealed that a village with such a name is shown on maps to the west of the town of Ikela, about 400 km in a straight line to the south-west of Kisangani. There is a road from Kisangani to Ikela on the map. However, this road was in disrepair as it had not been maintained during the civil war, and it was already bad before that. Moreover, we were informed that there was not even a road beyond Ikela. In the end, it was decided to take a UN military helicopter to the site. For the time being, we had to fly a reconnaissance flight, in other words, to check whether there were really indigenous people there, whether it was possible to land at the village, and whether the flight route was safe. I was to accompany the reconnaissance flight on behalf of the Inspection Panel. I was excited because it was a great opportunity to see the forests of the Congo Basin from a low altitude.

The flight took off from Kisangani airport on a cool, early morning in a Russian-made helicopter, piloted by a Ukrainian. The helicopter was escorted on board by seven strong-looking Senegalese soldiers who had been deployed by MONUC (United Nations Forces), armed with automatic weapons and bulletproof vests. As soon as we took off from Kisangani airport, the Congo River came into view. The river, which stretches like a serpent all the way to the horizon, is a sight to behold. The forests of the Congo Basin could also be seen all the way to the horizon. White smoke from slash-and-burn fields was rising in places. After a while, we saw a village in the middle of a vast forest that seemed isolated from its surroundings. Only the area around it was cultivated, but the forest continued unbroken around it. I wondered what kind of life the people there were living, as I had spent time some 30 years ago in a similarly isolated forest. Thinking of this warmed my heart.

After a little over three hours' flight, the helicopter reached the airspace above the village of Samanda, the intended destination. The village was open for its remote location, with a white sand road running right through the middle of two rows of houses. The houses were relatively fine. It appeared to be a Bantu farming village rather than a hunter-gatherer settlement. However, there were no large open spaces in the village where helicopters could descend. The pilot said that if we tried to force a landing, the wind generated by the helicopter's rotor blades would blow off the roofs of their palm-thatched houses. The pilot did not agree to land, as that would be a big problem.

In the end, we were unable to land in the village of Samanda, which we had aimed to do, and were unable to meet the people of Batswa. We had also prepared a message that if we landed successfully and met them, the main survey team would come the next day to interview them, but we could not do that either. However, that was all right. The village of Samanda on the UN force's map was a completely different village from the Batswa village that we were looking for. The next day, after a satellite phone call with the pastor of a church supporting the Batswa people, we discovered that the village they were in was on the banks of the Chuapa River, more than 100 km east of the village we had flown over, in the opposite direction, across the town of Ikela. Samanda there was not on the map, probably because it was a newly established village. As is often the case in Africa, there are several villages with the same name, and we mistook the one on the map for the village we were seeking.

On returning to Kinshasa from Kisangani, the team now flew to Mbandaka, the capital of Equateur Province. The plan was to conduct interviews with the Batswa people living around Mbankaka and the Batswa people at Ingende in the east, up the Ruki River, a tributary of

Chapter 1

Photo 1.2 The Congo River near Kisangani

the Congo River. After a routine evening meeting, we left the hotel at 4 am before dawn the next morning for the Kinshasa airport to catch the morning flight to Mbandaka. I recalled that when we did research in this country in the 1980s, we would have to go to the airport at midnight to catch a morning flight. Back then, the flight we were waiting for was often cancelled when it was past boarding time, and we had to return to town disappointed. Even when we used the UN planes on World Bank missions, we still had to get to the airport very early. I was surprised at the fact that things had not changed much. Fortunately, unlike the situation in the 1980s, the UN plane took off from Kinshasa airport at around 08:00, only a little later than scheduled. After two hours of flying in an old UN Forces aircraft with rows of seats facing each other, the plane landed in the suburbs of Mbandaka.

We headed directly from Mbandaka Airport to the venue where the indigenous Batswa people were waiting to attend the meeting. First, Dr Kiene of the Inspection Panel explained the purpose of the mission, and then each member of the mission, including the indigenous representatives from other regions who had accompanied us from Kinshasa, introduced themselves. I introduced myself in Lingala language I had learnt during my previous research in the neighboring Republic of Congo. A representative from Batswa people then read out

Photo 1.3 Forest near Lomami river

a written request in French for assistance with the adverse effects of the logging operations and their welfare. After a few exchanges between the Batswa representatives and the Inspection Panel members, the mission representative, Dr Kiene, received the handwritten letter with a short comment that he understood their appeal. Thus ended the first meeting with the indigenous people in Equateur Province.

After the meeting, the two members of the Inspection Panel Secretariat immediately set out to arrange for a canoe up the river, an outboard motor, and fuel. We checked-in at an auberge (inn) on the banks of the Congo River. From the bar of the auberge overlooking the river, we could see the boats coming and going. Fortunately, we were able to arrange for a large wooden canoe and fuel by evening. The next morning, while it was still dark, we boarded a canoe attached to the riverbank below the auberge and headed up the Congo River. Vessels of all sizes passed by in the dim light. There were several large wooden boats looking like a houseboat with a roof, flowing slowly from upstream. Soon we entered the Ruki River, which parted from the mainstream of the Congo River and joined the river from the east. Houses on piles, built a few meters above the ground, lined the riverbank. The water level probably rises considerably during the rainy season. We guessed that the residents were engaged in fishing using the difference in the water level. As I had also

Chapter 1

Photo 1.4 Fishing camp on the bank of Ruki river

conducted fishery research before, I was interested in how they caught fish, but we did not have time to investigate this. The large wooden canoe with a 40-horsepower outboard engine was flying briskly, passing several villages along the riverbank. After about four hours on the river, we arrived at our destination, Ingende. At the landing site, we found the local inhabitants of the area, including the indigenous Batswa people.

We listened to the peoples' complaints in a vacant lot near the landing site. The logging company had started logging without consulting the local Batswa people; logging roads were built, destroying their fields, villages, and burial sites; the Batswa people could no longer hunt in the logging areas; and they had been losing more and more species of trees (such as *Entandrophragma* of the family Meliaceae) that fed important edible caterpillars (one of their important sources of protein). The Batswa representative read out a written statement about how logging operations were threatening their livelihoods, including the fact that the trees important to their livelihood were being cut down.

Although these were all expected complaints, hearing the voices of the people face-to-face and in situ reminded us of the seriousness of the situation.

On our return from Ingende, we were hit by a heavy squall. The river is wide, so when a gust of wind blew, the surface of the river became rough and rippled, causing the canoe to rock violently. The waves would have subsided if we had approached the riverbank, but there was a danger of hitting a fallen tree hidden in the water, so we dared to go through the middle of the river, where the waves were high and visibility was poor due to the rain. The outboard driver (*pinasse*) had been drinking a slightly stronger beer called "Turbo" since we left Ingende. He was so drunk that the canoe finally ran into a floating grass bush in the storm and got stuck. Having no choice, everyone except women got out and pushed the canoe back from the floating grass bush, soaking wet and waist-deep in water. When we managed to get back into the open river again, the squall stopped. It was already dark. I was wearing rain gear, so I did not get too wet when it rained. However, Dr. Lalas, who was soaked through without rain gear, developed a high fever on the night we returned to Mbandaka.

Despite these developments, there were no other major incidents, and the inspection generally proceeded as planned. The Inspection Panel requested that I submit a report on the field investigation within a month. By this time, I had already reviewed most of the relevant materials, so I had to compile the report by comparing them with the results of the observations and on-site interviews conducted in DRC.

The following is a summary of the draft report I submitted.

1.4. Draft Report on the Impacts on Indigenous People

1.4.1. The situation after the Peace Agreement and the World Bank's programs

In DRC, which had been in a state of civil war since the late 1990s, a peace agreement was reached in Pretoria in 2002 between the main rival forces. In fact, although fighting continued in the eastern part of the country between government forces and various militias that had taken up arms during the civil war, chaos had subsided in the rest of the country, and peace had been restored. In response, various aid projects by the World Bank were initiated. Among them was a project for institutional reform related to forestry. In DRC, various forces continued to usurp the country's abundant natural resources amid the chaos of the civil war. While the most important resources were minerals such as gold,

Chapter 1

diamonds, and rare metals, timber resources which had not been fully developed, were no exception. When the peace agreement was signed in 2002, various forms of "concessions" had been established for 43.5 million hectares, or half of the country's forest area. Many of these were granted without the agreement of the local people who had been using the forests, and without any reasonable return to them. Moreover, these logging areas were arbitrarily established on maps and often overlapped with existing villages, farmlands, and protected areas (Debroux et al., 2007).

In most of these concessions, there were no logging operations due to the civil war and the resulting devastation of the infrastructural and distribution systems. Some of the logging concessions were acquired for speculative purposes. Once peace was achieved, however, large-scale logging operations began almost immediately. It was obvious that this would cause serious problems for the inhabitants of the region, who depend on the forests for a wide range of resources, including fuel, food, folk medicine, and cash income (Debroux et al., 2007). The most affected people are the indigenous Pygmy hunter-gatherers, who heavily depend on forests for their livelihood.

In 2003, the UN Security Council adopted a resolution (UN resolution 1457) calling for the assistance of international organizations to form institutions to ensure that the abundant resources of DRC are properly used for the benefit of its people. On this basis, the World Bank has embarked on an institutional reform project for the country's forest sector. It was also in line with the World Bank's "Forestry Strategy" (World Bank, 2002), which integrates forest development and conservation for poverty alleviation among the people in the country.

The Bank's assistance project on DRC's forest sector consisted of two projects. The first was the Emergency Economic and Social Reunification Support Project (EESRSP), which included institutional reform of the forest sector. The second was the Transitional Support for Economic Recovery Credit Operation (TSERO). The purposes of these two projects were to (1) implement the *Code Forêstier* of 2002, (2) classify forests (zoning) according to the uses specified in the *Code Forêstier*, (3) establish transparency in the forest concession granting system, (4) extension of the Presidential Decree establishing a moratorium on granting new concessions, (5) legal review of concessions granted to

Conservation of Tropical Rainforests and Indigenous Peoples

date, (6) invalidation of illegal logging contracts and conversion of valid contracts into a new concession granting system; (7) a three-year plan for granting new concessions; and (8) capacity building related to the forest sector in the DRC (World Bank, 2006a).

In 2002, the DRC government followed the World Bank's advice and invalidated as illegal 168 contracts (totaling 25.5 million hectares) covering more than half of the 43.5 million hectares of forests that had previously been granted concessions (Debroux et al., 2007). This allowed for a legal review of the remaining 18 million hectares of logging concessions. Zoning of the forests (forest classification by use) where no concessions had been established was also made possible. After the EESRSP was approved in December 2003, a draft Terms of Reference for a forest zoning pilot project in the Maringa-Lopori-Wamba triangle in the Equateur Province of central Congo was prepared in 2004. According to the new *Code Forêstier*, forest types are classified into (1) classified forests (*forêts classées*), (2) protected forests (*forêts protégées*), and (3) permanent production forests subject to sustainable forestry (*forêts de production permanente*) (*Code Forêstier*, Government of DRC, 2002)[1] and forests were to be zoned according to this classification. In addition, the TSERO funds approved by the World Bank Board of Directors in 2005 initiated a review of the concession contracts previously granted. However, prior to the start of these projects, large-scale logging had already begun in some forests under the rights granted during the civil war.

1.4.2. Indigenous peoples request an inspection

In October 2005, the *Organisations Autochtones Pygmées en République Démocratique du Congo* (Indigenous Pygmy Organizations in DRC) and their supporters announced that the two projects (EESRSP and TSERO) would have negative impacts on local people and their environment and requested the Inspection Panel to review them. They complained that these projects violated their rights of access to the land and resources they had been using and living on. They further stated

---

1   Although confusing to us, forests subject to protected forests belong to category (1), not (2). The *"forêts protégées"* in (2) are not so-called forest reserves, and forests used by local people are included in this category.

Chapter 1

that the Congolese Forest Law (*Code Forêstier*), on which these projects were based, was adopted without any consultation or agreement with them. They claimed that the Bank's projects implemented under these circumstances were in violation of the Bank's own Operational Policy regarding "environmental assessment," "indigenous peoples," and "poverty alleviation" (World Bank, 2006b). This was probably the first time such an appeal has been filed by an indigenous people in DRC. Signatories to this request were representatives of so-called indigenous Pygmy organizations from a wide range of the DRC, from the provinces of Kasai, Oriental, North Kivu, South Kivu, Equateur, Bandundu and Maniema. This was also the first time that so many indigenous people, who until then had been living in small, dispersed groups in different parts of the Congo, had come together to make their voices heard in a wider, international context. The substance of their appeal was as follows.

First, the *Code Forêstier* on which the two projects in question relied was passed in 2002 with the assistance of FAO and other organizations, but it was decided without any consultation with the forest inhabitants who are most affected by it, and in this sense is likely to have negative impacts on their lives. Second, while the forest zoning to be promoted by this project would lead to the establishment of logging areas and the promotion of large-scale logging operations, the local indigenous people, who had long been depending on the forests in this area, have not given an opportunity to have "free, prior and informed consultation" with the zoning program. And third, although the *Code Forêstier* and logging contracts stipulate the distribution of tax revenues from logging operations to local communities and *cahiers des charges* (logging companies' responsibility for social contributions such as building and repairing schools, clinics, bridges, and roads), many of those promises have not been realized in areas where logging had begun. In other words, logging operations have made little or no contribution to poverty alleviation among the local people.

The question is, therefore, are there better ways to reduce poverty among the local people than logging projects? We will examine this question in more detail below.

1.4.3. Problems in the Code Forêstier

1.4.3.1. Innovations in the Code Forêstier

According to the World Bank Management, the new *Code Forêstier* introduces various innovations for protecting traditional user's right and for contributions to rural development (World Bank, 2006a). The major innovations include:

- Mandatory implementation in all production forests of sustainable management plans including the protection of biodiversity (Art. 71, 99, 100).

- Preservation in all production forests of traditional users' rights, including those of indigenous people (Art. 44).

- Transfer of 40% of forest area fees to decentralized administrative entities (Art. 122).

- Mandatory in-kind contributions by forest companies to rural development in neighboring villages (*"Cahiers des Charges,"* Art. 89).

- Direct management of forest by local communities ("concessions des communautés locales," Art. 22).

- Provisions for new non-extractive uses of forests and the valorization of environmental services (Art. 72, 87, 96, 119).

Among these, preservation of customary rights (traditional users' rights) is of extreme importance. As stipulated in the Articles in the *Code Forêstier*, the customary usage rights to the forest are formally established for the first time in the DRC forestry history, and in this sense the new *Code Forêstier* is expected to have some positive influences on the forest communities.[2] Moreover, as Articles 36 and 38 stipulate, only the people living in or adjacent to the forest are given usage rights as

---

2   However, these rights are not restricted to "indigenous peoples." The rights limited to indigenous peoples were established later.

Chapter 1

"the result of customs and local traditions." Such rights will provide the local community with a foundation for managing forest resources on a long-term basis, by preventing outsiders from encroaching on the forest, which would eventually lead to over-exploitation and deterioration of forest resources through pursuing short-term benefits at the expense of long-term sustainability.

Therefore, if these innovations on the customary rights are firmly established for the indigenous people, their customary use of forest resources can be secured to some extent. While forest resources were used until recently with *de fact* right by the forest-dwelling peoples, there was no legal basis for preventing outsiders from encroaching and exploiting the forest in which indigenous people have been living for many centuries. Due mainly to these shortcomings, there have often been an influx of migrant hunters into the forest, and in some other areas of the Congo Basin it has resulted in over-exploitation of forest resources. The forest people, in particular Pygmy people who are most heavily dependent on the forest, were unable to manage forest resources on a long-term sustainable basis, which would have been possible if there had not been encroachment by outsiders.

1.4.3.2. Commercial Use

However, there is a problem in Article 37, which states: "commercialization of forest products removed under this title is not authorized..." Article 39 further stipulates that:

> in the classified forests [i.e., nature conservation area], usage rights are restricted to …a) collecting of dead wood and straw, b) gathering of fruit, food and medicinal plants, c) the harvesting of rubber/gum, resin, and honey, d) collecting of caterpillars, snails or frogs, e) removal of wood for construction of homes and for artisan work.[3]

Previous studies in DRC showed that a variety of forest products were used not only for their own consumption, but also for earning cash (Ichikawa, 1992). These include forest products such as the sweet

---

3   Most parts of the *Code Forêstier* relevant to this study were translated into English by the Inspection Panel.

Photo 1.5 Bushmeat sold at local market

and sour fruit of *Landolphia* spp. and olive-shaped energy-rich fruit of *Canarium schweinfurthii,* the cola nuts which are eagerly sought after as stimulants, oil-rich *Irvingia* nuts, various mushrooms, and a variety of edible insects, including caterpillars, grubs and termites. Most of these products are also sold at local markets in their seasons. Honey is highly valued forest food and eagerly sought after by all the people in the forest region. Other than food, there are important materials for manufacturing and construction, such as young leaves of raffia palm (*Raphia* sp.) for weaving mats, large Marantaceae leaves (*Megaphrynium macrostachyum*) for thatching and wrapping materials, and palm liana (*Eremospatha haullevilleana*) for making baskets and as binding material. All of these comprise important trade items at local markets (Ichikawa, 1992).

In particular, bushmeat was one of the most important sources of protein for the region's forest inhabitants and comprised an important trading good. As described in the next chapter, in the Ituri Forest where we conducted our research, the trade of bushmeat in this region activity had started in the 1950s as a source of protein for workers in mines and plantations, where livestock were scarce. The meat was also transported

Chapter 1

Photo 1.6 Edible caterpillars sold at a local market

to Butembo, Beni, and other local towns in densely populated areas to the east of the Ituri Forest, for consumption by town residents. Today, wild game is valued as more than just a source of protein; it is valued as a source of "wild power" for urban residents who have lost contact with the "wilderness" of the forest (see Chapter 3). In addition, especially since the late 1970s and 80s when the economy deteriorated drastically due to the failure of hasty "Zairianization" policy (Young and Turner, 1985), or since the late 1990s when civil war devastated roads and river transportation systems and other infrastructure, the trade in bushmeat expanded rapidly as an affordable way to generate cash income. In the Ituri Forests, the meat hunted by Mbuti was exchanged for cassava flour, rice, and other crops, as well as clothing, cooking pots, and other items. Alternatively, it was sold for cash in order to pay taxes and fines, and for marriage (as part of bridewealth), childbirths, funerals and for other social and cultural needs (Hart, 1978; Ichikawa, 1991a). In this view, the strict enforcement of Article 37, which prohibits the commercialization of these forest products, would have enormous adverse effects on the extractive activities which have been practiced for earning cash by the forest-living people.

Conservation of Tropical Rainforests and Indigenous Peoples

1.4.3.3. Customary rights in production forests

Article 44 of the *Code Forêstier* stipulates that "the forest residents of a concession continue to exercise their traditional usage rights for that concession, insofar as it is compatible with the forestry exploitation." While most of the high, hard-wood trees, the targets for logging, are not directly used by the forest people for subsistence purposes, they are important sources of edible insects and honey, such as *Entandrophragma* spp. which accommodate a large quantity of edible caterpillars in their seasons, and *Caesalpinioidseae* tree species which comprise major nectar sources in the forest. One of the most frequent complaints about logging operations made by the forest people is that logging destroys the sources of edible fruit, honey and caterpillars, and seriously affects their livelihood in the forest. Furthermore, although "forest residents" are allowed to collect honey, edible insects, and useful plants in the logging area free of charge, some logging companies restrict access or charge entry fees. Other adverse impacts of logging include over-hunting of animals by outside poachers who access the interior forest using logging roads, rapid infiltration of cash economy and consumerism, alcoholism accelerated by the sale of bushmeat, disappearing of game animals from the forest, and other indirect influences of logging operations. If these negative influences are taken into consideration, active logging operations impose adverse impacts on, and are generally incompatible with, the customary use of the forest by local and indigenous peoples, if they take place simultaneously in the same area.

1.4.3.4. Concession granting process: Free, prior and informed consultation

Article 84 of the *Code Forêstier* stipulates that "the forest concession contract is preceded by a public investigation... The investigation has the goal of laying out the rights of third parties in the forest and figuring out their eventual remuneration." However, as anthropologists who had previously studied the region pointed out,

> ...it is safe to say that there is rarely a forest in central Africa that is not occupied by humans. Whether considering development or planning for nature conservation, one must first assume that a particular individual,

Chapter 1

clan, lineage, or other group will occupy and claim rights to any forest. (Bailey et al. 1992)

Indeed, many of the logging areas that have already been granted concessions and are subject to the World Bank's review work include roads, villages, crop fields, and fallow areas, which will inevitably involve existing rights and compensation for violating them (Deveroux, et al, 2007). As to the remuneration, the report prepared by the experts of World Bank Management estimated the total economic value of bushmeat, honey and caterpillars procured from the forests of the DRC amounts to well over two billion US dollars per annum, which is much more than the total economic value of the expected annual timber production, which was estimated at USD 160 million at most in DRC at the time of inspection (Debroux et al., 2007). Compensation for the total loss of access to these resources would cost an enormous amount.

The *Code Forêstier* clearly mentions that a forest concession is granted after consultation with local community which has customary rights to the forest (Article 84). However, there is often little or no real consultation. This failure is partly due to the formal and customary land tenure systems in DRC. In formal legal terms, DRC established state ownership over the forest lands by a series of legislation; Forest Law of 1949 in the colonial period, Bakajika Land Law of 1966, the 1973 Land Law, and the 1980 revised Land Law, all stipulates that the forest land belongs to the State. The new Forest Law (*Code Forêstier*) also stipulates the state ownership of the forests (FAO, 2007; Counsell, 2006). There are, however, customary land tenure and usage systems in the Congo Basin. In spite of the widespread belief that Pygmy hunter-gatherers are the first inhabitants of the forest (whether or not it was actually the case, many Congolese people understand this to be the case), and that first occupants usually claim the customary rights to the forests, it is not the hunter-gatherer groups, but agricultural people, who have the stronger rights to the forest land in most customary land tenure systems in DRC.[4] And according to the agricultural villagers, under

---

4   According to the agriculturalists in the region, the hunter-gatherers have no rights to the land because they lead a nomadic life and make little 'investment' in the land. But as shown in the next chapter, they have positively impacted the forest environment in various ways.

this umbrella the Pygmy hunter-gatherers are allowed to use the land. At least this is the understanding of the agricultural villagers who are "masters" or "patrons," though the Pygmy people naturally oppose this view of villagers. The Pygmy people insist their own rights to the forests, but their rights are not properly recognized, due mainly to their weak power and lack of representation in a wider political system. Based on this understanding, government officials, logging companies, and agricultural villagers are liable to think that consultation with Pygmy people may not be necessary when making logging contracts.

The overlapping or hierarchical land right of the Pygmies and the agricultural villagers did not make much trouble, when the forest areas were large enough for the people to use them, or when the economic opportunity for exploiting forest resources was limited. However, when the forests are allocated to logging concessions and part of the concession fees is distributed to the local community, the overlapping rights to the forests often develop into extremely severe conflicts. And in most cases, Pygmy people are in a disadvantageous position against more powerful agriculturalists, who try to monopolize the benefits from new opportunities. The case the Batswa people in Ingende, Equateur region presented to the World Bank Inspection Panel investigation clearly illustrates the underprivileged position of the indigenous people (World Bank, 2007a).

When I visited the area with the Inspection Panel, the Batswa people complained that they had not been consulted at all by the logging company operating in the forest which they had been inhabiting for hundreds of years, and that consultation about the logging concessions and negotiations of the *cahier des charges* were made only between the logging company and Bantu agriculturalists (of the Mongo group). Without any consultation with, or compensation for, the indigenous Batswa people who occupy the majority of the population in the area, the logging company built roads penetrating their settlement sites, and cut useful fruit- and caterpillar- bearing trees, even in burial sites and sacred parts of their forest. The Batswa also complained that the logging company does not provide them with any job opportunities. When they complained to the loggers about these ill-mannered acts, the loggers said that they (the Batswa) should go to Kinshasa and appeal to the

Chapter 1

administration, as the formal dispute settlement procedure requires. They cannot, however, afford to do that.

The indigenous people are at an overwhelming disadvantage when it comes to consultation with logging companies and government agencies. As previous studies have shown (Ichikawa, 1978), the Pygmy hunter-gatherers have long maintained an inter-dependent but unequal relationship with their agricultural neighbors, who are called "*kpala*" among the Mbuti in the Ituri Forest, and "*nkolo*" among the Batswa in Equateur Province. Both words literally mean "man," but also have a connotation of "patron" or "boss," who represent the hunter-gatherers and play intermediary roles between the hunter-gatherers and external society. These long-lasting unequal relationships (as described in Chapter 5) remain in the political structure of the region to this day. Moreover, most of the central African hunter-gatherer societies are characterized by non-hierarchical, egalitarian social relationship (Ichikawa, 2005), which are at odds with a modern representation system that requires a leader or spokesman to express their voice. They are thus often represented by more powerful agricultural neighbors in a wider political context, and rarely have a chance to have their own voice heard in wider society. This, coupled with overlapping, hierarchical customary rights to the same forest areas, makes it more difficult for indigenous people to express their interests.

1.4.4. Forest reforms and poverty reduction: alternatives to logging

Concerning the problem of poverty in DRC, the Chairman of the Forest Forum held in November 2004 stated: "The Congolese forest is the world's second tropical forest block and an incomparable biodiversity reservoir. But the Congolese people are also among the poorest in the world. It's a paradox that needs to be reconciled" (World Bank, 2006a; Swing, 2007).

According to the World Bank, the DRC's forests have been managed poorly in the past and have yielded few benefits to the Congolese people as a whole. Therefore, the Bank included forest issues in the reform agenda which was a strong signal of its engagement in natural resources. However, the indigenous Pygmy people claim that the projects would not alleviate their poverty. Instead, they stated that the project's negative

Conservation of Tropical Rainforests and Indigenous Peoples

impacts would further impoverish the poorest and most marginalized segments of the Congolese population.

The World Bank Management stated that the impacts of forest reforms on poverty alleviation would be brought about through the economic benefits of logging concessions and community forest programs and analyzed the impact of forest reforms on poverty alleviation. A report by Bank consultants (Debroux et al., 2007) estimated the likely economic benefits of the timber sector as follows:

(1) Employment: 10,000–15,000 jobs produced for the forest sector plus 9,000–15,000 more jobs in the informal sector,

(2) Spill-over effect on the economy: stimulate consumers of services and transportation,

(3) Revenues to the State and local entities: Forest revenues (tax) may reach 10 million US\$ in 2007, reaching 20–40 million US\$ within 5–10 years, from the tax of 20 US\$ /m3 for a total of 1–2 million m³ of timber production. Through the revenue sharing system established by Article 122 of the Forest Code, forest could also become a significant source of revenue for local entities; for example, each of the provinces of Bandundu, Equateur and Orientale could receive approximately half a million US\$ per annum, obtained from 40% of concession fee, which is 0.5 US\$ /ha for 2–3 million ha concession area in 2007,

(4) Direct support for rural development (*cahier des charges*): Obligation of concession holders to improve infrastructure (school, health care center, roads, etc).

However, there have often been cases where local people have not really benefited from logging industries, except for a short-term benefit limited to a small number of people. We have seen elsewhere in central Africa that local people suffer from increased poverty, resulting either directly or indirectly from logging operations. For example, in Cameroon, where large-scale logging has been underway since the 1980s, indigenous Baka hunter-gatherers have suffered from the decreased animal population

Chapter 1

caused by influx of traders and poachers arriving through newly opened logging roads (Yasuoka, 2006a), restricted access to the newly established protected areas and sport hunting zones (set in the production forests, i.e., logging zones) reserved for wealthy Westerners, which had long been used for their hunting and gathering grounds (Ichikawa et al. 2016). The concession fees were often not properly distributed to the local entities, nor used for the benefits of local people, as was the case in Cameroon (See, Debroux et al., 2007; Box 6). Without taking concrete and strong measures to prevent these outcomes, logging could hardly be expected to alleviate the peoples' poverty.

We should also note that economic value from timber production comprises only a minor part of the total economic value produced from the forest. As mentioned above, the report by the Bank management's experts estimated the market value of timber production at the time, both formal and informal production combined, at USD 160 million per annum, whereas the total economic value of the resources used by local people, such as firewood, bushmeat, forest fruit, honey, plant medicines and other NTFPs (non-timber forest products) amounted to well over USD 2 billion per annum, and is by far the more important (Debroux et al., 2007). Therefore, if access to these resources was considerably restricted by the logging operations, the compensation necessary for the local people would be enormous and unaffordable.

For forest-living people who experience difficulties in satisfying their subsistence needs, promoting logging or commercialization for export products is by no means the only, nor the best way to solve the problem of poverty. Instead, it is of vital importance in the first place to secure ample subsistence-oriented life. The people need, by all means, healthy life with nutritionally adequate food supply, which is obtained in culturally appropriate ways. What they want first is an ample subsistence base that can also support their social and cultural needs, rather than short-term economic benefits from industrial logging and related activities, which may risk their subsistence base in the longer term.

The World Bank supported projects for forest institutional reform have certainly played a role in getting forest management back on track after the chaos caused by the civil war. However, our conclusion was that there were still problems with the project. First, the *Code Forestier* on which the reform project was based, and its implementation lacked consideration for the local people (especially indigenous Pygmy people) whose livelihoods depend heavily on forest resources. The World Bank's intention to reduce poverty among the local people has not only had little effect but has even had negative impacts. In order to mitigate the negative impacts of the project, especially on the indigenous people who are heavily dependent on forests, safeguards such as the Indigenous People's Development Plan (IPDP) had to be triggered. A proper assessment of the impact on the forest environment is also needed. Logging activities are trampling on indigenous villages, sacred sites, and cemeteries, and destroying trees that are important for the ritual and material life of the indigenous people, with significant negative impacts on cultural properties. We concluded therefore that the Bank's Forest Reform Projects did not comply with the Operational Directive on "Indigenous Peoples" (OD 4.20), the Operational Policy on Poverty Reduction (OP 4.15), OP 4.01 on Environmental Assessment, OP 11.03 on Cultural Property, and that the safeguards needed to be triggered.

1.5. Progress following the Investigation Report

I submitted a draft report to the Inspection Panel a month after returning from the visit to DRC. The Inspection Panel spent several months internally reviewing the report, together with reports and materials from other consultants, Panel members, and Secretariat members, and compiled them into the Investigation Report, a 200-plus page document that includes the text, summary, and appendix (World Bank, 2007a) and submitted it to the Bank's Board of Directors for discussion on August 31, 2007. Almost four months later, in early January 2008, the Investigation Report on DRC was scheduled to be discussed at the Bank's headquarters in Washington, DC.

In response to the Inspection Panel's report, the following responses and action plans were to be taken on the part of the Bank's Management (World Bank, 2007b).

– The project was an "emergency support" after the end of the civil war in DRC, but even so, the Bank should have properly implemented its operational policy and strengthened safeguards as necessary.

Chapter 1

- Special attention should be paid to indigenous peoples in the region as a cross-sectoral theme of the upcoming Bank's projects concerning the forest, road, and agriculture, including the application of the Indigenous People's Development Plan (IPDP), dialogue with indigenous peoples, and their capacity building.

- Continue the moratorium suspending the granting of new forest concessions and complete the legal review of existing concessions.

- Introduce new projects related to the forest sector, such as a forest conservation plan by the Global Environment Facilities (GEF), a new approach to alternative forest uses and the establishment of concessions for nature conservation.

- Encourage participation in the Forest Carbon Partnership Facility (FCPF).

- Outreach activities.

At the January 2008 meeting of the Bank's Executive Board, both the Report of the Inspection Panel and the Management's Action Plan were approved, and the Action Plan was put into action. A year later, the Bank's progress report was released. First, safeguards on "indigenous people" and "cultural property" were put into effect. Specifically, in combination with the projects of REDD+ (Reducing Emissions from Deforestation and Forest Degradation) and the Global Environment Facility (GEF), a plan called the "Pygmy Development Strategy" was developed. It aims to contribute to the preservation of their at-risk cultural identity and to alleviate poverty. Two years later, in a progress report (World Bank, 2009), based on discussions with stakeholders, the DRC government and development partners (consultants), developed a "Framework for a National Development Strategy for Pygmy Communities." Through these various efforts, it can be said that awareness of the existence of Pygmy indigenous peoples and the problems they face have at least increased.

With regard to the forests, only 65 of the 156 concessions, excluding those deemed illegal at the start of the Bank's operations, were found to be legally sound and eligible for conversion to the new concession scheme. Even if social and environmental conditions could be agreed upon with local communities, including indigenous peoples, for all of these, only a total of 9.7 million hectares of concessions would remain. This is less than a quarter of the total of 43.5 million hectares at the end of the civil war in 2002, and less than half the 22.1 million hectares at the beginning of 2002, when the review of logging concessions by the World Bank project began. The Bank also reports that it has supported community-based forest management, including innovative forest use models for existing forest use rights and a range of ecosystem services as alternatives to logging, and participation of local communities in decision-making processes related to forest management (World Bank, 2011).

However, according to the third and final progress report submitted in 2012, there were 80 concessions remaining as of 2011, when the legal review of concessions was completed, with a total area of 12.2 million hectares. and the remaining 91 were invalid or questionable contracts. This means that the number of valid contracts has been added since the first progress report in 2009 (World Bank, 2012). Even more problematic is that since the 2002 presidential decree suspending the granting of new logging concessions, 33 new concession plots have been established. Their validity has been the subject of legal review. Such a situation raises questions about the effectiveness of the law in the DRC. The question now is whether the 12.2 million hectares of forest that have been determined to have valid concessions will be logged in accordance with the approved forest management plan. It is also necessary to determine whether the logging concessions that were supposed to have been canceled have really been extinguished.

Thus, there is no doubt that various challenges remain in the forest reform projects supported by the World Bank. However, it is also important to point out that various improvements have been achieved in the process of attempting to reform the forestry system and reviewing logging concessions as described above. First, capacity development of the DRC forestry sector should be mentioned. Until then, the DRC did not have the technology to monitor the condition of its forests and use this information for forest management. The projects supported by the Bank, provided the Ministry of Forestry and Water Resources, which

Chapter 1

has jurisdiction over the forest sector, with training in the use of satellite data and geographical information systems (GIS) under the guidance of Western experts. Second, there was an increased awareness of the involvement of the local people in forest policy and administration. In particular, involvement in forest reform issues led to the organization of indigenous Pygmy hunter-gatherers, who are strongly dependent on forests, and recognition of the need for "free, prior and informed consultation" with them regarding forest-related projects. On the one hand, of course, there are various problems with the way this "free, prior and informed consultation" is implemented, and in many cases, it is nothing more than a supercilious briefing session (Ichikawa, 2006). However, the fact that this has begun to be advocated may itself be a noteworthy change. On the other hand, participatory mapping of forest use has been attempted, as a basis for asserting their customary rights to the forests. This is also based on the new forest law, which states that logging and conservation plans require clarification of existing rights over the area (*Code Forestier*, 2002). In addition, the Bank's operational policy also provides for special safeguards for indigenous peoples, such as Indigenous Peoples' Development Plans (IPDPs), to be combined with new forest projects when there are concerns about the impacts of new projects on indigenous communities. Moreover, in the recent projects supported by the Bank, forests are not only considered for harvesting timber, but also for use of so-called "minor products" (see Chapter 4), such as non-timber forest products, which are produced by trees in their living state. There are also rapidly growing interests in the carbon sequestration, water source protection, and other environmental services of forests. The recent Bank projects are encouraging the pursuit of these alternative forest uses to timber harvesting.

Of course, these changes are not brought about by impacts of the Inspection Panel alone. These changes have been driven by the interaction of various stakeholders, including the World Bank, the governments of the countries concerned, civil society, various NGOs including indigenous peoples' organizations, and the Inspection Panel. It is worth pointing out that the activities conducted by the Inspection Panel played a role in facilitating and modifying this process of change.

1.6. Recent trends: Combining global interests with local needs

1.6.1. Global interest in tropical forest conservation

I would like to briefly touch on recent developments regarding the conservation of tropical rainforests. In the early 2000s, when I was involved in the World Bank's inspection activities, there were two international developments on this issue. One was the "Stern Review" (Stern, 2006), a report on the economics of climate change led by the British economist Nicholas Stern. The other was the "Declaration on the Rights of Indigenous Peoples" (UN, 2007) adopted by the UN General Assembly in 2007. They are of particular importance to researchers working on the relationship between nature and culture in the African forest region. With various indigenous peoples whose livelihoods and cultures are strongly dependent on the forests, central Africa faces a serious challenge in how to deal with these two issues in an integrated manner.

According to the Stern Review (2006), economic loss from climate change would reach 5–10% of global GDP for the next century if global warming continues. In contrast, the cost of reducing greenhouse gases would be limited to about 1% of GDP. This means, reducing greenhouse gas emissions is both necessary and economically viable. While "environment" and "economy" have traditionally been perceived as a trade-off relationship, in which environmental protection has been presumed to have a negative economic impact, environmental protection is more advantageous from global economic standpoint. According to a report by FAO (2010), one of the main sources (next to the fuel use) of greenhouse gas (carbon dioxide) emissions was the destruction of surface vegetation (see also Stern Review), especially destruction of tropical forests in developing countries such as South America and Africa. Between 2000 and 2010 ce, 7 to 8 million hectares of forest were lost each year, with nearly half of the forest loss occurring in Africa. While large-scale logging is the primary cause of this loss, the expansion of agricultural land due to population growth is also considered a culprit in deforestation. African forests have been mainly used for slash-and-burn agriculture, in which forests were cleared, cultivated for one or two years, and then abandoned and left to fallow for 10–20

Chapter 1

years. With a thin population and little incentive to expand agricultural production, this type of slash-and-burn agriculture with long-term fallow was an adaptive method in a tropical rainforest environment with generally poor soil. However, the recent rapid population growth and the commercialization of agricultural products have jeopardized the sustainability of such slash-and-burn systems. In the past, the expansion of cultivated land in tropical rainforest areas has also been restrained by a lack of labor for the heavy work of clearing the forests. In recent years, however, the introduction of chainsaws has facilitated cutting large forest trees, while at the same time the commercialization of agricultural products has stimulated the agricultural production and expansion of crop fields.

A huge amount of carbon is sequestered in tropical rainforests, estimated at around 250–300 tons per hectare (Debroux et al., 2007; FAO, 2010). When forests are destroyed, the ability of trees to absorb carbon dioxide is lost, and the carbon stored in the trees eventually oxidizes and is released as carbon dioxide, fueling global warming. Greenhouse gas emissions from deforestation account for nearly one-fifth (18%) of total emissions, second only to energy-related emissions (FAO, 2010). Incidentally, during the five years since 2005, the carbon stored in forests has decreased by about 0.5 gigatons per year (FAO, 2010), which means that greenhouse gas emissions have also reached a significant amount.

Against the backdrop of recognition of such problems, new approaches have been considered for the protection of tropical rainforests. This approach focuses on the "environmental service" of forests. While the timber produced by tropical rainforests is an important source of revenue for developing countries, these countries receive only one to a few USD per ton of carbon equivalent. However, each ton of carbon emitted into the air as carbon dioxide causes loss of USD 85 to the global economy (Oliver, 2008). Thus, the cost of protecting forests is economically beneficial both to developing countries and the global economy as a whole. From this perspective, the World Bank and other international organizations have promoted measures such as the Forest Carbon Partnership Facility (FCPF). This is an effort to promote "Reduced Emissions from Deforestation and Forest Degradation (REDD)" by assigning economic value to remaining

Photo 1.7 Logging base in southeatsern Cameroon

forests. In other words, if developing countries protect their forests, they will receive payments from the Forest Carbon Partners Facility. In the DRC, for example, 580,000 hectares of forest were logged annually when the pilot project under this scheme was introduced (Debroux et al., 2007). If we assume that 20% of that was protected and that the country would receive USD 4 per ton for it, that alone would bring the revenue of more than USD 100 million for the country. Furthermore, in 2010, the Conference of the Parties to the United Nations Framework Convention on Climate Change (COP16) decided to establish the Green Climate Fund (GCF) (see Ministry of Foreign Affairs, 2020). This fund will support climate change mitigation and adaptation programs by certified national and private organizations. Thus, it appears that efforts are underway to incentivize countries to conserve forests. However, all of these efforts have been made from international movements or prompted "from above" initiatives.

1.6.2. Problems experienced by indigenous forest people

There is, however, a forgotten problem in these programs. The tropical rainforests in central Africa have long been inhabited by indigenous peoples who have been depending on the forests and developed their own unique culture. For them, the forests are the place where they

Chapter 1

obtain food, fuelwood and materials for tools and construction. The forests are the treasure trove of resources commonly referred to as Non-Timber Forest Products (NTFPs), including fruits, tubers, leaves, mushrooms and other foods, folk medicines to treat various diseases, and bushmeat as a source of protein, edible insects and honey. The roles played by the rich vegetation in environmental services, such as soil conservation and water source maintenance cannot be ignored. In the Congo Basin alone, there are between 60 and 75 million people who depend on a variety of resources and services provided by the forests (Debroux et al., 2007; WWF, n.d.). For the indigenous hunter-gatherers, whose livelihoods depend heavily on forest animals and plants, access to forests is indispensable.

It is important to note, however, that the use of non-timber forest products (NTFPs) can be compatible with environmental services such as carbon sequestration. As timber is the dead form and end product of trees, the impacts of logging on forest ecosystems are inevitable. Non-timber forest products (NTFPs), however, are predicated on the presence of living trees; the fruits, leaves, and bark are produced by trees in their living state, which the animals depend on for survival. It is a way to "use the forest without cutting down the trees." In other words, it utilizes the "interests" the trees generate, without damaging the "capital," the trees themselves. Therefore, their use is compatible with the carbon sequestration function and a variety of other environmental services. Indigenous peoples are not the only ones benefiting from non-timber forest products. A report by World Bank prepared by a team of consultants from various fields noted that "40 million people, or about 70% of the DRC's population of 60 million, obtain a modest income from non-timber forest products (Debroux et al., 2007)." Therefore, ensuring these people have access to forest resources is crucial to addressing social issues such as "alleviating poverty" and "human security."

In fact, the economic value derived from timber harvesting is only a small part of the economic value of the forests. As mentioned, according to a report on the forests in the DRC conducted immediately after the civil war, the economic value derived from timber production at that time was only about USD 160 million per year, including that of the informal sector. In contrast, the value of non-timber forest products such as fuelwood, bushmeat, wild fruits, honey, and medicinal plants collected by the local people was much higher, amounting to more than USD 2 billion per year in monetary value (calculated from market value, replacement value, willing to pay, etc., see Debroux et al., 2007). If access to these non-timber forest products were prohibited, the compensation would be enormous. Timber harvesting for export is neither the only nor the best way to ensure the welfare of the forest peoples, who currently face difficulties in securing the means of survival. For them, it is essential to first make sure that they can lead a comfortable, self-sufficient life. The most important thing is to ensure a nutritious diet can be obtained in a culturally appropriate manner. What they want is a subsistence base that is ample to meet their dietary as well as social and cultural needs. Any short-term benefits from logging operations will be meaning-less in the long term if they jeopardize the people's survival through forest destruction.

Moreover, any potential income generated from protecting the forests to provide a "carbon sequestration function" is unlikely to contribute much to the welfare of the forest peoples. Government control over the forests that would generate huge compensation payments would be tightened, and the resultant restricted access to the forests would make the life of local peoples increasingly difficult. This is not merely a groundless fear. Forest policies in central African countries were generally not well received. Whether they aimed at sustainable logging or biodiversity conservation in the forests, they have prevented forest people from using the forests in their customary ways, threatening livelihoods and cultures. Forest policies have also led to speculation in forests, conflicts over forest resources, and increased social inequality in the country (Debroux et al., 2007). Most previous programs for forest protection and utilization were indeed "green grabbing" (Fairhead, et al, 2013) by the state, international organizations and overseas capital. We must avoid creating a situation in which the local people, who best know the needs of the forests, "suffer under the guise of avoiding deforestation (Ernsting and Rughani, 2007)." The forests to be protected or exploited are forests that were originally inhabited only by them.

However, some forest resource uses, especially the hunting of animals, do not allow for optimism. Bushmeat hunting pressure in the DRC is currently too high for many game species to keep up with reproduction (Debroux et al., 2007). As will be discussed in detail in

Chapter 1

Chapter 3, excessive hunting pressure is largely due to the impact of the commercialization of wild game (bushmeat), especially the involvement of poachers and traders from outside the forests. Unlike the local people, outsiders who enter the forest in search of bushmeat seek to maximize their catch in a short period of time, without regard for the long-term sustainability of the resource. As a result, the local resource base will deteriorate. Therefore, to enable sustainable hunting, local people must be given exclusive forest use rights to prevent the intrusion of outsiders who pursue short-term gains. If this can be done, management by the local people, with a view to sustainable use, may pave the way to prevent over-exploitation of animal resources.

Under the laws of DRC and Cameroon, forests are owned by the state, and until recently there were no legal provisions defining the people's customary use rights. Although the new Congolese forest law (*Code Forestier*) clearly stipulates the use of forests by local communities, there are still many challenges to its effectiveness. As a result, outsiders have often entered the forests and continued poaching with the involvement of the local people. Without the intrusion of outsiders, local forest people could manage their resources from a long-term perspective. Therefore, it is essential to first establish the effective rights of local people to the forests. To prevent the degradation of forest ecosystems, it will be necessary to grant customary rights to forest peoples who have lived there for a long time and are highly sensitive to the dynamics of animal populations.

1.6.3. Indigenous peoples in Africa

In Africa, the "principle of indigeneity" is often recognized with regard to customary land use rights. The first settlers have rights to the land, and latecomers must ask their permission to use it. However, as mentioned earlier, in the case of hunter-gatherer Pygmies, the rights to the forest lands are held by their "patron" agriculturalists, even when they are regarded by the agriculturalists as "indigenous" to the area. They are then supposedly allowed to reside in the forest and use its resources under the patronage of, or through the authority of, the agricultural patrons. This is the view of the agricultural people who form the dominant group in the area. Of course, the Pygmy people objected to this view, but their complaints were rarely accepted by the wider society. This is, according to the agricultural people, due the lifestyle of hunter-gatherers who lead nomadic lives without permanent villages, with little "investment" in the land. There is clear discrimination here against hunter-gatherers.

The Declaration of the Rights of Indigenous Peoples, adopted by the United Nations in 2007, states indigenous peoples' rights to land and resources. There are examples in Africa, such as some of the San people in Botswana, who, after being forcibly displaced, managed to win rights to their traditional land, albeit with conditions, through a court case (Maruyama, 2018). The Hatza hunter-gatherers of Tanzania were also given the right to use their land on the foot of Ngorongoro Mountain (Yatsuka, 2018). However, the laws of many central African countries stipulate that forest land belongs to the state. Few countries in this region have yet actually implemented the non-binding UN declaration. In central African countries, even the concept of indigenous peoples, not to mention their rights to land, were not recognized by effective laws until recently.[5]

The UN Declaration on the Rights of Indigenous Peoples does not clearly define who are "indigenous people." The World Bank has stipulated in its Operational Directives (ODs) that special consideration must be given to "indigenous peoples" in the implementation of the Bank-supported projects. When I worked for the Inspection Panel, Operational Directive (OD 4.20) stated the following about "indigenous peoples." Indigenous peoples have:

(a) close attachment to ancestral territories and to the natural resources in these areas;

(b) self-identification and identification by others as members of a distinct cultural group;

(c) an indigenous language, often different from the national language;

---

5   The DRC government recently adopted a new law on "Indigenous Pygmy Peoples" in which the customary rights of its indigenous population were recognized. It is expected to secure land rights of the indigenous peoples and integrate them in conservation initiatives (Gauthier, 2022). We need to carefully monitor how this new law is implemented in practice.

Chapter 1

(d) presence of customary social and political institutions; and,

(e) primarily subsistence-oriented production (OD 4.20).

Around the same time, the Bank was reviewing its operational policies and directives. The revised operational policy on "Indigenous People" (OP 4.10), approved in 2013, describes the following (World Bank, 2013).

After stating that "Because of the varied and changing contexts in which Indigenous Peoples live and because there is no universally accepted definition of 'Indigenous Peoples,' this policy does not define the term," it explains:

...the term "Indigenous Peoples" is used in a generic sense to refer to a distinct, vulnerable, social and cultural group possessing the following characteristics in varying degrees:

(a) self-identification as members of a distinct indigenous cultural group and recognition of this identity by others;

(b) collective attachment to geographically distinct habitats or ancestral territories in the project area and to the natural resources in these habitats and territories;

(c) customary cultural, economic, social, or political institutions that are separate from those of the dominant society and culture; and

(d) an indigenous language, often different from the official language of the country or region. (World Bank, OP4.10)

Besides acknowledging the difficulty in defining the term "Indigenous People" and identifying them with "customary cultural, economic, social, or political institutions that are separate from those of the dominant society and culture," the most significant change from the previous OD 4.20 was the removal of the phrase "primarily subsistence-oriented production." These changes reflect the reality of indigenous peoples and recent development of research on indigenous peoples.

However, unlike nations created by immigrants in the Americas or Australia, it is not self-evident who are "indigenous people" in Africa. It is not appropriate to consider "indigenous issues" solely from such "essentialist" definitions. The reason many African countries hesitate to recognize the existence of "indigenous peoples" as distinct from other citizens is that "national unity" and "nation-building" have been important issues in Africa, where there are many multi-ethnic nations. It may be difficult for the government to readily accept the concept of "indigenous peoples," which may lead to the fragmentation of the "nation." Furthermore, under the World Bank's definition, many other African ethnic groups can be considered "indigenous" as well. The 2007 UN Declaration on the Rights of Indigenous Peoples does not provide a definition of "indigenous peoples" either. It is, therefore, necessary to consider the issue of "indigenous peoples" in the African social context.

The African Commission of Human and People's Rights (headquartered in Banjul, Gambia) issued the following statement on "indigenous peoples" in 2006:

> ...almost all African states host a rich variety of different ethnic groups... Basically all of these groups are indigenous to Africa. However, some are in a structurally subordinate position to the dominating groups and the state leading to marginalization and discrimination. It is this situation, which the indigenous concept in its modern analytic form, and the international legal framework attached to it, addresses. (ACHPR and IWGIA, 2006)

In this context, the Pygmy hunter-gatherers of the Congo Forest, who are in a structurally subordinate position, can be called "indigenous peoples." They are subject to the World Bank's "Safeguard on Indigenous Peoples" (OP 4.10), which was to be triggered. In fact, as mentioned earlier, in the DRC, the World Bank-supported forestry reform projects resulted in the reconsideration of the projects and triggering safeguards following a Pygmy indigenous organization's request for investigation submitted to the Inspection Panel. Along with this request and the subsequent review process, the various (Pygmy) indigenous groups in the Congo Basin were rapidly interacting and organizing themselves.

Chapter 1

The difficulties that the indigenous Pygmy people are facing today have mainly derived from their past relationships with other, dominant groups. Most of these Pygmy groups have maintained exchange relationships with neighboring agricultural groups. The relationships probably date back centuries, or even millennia (Bahuchet and Guillaume, 1979; Guillaume, 2001). Through these long-standing relationships, Pygmy people have specialized as hunter-gatherers, and in that role have connected, though loosely, with the broader society (see also Chapter 5).

But this relationship is not formed on equal terms. While central African people were gradually incorporated into the modern state system during colonization and independence (Grinker, 1994; Guillaume, 2001), the opportunities for the indigenous Pygmy people to participate in the activities in a broader society have been limited, as discussed in more detail in Chapter 5. Few Pygmy people are employed as civil servants. The political representation in the broader society has been almost monopolized by the dominant agricultural villagers.

Moreover, as mentioned, they have had no legal rights to the forest lands. In the forest laws of central African countries, the forest lands officially belong to the state, but there are also customary rights by which local people regulate the use of forest land. In Africa, customary rights are acknowledged on the principle of "first come, first served." Namely, in most African customary systems, land ownership belongs to those claiming prior occupancy (Colchester, 2001). However, in the case of Pygmy people, even if they are acknowledged as first inhabitants of the area, customary rights to the forest belong to their "patron" agricultural people. In the Congo Basin, the governments have ignored politically weak hunter-gatherers because they do not make investments in land, such as clearing and farming (Wilson/Survival, 2006). Hunting and gathering is not considered a legitimate or sustainable use of land, unlike agriculture practiced by dominant people. This is clearly discriminatory against nomadic hunter-gatherers. While the constitution of central African countries guarantees the fundamental rights and equality for all citizens, including culturally minority peoples, the reality is quite different. They are in fact underprivileged, as seen in these cases.

Around the time of the UN Declaration on the Rights of Indigenous Peoples, an international forum was held in 2007 in the town of Impfondo, on the right bank of the Ubangi River (a tributary of the

Congo River) in the Republic of Congo, bringing together the various Pygmy peoples of the Congo Basin (James, 2007). While they had lived in small groups of a few dozen scattered throughout central Africa and had little mutual contact until then, they held a large gathering in search of a common identity as "forest people" and their customary rights to the forest. They discussed discrimination by dominant groups against marginalized minority groups in various parts of the Congo Basin, and appealed for the necessary protection of the forests they have been living in. The gathering brought together Pygmy groups not only from the DRC and the Republic of Congo, but also from Cameroon, Gabon, and the Central African Republic. Some of them traveled 2,000 kilometers overland to attend the meeting. They called the indigenous Pygmy groups in the region "the third world of the third world," and appealed to the world about the hardships they were facing (James 2007). This was the first opportunity for the Pygmy people to assert their identity and their rights to the forest to the outside world. Since that time, a network of indigenous Pygmy organizations has rapidly developed, and NGOs have been established in various regions of central Africa. These organizations also became linked to global indigenous networks, where they began to make their voices heard.

The future of humanity depends on how we can maintain and develop rich cultural diversity while coexisting with the natural environment. It will be a touchstone for the future of humanity, to find and implement solutions to the problems currently occurring in the African rainforests, that is, to integrate forest conservation with the livelihoods and cultures of indigenous peoples. The success of the indigenous peoples' movement, which is being driven by the UN Declaration on the Rights of Indigenous Peoples, will depend on the international support and the understanding of the governments of these countries.

Chapter 2

Where Humans Coexist with Forests

Chapter 2

Photo on the previous page: Mbuti forest camp

2.1. Contemporary environmental problems and "infinite nature"

As humanity enters the 21st century, environmental problems are considered to be an issue that must be addressed by all of humankind, along with issues such as social disparity and ethnic conflicts. Many international conferences, academic societies, and journalists have devoted a great deal of time and space to discussing the progress of environmental destruction and nature conservation, as well as technical and policy responses to these issues. However, in contrast to the increasing threats of environmental destruction on a global scale and the growing awareness of the problem, the reality of the relationship between humans and the environment in local communities has only recently begun to attract attention. In particular, the economic activities of local people are greatly affected by the local environment and in turn, impact it in various ways. Nevertheless, there are still many issues to be clarified regarding the relationship between humans and the environment in such local contexts. Understanding environmental issues in particular areas and cultures is now one of the main interests of anthropology, which explores the cultural relationship between humans and nature, and especially ecological anthropology, which deals with the interaction between humankind and the environment.

The contemporary environmental problems are manifested in two ways: resource depletion and environmental pollution (including carbon dioxide emissions). This indicates that the illusion that the natural environment is a "never-ending fountain" and at the same time a "vessel that swallows everything" has collapsed. What was thought to be an "infinite environment" is in fact a "finite" and fragile one. The illusion of an "infinite environment" has been supported by conventional economic activities and perceptions of nature.

Human economic activity involves (1) extracting resources from the environment and (2) consuming them to produce a variety of goods, (3) consuming the goods thus produced and producing new goods, and finally (4) disposing of the residues of this consumption. So-called production means converting the Earth's "resources" into various forms of "goods," consuming large amounts of resources in the process and emitting "waste" as a result of such consumption. Production consumes resources, and consumption produces waste. However, until

Chapter 2

recently both ends of this system had been largely neglected. Only the middle two have been separated, and production has expanded. The global expansion of "mass production-mass consumption" has been promoted by the capitalist market economy as a self-generating system which entails the creation of demands. Contemporary environmental destruction results from this expansionary movement in pursuit of wealth, supported by the illusory perception that nature is infinite. This "view of infinite nature" underpins modern economics, which considers the natural environment to be "external to economies" or "non-essential givens." The problem lies in the assumption that the activities conducted inside the market – the center of economic activity – have no effect on nature outside the market. This is the basis of the illusion that resource depletion and pollution will not occur due to economic activity (Murota et al. 1995; Mita, 1996; Nakamura, 1996).

In the past, however, in many parts of the world, the natural environment could be considered to be effectively "infinite" or "unlimited." This view of "infinite nature" had a certain background. One of the factors for such a view of nature was the fact that the pressures to extract resources and the scale of production were extremely small compared with the vast resources available in the environment. While many of the Earth's resources, especially fossil fuels and mineral resources, are non-renewable, solar energy is almost inexhaustible, at least as far as the time scale of a human life or history is concerned. Thus, biological resources and environments which are produced and maintained by solar energy, can be consumed, polluted, and degraded, but also have the potential to regenerate and to some extent, cleanse themselves. Within the range of such self-sustaining capacity, or tolerance, nature appears as if it were enduring. In fact, it sometimes even appears to grow richer with time.

The notion of "nature" as infinitely large and inexhaustible probably arose from trust in the sustainability of nature. Such trust in nature's abundance was a rather common view for people whose livelihoods were dependent upon the "giving environment" (Bird-David, 1990; 1992). For example, when the San (Bushmen), hunter-gatherers of the Kalahari Desert, were encouraged to adopt agriculture, they asked, "Why should we sow the seeds when we have more than enough *mongongo* nuts?" (wild nuts of *Schinziophyton rautanenii*, Euphorbiaceae) (Lee, 1989). Trust in the abundance of nature is based in the belief that the resource will regenerate. A similar perception is shared by rainforest hunter-gatherers such as the Mbuti, for whom the idea of forest protection or the exhaustion of its resources by humans had never arisen. Before the rapid degradation of forest resources in recent decades, in particular, the loss of animals due to deforestation and excessive hunting pressure, they would probably have perceived that it is humans who were protected by the forest (not vice versa) and that animals have disappeared because the "Apakumandura" (i.e., master of the forest) had "closed the forest." Otherwise, they would say that the animals were no longer being caught easily as the animals had simply moved to other areas (Ichikawa, 1996).

2.2. Human impacts on vegetation

It is not just that they have a vague trust in nature. In certain areas, human activities have contributed to environmental sustainability and even to the nurturing of a richer environment. Recently, there have been a series of reports from the regions far from modern civilization on the positive impacts of human activities on the environment. Here I would like to give some examples of indigenous societies in South America and agricultural societies in West Africa that have attracted attention in the 1990s.

The Kayapo Indians in South America are slash-and-burn agriculturalists who live in a mosaic environment of forest and savanna in the eastern Amazon region of Brazil. They utilize the forest resources of the region in a variety of ways, but also "cultivate" the environment. The "forest islands" called *apete* scattered throughout the savanna are particularly noteworthy examples of such efforts. In fact, 85% of the plant species on *apete* was planted by the Kayapo, rather than originally growing there. They first create green manure in the existing *apete*, then take it to a depression in the savanna area and mix it with mineral-rich soil from termite mounds to create a small mound. There they plant useful plants such as for food, medicine, and material culture, as well as food for animals they hunt. When fully grown, the *apete* created in this way would cover an area of 5 to 10 hectares, where plants gathered from an area as large as Western Europe were planted. In addition to these *apetes*, forests with particularly useful plants are scattered along their travel and migration routes. In the Kayapo territory, the network of

Chapter 2

such migratory routes extended for 500 kilometers, along which various wild fruit trees and medicinal plants were planted together with crops such as wild yam (Posey, 1992).

A similar case has been reported from west Africa. Forest patches known as "forest islands" are scattered throughout the transitional zone between rainforest and savanna in Guinea (Conakry is the capital). These forest patches are round in shape, roughly one to two kilometers in diameter, and within each is an agriculturalists' village surrounded by the forest. Since the early colonial period, these forest patches had been considered by administrators, scientists, and others to be the last remnants (relics) of the vast forests that had once covered the region, and which had barely survived destruction by burning and cultivation by the inhabitants. Until recently, this view prevailed and the landscape was considered to be in the final stages of "anthropogenic savannahization." With the growing concern for global environmental issues, the rehabilitation of these "relic forests" became a target of international assistance.

However, Fairhead and Leach (1996), who studied the area, showed from historical documents, old photographs, and oral traditions of local people that these forest islands had in fact increased due to human intervention. They also showed that the local people were fertilizing the land through various daily activities, controlling wildfires to prevent grassland expansion, and converting fallow areas into forests. Thus, they corrected the misreading of the landscape by previous scientists and administrators and criticized forest protection policies based on such misconceptions of the landscape.

Recent examination of human history in the forests on a global scale (Roberts, 2019) revealed extensive human impact on tropical forests which had often been thought to have contained few human traces. It has also been demonstrated that Aboriginal peoples in Australia have long practiced land burning to encourage the growth of certain useful plants or to attract animals to newly sprouting plants. Traces of such interventions into the vegetation are found over extensive areas of Australia, which has been called "the biggest estates on earth" (Gammage, 2011). The practice is called "cool burning" (small-scale controlled burning), or "cultural burning" and is presently being re-evaluated for better land management in modern Australia. In North America, there is evidence that indigenous peoples in California modified the flora and fauna of their areas for more than 10,000 years through fire burning, tilling, weeding, and other works on the land (Anderson, 2005).

It is thus mistaken to assume that human activities are invariably harmful to the environment, and that only those who are aware of their harmful effects would make efforts to preserve the environment. It is not human production and consumption, or even human existence itself, that is a problem for the environment, but rather the "social system" of unlimited expansion of production and consumption that results in environmental destruction. Such a "social system" has institutionalized certain forms of interaction between humans and the natural environment.

Today we see the phenomenon of "landscape polarization" as the Earth is divided between "wildlife sanctuaries" (protected areas) that exclude humans and "human-made spaces" created by economic and social development. In the future, nature reserves may be reduced to small areas scattered around the globe, while everything else will be developed into artificial spaces such as cities, farms, and neatly planted parks. Is there a path between these two extremes where nature and humans can coexist harmoniously? As a researcher who has long been interested in the relationships between humans and nature in Africa, I would like to look at the life of indigenous peoples in the central African rainforests, with the hope that there may be a world in which humans and nature coexist in a desirable way.

2.3. Development and conflicts in the forests of central Africa

The forests of the Congo Basin comprise one-fifth of the world's tropical rainforests, or about 150–200 million hectares. The tropical rainforests in central Africa had been logged since the contact with the West along the Atlantic coast, while the central parts of the Congo Basin had not been logged on a large scale until recently, partly due to the lack of transportation access along the Congo River. A major obstacle was the great waterfalls downstream of the Congo River, where the explorer Stanley had suffered when he was the first Westerner to travel down the river (Stanley, 1890). The present Democratic Republic of the Congo

Chapter 2

(DRC) became the private property of King Leopold II after the Berlin Conference at the end of the 19th century. From then until the early colonial period by Belgium in the 20th century, the extraction of forest products such as wild rubber, ivory, and copal (resins) was promoted in the interior of the Congo Basin (see also Chapter 5). When full-scale Belgian colonial management was introduced around World War II, mining and plantation development progressed, but the vast forests of the interior remained untouched. More recently, however, with the development of roads, water transportation, and other infrastructure, and with logging in Asia and South America becoming more difficult due to depletion of easily accessible timber resources, the timber harvesting has rapidly spread to the interior of Africa. In the northern part of the Republic of Congo (capital Brazzaville), for example, hundreds of thousands of hectares of forest were targeted for logging programs in the 1990s. In the southeastern part of Cameroon, large areas of forest have been designated as logging areas or nature reserves based on the revised Forest Law of 1994, which restricted the Baka hunter-gatherers' and other local people's access to the forests they have long been dependent upon (Ichikawa et al., 2016; 2020; also see Chapter 4).

In the Ituri Forest of the DRC, large-scale logging had not yet begun in the 1970s and 1980s, when I was conducting my fieldwork, because the road conditions were extremely poor. However, in the 1980s, when the extraction of mineral resources such as gold, which had been prohibited in the Ituri Forest, was legalized, many people moved into the forest. The people of Ituri, including some of the Mbuti, were also engaged in collecting gold dust. In the 1990s, the extraction of columbite-tantalite (commonly known as coltan), a mineral used to make capacitors in electrical appliances, began to draw more and more people to the forest. Many of these migrants were farmers from the densely populated and land-scarce hills of the eastern Congo. They cultivated farmland in parallel with mineral extraction. Moreover, many of them expanded their cultivation not only for subsistence but also for sales of the crops. Hunting pressure on wild animals increased as they sought bushmeat, an important source of protein in this region where livestock were scarce. This rapid population influx and the accompanying subsistence and other activities in the forest resulted in major changes in the forest ecosystem.

Where Humans Coexist with Forests

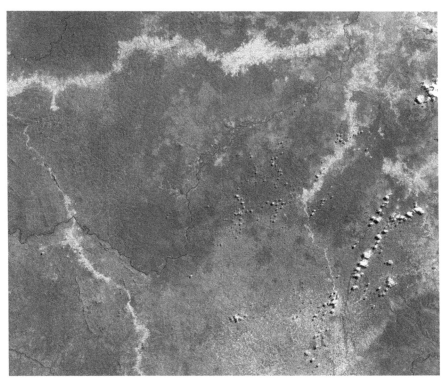

Photo 2.1 Satellite image of the southeastern part of the Ituri Forest. Forest destruction promoted by the influx of migrants seeking for land and minerals, as shown in the lower part

The civil war in the DRC that began in the latter half of the 1990s caused great turmoil for the people in the region. The abundant mineral resources became a source of funding for rebel forces and militias. As a result, conflicts over resources continue today. The abundant natural resources would have enriched people's lives, but in this region, the resources have been the reason for constant conflict. The situation is paradoxical and tragic. Then logging for commercial purposes started, and the wood harvested from the forests was transported to cities in the densely populated eastern part of the country, as well as outside the country.

In the following, I will look at the relationships of the Mbuti hunter-gatherers with the forest world and their way of life during my visit in the 1970s and 80s, before the Ituri forest became what it is today.

Chapter 2

Photo 2.2 Gold miners dug up the former river course and stripped the bark of giant trees to create flumes for gold sorting

2.4. Cultural dependence on forest diversity: Cultural ecology

In order to see how heavily dependent the Mbuti people were on the forests, we need only to take a glance at their forest camp. Their hemispherical huts are made of the thin trees and leaves of *Marantaceae* plants collected in the forest; their simple wooden chairs and beds, and tools such as baskets and vines for transport, are all made of forest plants; a woman grates and cooks forest nuts, called *mbau* (*Gilbertiodendron dewevrei*, Caesalpinipoideae), in front of a small single-family hut. Material culture, such as the comb that the woman sticks in her hair and the container for the nuts, is also made of plants. The children's playthings and the fruit juice for coloring their faces are also products of the forest. Here and there in the camp, remains of wild fruits, tubers, and other food are found scattered on the ground. After sunset, they sing and dance until late at night with the spirits that appear from the forest in response to the booming polyphonic chorus. The forest is closely connected to all aspects of their life, not only in terms of food, shelter, tools, and other material things, but also in terms of plays and rituals. Their culture uses the various possibilities that the forest provides.

Where Humans Coexist with Forests

Photo 2.3 A Mbuti forest camp. Various forest plants are used for food, materials for tools, ornaments, dwelling and other purposes

During our research in the Ituri forest, we collected extensive forest plants and recorded their ethnobotanical knowledge. We collected over 1,000 plant specimens, comprising a total of nearly 600 species, and interviewed the Mbuti and Efe people about their names, various uses, and other ethnobotanical knowledge (Terashima and Ichikawa, 2003). Although 600 species represent only a small part of the total, given the vast plant world in the tropical rainforest, it is a reasonable number to get an overview of hunter-gatherers' relationship with plants. In the Ituri forest, about 200 species of woody plants can be easily collected in the nearby forest. However, collecting more than 300 species takes time. The majority of the 600 species we collected were woody plants, but for an amateur botanist to collect that number of species, it took nearly a month of searching.

Although tropical rainforests have often been considered as "green desert" where little human food is available, central African forests, in fact, offer a sort of "cornucopia of food." Of the plants collected, more than 100 were used for food. While a considerable proportion (60 % in weight) of their current diet is comprised of cassava, plantain banana and other agricultural crops obtained from the agricultural villagers and their own small fields (Ichikawa, 1986), they still use dozens of wild

Chapter 2

2.4.1 Nuts of *Irvingia robur*

2.4.2 Fruit of *Landolphia jumellei*

2.4.3 *Canarium schweinfurthi*

2.4.4 *Aframomum sanguineum*

2.4.5 *Anonidium manni*

Photo 2.4 Forest as cornucopia of food plants

plants which are highly prized. These include various nuts with high lipid contents such as *Irvingia gabonensis* (called *esele* by the Mbuti, and *ambele* by the Efe), starchy food like wild yams (*Dioscorea praehensilis*, called *aduaka* by the Mbuti, *kango* by the Efe) and fruit of *Canarium schweinfurthii* (called *nbe* by the Mbuti, *opi* by the Efe), all of which are an important energy source, sweet and sour fruits of *Landolphia* spp. and *Aframomum* spp., which are a source of vitamins and refreshment, and narcotics like cola nuts (*liko* by Mbuti and *eme* by Efe). Other plants were widely used as spices and seasonings, such as African pepper *(Piper guineense,* called *abeka* by the Mbuti, *beka* by the Efe) and African ginger (*Aframomum* spp.). The fruit of *Dioscoreophyllum cumminsii* (*kisombi,* belonging to Menispermaceae; the tubers are also eaten) contains natural sweet substance called "monellin," up to 3,000 times sweeter than sucrose, and the fruit *Thaumatococus daniellii* has another

2.5.1 Making a hunting net

2.5.2 Coloring with *Rothmannia* fruit juice

2.5.3 Making bark cloth of Ficus Lianas

2.5.4 Decorated bark cloth

Photo 2.5 Plants used for material culture

natural sweet substance called "thaumatin." Many of these are being examined as future food or medicinal resources. As will be described below (Chapter 4), these forest products are sold at town markets as condiments along with consommé cubes and other products used for cooking. It is evident that these forest condiments are valued by town dwellers as a "taste of their homeland."

A tropical rainforest is much like a chemical factory. Many plants in tropical rain forests accumulate various toxic substances, called "secondary compounds," as adaptation against herbivorous animals' feeding. Some of these, if administered properly, could be used as medicine for curing diseases, or as poison for hunting and fishing. The Mbuti people are careful observers of plant properties. They explore the potential use of plants for medicinal purposes by examining the color, texture, smell and taste of the leaves, bark, roots, and resins of plants and guess their applicability for medicinal uses. In the Ituri Forest, we recorded more than 100 species that are used for medicinal or poisonous purposes.

Chapter 2

Photo 2.6 Plants used for arrow poison

Photo 2.7 Honey collecting

There were more than 300 species of plants used as materials for a wide variety of tools, decoration, and construction. An average Mbuti family possesses less than 100 pieces of tools, ornaments, household utensils and simple furniture, which is a very small number. More than 80% of them were made, either totally or in part, of plant materials (Tanno, 1981; Ichikawa, 1992). Leading a nomadic life in the forest, material wealth such as household goods is literally a burden. Their lifestyle is to procure necessary materials wherever they go and process them into the tools and other things they need. Things that cannot be

Where Humans Coexist with Forests

carried, such as huts, and simple chairs and beds are made on the spot, and either abandoned or burned when moving on to the next camp. Their material culture is literally a "forest culture" that makes full use of the abundant plants in the forest.

Plants are also used in various rituals. Small seeds or wooden pieces of certain plants on which forest animals feed are put on the body as ritual medicine for good hunting. Conversely, other plants are used for protection from diseases that are believed to be caused by wild animals (see Chapter 3). Mbuti hunters smother their bodies with the smoke of certain forest plants to hide their odor so that they will not be noticed by the animals. Or, they smear their faces with charcoal from burning the plants so that their bodies would not be visible to the forest animals. In other words, they try to assimilate their bodies with the forest by using forest plants. There are more than 150 different plants used for such purposes.

In addition to these direct uses, many plants have indirect significance for the Mbuti. The animals that are hunted feed on the plants of the forest. They know the plants on which wild animals feed, their fruiting seasons and their distribution. During fruiting seasons they build scaffolds on the trees to ambush animals that come to feed on fallen fruit. While the large trees that make up the canopy of mature forests may appear to be of little value to them, many of them are important as nectar sources, providing homes for wild bees. Honey is their favorite food. During the season they depend on honey for more than 80% of their caloric intake (Ichikawa, 1981). In addition, a variety of edible insects feed on the forest plants.

The forest is home to a supernatural being called Apakumandura, literally meaning "master" or "father" of the forest, who controls the forest world. When the hunt failed, they said it was because this master of the forest "closed" or "chilled" the forest. The *akobisi* (*Uvariopsis congolana*, Annonaceae) tree, a small cauliflory tree (with flowers and fruit grown directly from the main stems) of several meters in height, which grows only in deep, dark forests is said to have a special relationship with the Apakumandura. It is taboo to break or cut this tree. If the tree is accidentally cut, Apakumandura will be offended, and it is necessary to beat the buttress roots of a large nearby tree in place of a drum and dance to appease his anger.

Chapter 2

The forests are thus used in various ways by the Mbuti. They do not, however, have only positive images of the forest. For example, they feed on a wide variety of wild animals, numbering more than 200 species (Ichikawa, 1982; 1987). While these animals are indeed their favorite food and an important source of protein, some of them, called *kuweri*, are thought to be dangerous, bringing diseases and other misfortunes. For example, genets and black Guinea fowls are avoided by parents of small children, because eating them can cause febrile illness in their children (see description in Chapter 3). Of about 60 species of mammals documented as food, nearly 60% (34 species) are considered *kuweri* animals, which may bring disease to the person who eats them or their children. Eating them is avoided by parents with infants before they start walking (Ichikawa, 1987; see also Chapter 3). Therefore, when Mbuti parents give the meat of a new animal to their children, they pay attention to whether the children are sufficiently grown and strong enough to resist such dangers of wild animals. Forest animals thus have an ambivalent value, being both valuable food and a possible source of unidentifiable diseases and other problems.

In these ways, the forest has a variety of meanings for the Mbuti, both material and spiritual, direct and indirect, positive and negative. Their relationship with the forest is diverse and ambivalent. The forest is the source of a variety of values necessary for the maintenance of Mbuti culture and livelihood. Their culture depends on the diversity of the forest itself.

It should be noted that some of these forest resources are sold in local markets. The caffeine-containing kola nut (*Cola acuminata*, Malvaceae) has long been traded in the African interior as a stimulant. In the Congo Basin, the bitter, astringent fruit is chewed directly or pounded with the bitter fruit of *Solanum* sp. (called *ngbako* by the Mbuti) and red peppers in a mortar and added to boiling water to make a stimulant drink called *liboliko* (meaning "cola water," also called *bombolya* in Swahili dialect). Other forest products often found in local markets are: *Irvingia* spp. used for oily condiments, African ginger used for medicinal purposes and as a seasoning, edible insects and honey, which can be gathered in large quantities in their seasons, and especially the bushmeat from hunting. Some of them, such as *Irvingia* nuts are not only traded within the region but are sold in markets in other parts of Africa or transported

2.8.1 *Piper guineense* (lower) and African zinger (upper)
2.8.2 *Gnetum* leaves with rich protein contents
2.8.3 Forest nuts used for condiments

Photo 2.8 Non-timber forest products sold at local market

even to European cities and used by African immigrants to prepare their homeland's cuisine.

There is growing interest in these non-timber forest products. Plans for forest conservation by commercializing these products are underway (see Chapter 4). Although there are still many challenges to be overcome, it is important to understand that the central African rainforest is a treasure trove of resources about which we still have very little information. To obtain such information, we need to learn the traditional knowledge accumulated by the people who have lived in these forests for hundreds or thousands of years.

One thing should be noted here, however. Most of the forest plants and animals used by the indigenous forest peoples (hunter-gatherers) are not commercialized, nor exchanged with the people from the outside world. They are, however, used in a diversity of ways and have important meanings to the local people's life and culture. We should appreciate, therefore, the use values of these plants and animals. The culture of the indigenous forest hunter-gatherers is dependent on and inseparable from the diversity of forest plants and animals. It is essentially different from the market economy, which demands only a few resources with high market value, such as timber, ivory, bushmeat, etc., ignoring the cultural value of other resources. The commercialization of forest resources might therefore distort the people's rich forest-based culture, which can be seen as a criticism of our own, overly practical and commercially

Chapter 2

oriented use of the forest. We should always keep this in mind when considering the commercialization of forest products.

2.5. Human impacts on the forest environment: Historical ecology

2.5.1. Wild food plants in secondary forests

For the Mbuti people who depend on the forest in diverse ways, the forest as a whole, rather than individual resources, is essential to maintaining their lives and culture. Forest conservation is, therefore, necessary to sustain their lives and culture. What then are the impacts of their various activities on the forest environment? If forest resources are consumed and not adequately reproduced, their use of the forest cannot be sustainable.

While more than 100 plant species are used as food by the Mbuti people in the Ituri forest, about 10–15 of the major food species account for 60–80% of the wild plant food consumed (Ichikawa, 1992). We have noticed some interesting facts from examining the habitats where major food plants grow. Of the 13 major plant species used by a Mbuti group, 8 were so-called sun trees, which do not germinate and will not grow without sufficient sunlight. These include the oil-rich nut-producing *Antrocaryon nannanii* (called *essenge*, belonging to Anacardiaceae) and *Ricinodendron heudelotii* (*songo*, Euphorbiaceae). Although these plants are now found as high trees that make up the forest canopy, they are essentially sun trees that cannot grow in shade. The same is true of *Canarium schweinfurthii* (belonging to Burseraceae and called *nbe* by the Mbuti). These giant *nbe* trees are often found in deep forest at the site of a former village or campsite. *Landolphia* spp. (Apocynaceae) and *Aframomum* spp. (Zingiberaceae), which produce sweet and sour refreshing fruits, are also common in disturbed environments or forest margins with good light condition (Ichikawa, 1996). In other words, many of the major edible plants germinated and grew in open spaces or "clearings" which allowed sufficient light to reach the ground surface.

When walking through the forest, we find gaps where the forest canopy opens and light shines through. These gaps are often caused by fallen trees due to natural phenomena such as wind, rain, and lightning, but they can also be created by human activity. For example, if the Mbuti find a beehive in the hollow of a large tree, they will cut it down from the base if the tree has few branches to climb and the wood is of soft material. Thus, a gap is formed in the forest by humans, much like a natural gap. When a new campsite is opened, the small to medium-sized trees are also cut down, which eventually allows sunlight to shine in. Such human activity creates an environment favorable to the growth of sun trees.

In forest settlements, a new generation of edible plants may sprout from discarded food waste, such as the parts of wild yam tubers, fruits and nuts. The sweet and sour fruits of *Landolphia owariensis* (called *buma* by the Mbuti, of Apocynaceae family), for example, are eaten by swallowing the seeds whole, since the pulp and seeds are difficult to separate. The seeds, which become easier to germinate by passing through the digestive tract, are dispersed through excretion around the camp where light conditions are favorable for germination and growth. In fact, we can see many seedlings of edible plants germinating from such waste around the camp.

In addition, large quantities of organic matter and minerals in the form of firewood and food are collected and relocated to human settlements from a broad swathe of the forest. Through human consumption, these residues accumulate in the vicinity of the camp. Although few studies have properly measured these residues, according to Nishida (1997), an ethnoarchaeologist who studied the environmental modification effects of human habitation and activity, the annual consumption of food and fuel by a group of about 25 people in the prehistoric Jomon period in Japan was estimated at roughly 400 kg of nitrogen, 200 kg of phosphorus, 70 kilograms of potassium and 110 kilograms of calcium. This is equivalent to the fertilizer used in a chestnut orchard that produces 10 tons of chestnuts per year.

Mbuti hunter-gatherers in the Ituri Forest consume roughly three kilograms of firewood and one kilogram of food per adult per day in their forest camps. It is estimated that an average group size of 40–50 Mbuti living in one place for about a month would bring in 3.5–4.5 tons of firewood and would consume approximately 1–1.5 tons of animal and plant food. The residues accumulate around the camp as ashes and waste (and excrement). Not all of this remains in the soil, but the

Chapter 2

amount of nitrogen supplied by food alone is equivalent to about 200 kg of ammonium sulfate (Ichikawa, 2001), a frequently used fertilizer.

Soils in tropical rainforests are said to be poor, with little humus layer developed. Soil nutrients are quickly absorbed by plants, then by the animals that feed on the plants. Human settlements are places where such organic matter and minerals, which are only thinly distributed in the forest, are collected from a wide range and concentrated in the form of useful resources such as firewood and food. They are disposed of or excreted through human consumption and returned to the soil around the camp in the form of minerals and organic matters. Those soil nutrients thus continue circulating in the forest unless they are washed away by rainwater or carried to the outside world as forest products. Human habitation and activity have the effect of creating concentrations of these nutrients in the forest, which in their natural state are only thinly distributed.

There is a loose territorial system among the Mbuti of the Ituri forest. Each group of several tens to a hundred Mbuti people, related by blood or marriage, considered 150 to 250 km² of forest as their territory, and hunted and gathered within that area. Although the boundaries between groups were not clearly defined, forest paths connecting several campsites and hunting and gathering trails extending from the campsites formed the "skeleton" of each group's territory. In this way, most of the Ituri Forest is claimed by one of the Mbuti (and Efe) groups, although some places are frequently used, and others in remote places are rarely visited. In each territory, there are four to six camps, which they move between every two weeks to two months, depending on the availability of plant and animal resources (Ichikawa, 1978; see also Fig. 2.1). As time passes, old camps are abandoned, and new camps are opened. I recorded as many as 20 campsite names in one of the Mbuti territories, as far as they remembered. Most of the old sites I visited were covered with secondary vegetation that had flourished after the camps had been abandoned, but the lack of large trees and the tree species composition (dominated by fast-growing trees, characteristic of secondary forests) made them look different from the surrounding mature forest.

However, there are stronger impacts on the vegetation than that of the hunter-gatherers, that is, the activities of agriculturalists. At the time of my research in the Ituri Forest in the 1970s through 1980s, agriculturalists' settlements were concentrated along roads running east-west and north-south through the Ituri Forest. However, before the construction of these roads between the 1930s and 1950s, and their forced displacement by the colonial government for the road maintenance and tax collection, small settlements of agriculturalists were widely dispersed throughout the forest. Along the old trading routes there were trading posts and large villages in the early 1900s, such as Mawanbi post on the bank of Ituri River (see Powel-Cotton, 1907), which had already grown over with thick vegetation. Some of these old settlement sites can still be discerned as secondary forests in the satellite image shown as bright yellow patches. The distribution of the Mbuti, who maintained close exchange relations with the agriculturalists, was also likely dispersed accordingly (Ichikawa, 1996).

In the Ituri Forest, the traces of these former settlements and fields remain here and there as old secondary forest. The vegetation in these areas is dominated by species belonging to the Moraceae, Euphorbiaceae, and Ulmaceae families, and can be clearly distinguished from the mature forests dominated by tall trees belonging to the Caesalpinioideae. According to a study by ecologists Hart and Hart (1986), these secondary forests contained an average of 13 food tree species per hectare, compared to only about 6 per hectare in the mature (primary) forests, where there had been little human influence. In addition, the fields that have been abandoned recently still contain some crops, making them excellent feeding grounds for wild animals. Mbuti hunt animals that are attracted to these old fields and settlements and exchange the hunted meat for the agriculturalists' crops. In this way, the Ituri Forest, as a living environment for humans, has become more favorable for humans through interaction between the Mbuti hunter-gatherers, agriculturalists, wild plants and animals. Given these considerations, we think that understanding the Congo Basin Forest as a human living environment requires reconsideration of the ecological significance of human interactions with this forest, particularly the impacts of human habitation and activities on the forest over time.

Chapter 2

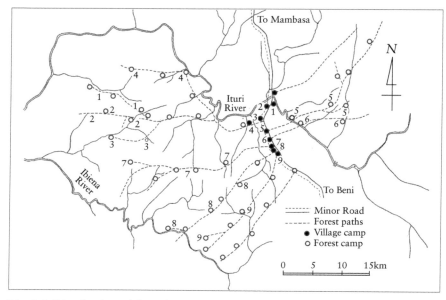

Fig. 2.1 Distribution of the Mbuti territories and camps in the Teturi area

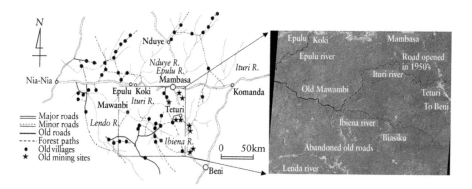

Fig. 2.2 Distribution of old village sites in the southern part of the Ituri Forest (Information of old village sites were obtained from the map published in the 1950s, *Zone de Mambasa*, 1:100,000)

2.5.2. Wild yam question: Re-evaluation of the secondary forest environment

As an example of the importance of vegetation modification to the living environment for humans, let us explore "wild yam question." This example illustrates how important the environment in which wild yams grow is to human subsistence, and how this environment has been modified by human activities.

Central African hunter-gatherers had long been considered to be the original inhabitants of the forest, having lived there long before the Bantu-speaking cultivators arrived in the region. In the late 1980s, however, questions were raised about this conception of indigenous forest hunter-gatherers. The questions arose from observations that: 1) there is virtually no hunter-gatherer group today that relies solely upon wild food resources (i.e., no group that exists without cultivated food obtained either from their own fields or from neighboring agriculturalists), 2) no archaeological remains of hunter-gatherers have been found in tropical rainforests (but see Mercader et al., 2000; Mercader and Brooks, 2001; Mercader, 2002), and 3) there is not sufficient wild food in the forest to sustain an exclusive hunting-and-gathering lifestyle, particularly in the dry season when little fruit, honey, or other food is available. In reference to this final point, and the fact that wild yams constitute a key food resource in humid tropical forests, the question is often called the "wild yam question" (Bailey et al., 1989; Bailey and Headland, 1991; Headland 1987; 1997).[1]

Such a view was apparently influenced by "revisionism," which dominated the study of hunter-gatherer societies in the 1980s and 1990s. What began as a review of the history of the San hunter-gatherers (Bushmen) of the Kalahari Desert in southern Africa spilled over into the study of hunter-gatherer societies in central Africa. The traditional view was that hunter-gatherers maintained their unique culture in isolation from other societies. Revisionists, however, argue that such peoples have rather been kept in the state of hunter-gatherers through repeated contact and interaction with other, dominant peoples. Revisionism therefore

---

1   Recent research in Cameroon has indicated that nuts of *Irvingia gabonensis* (*peke*) can be an important food resource during the rainy season (see Hirai, 2014 and Hirai and Yasuoka, 2020).

Chapter 2

argues that hunter-gatherer societies and lifestyles must be placed in the context of history (Wilmsen, 1986; 1989). From this perspective, there have also been doubts about the authenticity of hunter-gatherer societies in the rainforests (Bailey et al., 1989; Headland, 1997).

Several studies have been conducted on the food resource base in the central African forests, mainly on the availability of wild yams (Hladik et al., 1984; Bahuchet et al., 1991; Hladik and Dounias, 1993; Dounias, 1993). Sato (2001a) conducted an "experimental survey" to examine the potential of wild yams, and the possibility of a hunting and gathering lifestyle based exclusively on foraging among the Baka people in Cameroon. There was, however, no empirical study based on the actual foraging lifestyles of the hunter-gatherers in the region which includes agricultural goods bartered with neighboring peoples.

Progress was made on this issue from our research in the forests of Cameroon, located on the western part of the Congo Basin. We had begun an ecological anthropological study of hunter-gatherers (Baka Pygmies) living in the rainforest of the East Region of Cameroon in the mid-1990s, when the political turmoil in the former Zaire and Congo-Brazzaville disrupted our research. Yasuoka, who joined this study in 2001, accompanied the Baka people on their "*molongo*," a long-term hunting and gathering expedition for the entirety of the dry season, and collected quantitative data on their livelihood activities and diet during this period. He demonstrated for the first time that even in the dry season, when food resources are generally considered scarce, it is possible to subsist solely on the products of hunting and gathering (Yasuoka, 2006b). The *molongo* of the Baka consists of a "migratory phase," in which they repeatedly move from one camp to another every few days, and a "long-stay phase," in which they stay in the same camp for longer periods of time. During the *molongo*, Baka consumed an adequate energy source of 1800–2800 kcal per adult per day. In particular, the camps in the long-stay phase consumed food equivalent to about 2400–2800 kcal per adult-day (Yasuoka, 2006b), which is more than the food intake (2400 kcal) near the villages where agricultural crops were available. The food consumed during this period included the meat of about 20 species of mammals and reptiles, and about 10 species of plants, as well as river fish, honey, and edible insects. Of these, the yams with annual stems (the above ground parts die each year and tubers stored underground sprout in the next rainy season) were particularly important. The two species, *Dioscorea praehensilis*, called *safa* by the Baka, and *D. semperflorens*, called *esuma*, accounted for three-quarters of the energy consumed during the entire *molongo* period. As implied in the "wild yam question," wild yams were the most important energy food source in the dry season rainforest diet.

Yasuoka also conducted a study of the forest vegetation and distribution of wild yams, which yielded some very interesting points for considering the ecological history of the forest (Yasuoka, 2009a, b). He established several survey plots along the *molongo* migration route and in areas where wild yams grow in large, concentrated patches (i.e., long-term stay areas), and recorded the distribution and numbers of wild yam stems and all medium- to large-diameter woody plants that appeared in these plots. At the same time, at 10-meter intervals, he photographed the canopy from below and calculated the ISF (Indirect Site Factor, a measure of the sunlight reaching the ground). The vegetation environment was then classified according to Baka's definition into "*bi*," or open canopy environments (so-called gaps), and "*manja*," or closed canopy environments. The results showed that the yams with annual stems, safa (*D. praehensilis*) and *esuma* (*D. semperflorens*) were more common in relatively bright, open environments with an ISF of 8–10%, whereas the perennial yams (i.e., the above-ground parts, stems and leaves, do not die throughout the year), such as *D. burkilliana* and *D. mangenotiana*, were found in relatively more enclosed environments with less than 5% ISF. In other words, annual yams, the key food that supports *molongo*, were found to grow abundantly in what Baka people call "*bi*" (gap, i.e., environments where the forest canopy is open).

At the same time, however, the survey revealed an interesting fact. Whereas the "*bi*" or open environment, in the forest was found throughout the forest, albeit with somewhat different frequencies, the yams were not found in every "*bi*," but only in very limited places. In other words, these yams grow in large clusters in one location, but such clusters are only found in very localized areas. Compared to perennial yams, which are distributed relatively evenly throughout the forest, annual yams have a very limited distribution area. While there are large numbers of annual yams in some areas, many areas are completely devoid of annual yams, even in areas with favorable light conditions

Chapter 2

Table 2.1 The density of annual yams and light environment

Survey plots	1	2	3	4	5	6	7
Distance from village	13	17	22	28	33	37	32
Vegetation							
manja (%)	60	38	33	63	38	20	30
bi (%)	40	62	23	37	62	80	70
Density of yam stems							
safa (stems/ha)	0	0	0	0	0	28	0
esuma (stems/ha)	1.0	0	0	0	2.5	0	21

Note: Yams with annual stems are abundant in *bi*, but their distribution is localized to specific locations. (Data from Yasuoka, 2009b, partly modified)

for their growth. This fact is consistent with what the French ecological anthropologist Edmond Dounias (1993) has previously pointed out: "wild yams are very unevenly distributed."

This fact also indicates that the dispersal ability of wild yams is in fact limited. According to Yasuoka (2009b), most of the forest gaps in the region were quickly covered with pioneer plants, such as herbaceous plants and vines of *Manniophyton fulvum* (Euphorbiaceae) and fast-growing soft wood trees. The wild annual yams are, however, not found in most such gaps. How, then, were such huge colonies of yams formed that 50–100 people could depend on them for 2–3 months for food? While I was searching for the relevant documents in the National Archives in Yaounde, Cameroon's capital, I came across an old map of the East Region of Cameroon (published in 1910) by the German cartographer Max Moisel. It was a detailed map of the Dja River and its tributaries in the southeastern part of Cameroon, showing in detail the numerous tributaries, their names, the direction of confluence, river width, and main forest trails, as well as the location of villages at that time. Yasuoka added other old village sites obtained from the Baka people on the map and superimposed this map on the sites with abundant annual yams. He noticed then that all the annual yam sites he recorded during *molongo* were located within a few kilometers of the former (presumably agriculturalists') village sites. They are now located in a protected area (Nki National Park) more than 30 km in a straight line from the Baka's roadside village settlement. They know the yams are located near the former settlements, tens of kilometers away from the present settlements, and they travel those long distances to collect them.

The spatial proximity of the yam colonies to the former village sites does not seem to be coincidental. The clearing of the forests around the village created a favorable environment for light-demanding annual yams to grow, and the regeneration of wild yams was facilitated by "para-cultivation" (an intervention into regeneration, see Dounias, 2001 for details), in which some of the tubers are left behind or reburied in the ground after collection, or semi-domestication (Matsui, 1989), which is one step before cultivation. In any case, it would indicate that human habitation and activities in the past likely had a positive impact on the growth of the wild yams that are used intensively by the Baka people.

As described above, recent research in Cameroon has revealed the following points. First, 1) hunter-gatherers in the region can survive in the forest, depending solely on the products of hunting and gathering, even during the dry season when food supplies are generally thought to be scarce, in remote areas where there are currently no farming settlements or crop fields; 2) annual wild yams support their diet during forest life in the dry season; 3) annual wild yams prefer open environments (gaps) with sufficient sun light, 4) such open environments can be found anywhere in the forest, but annual wild yams are found only in limited areas and are concentrated there, 6) it is highly likely that some anthropogenic influences, such as modification of the vegetation environment and human intervention in yam regeneration process, contributed to the formation of wild yam patches.

Therefore, it is necessary to examine the human impacts on the forest environment if we are to understand the possibility of hunter-gatherers' subsistence in the forest. The "wild yam question" has thus been reframed as one concerning the historical ecology of human impacts on the forest environment.

I will add some remarks on the human impacts on forest vegetation from our recent research in Cameroon. The Baka in Cameroon today cultivate small crop fields near village settlements (Kitanishi, 2003; Yasuika, 2012), but they often move into the forest for foraging, leaving the unharvested crops in the fields. When they return to the village settlement, they harvest the crops from fields, which are covered with thick secondary vegetation. This form of cultivation is not entirely different from foraging. It is better to understand their simple cultivation as an extension and continuum of human intervention in the

Chapter 2

resource regeneration process, from partial vegetation modification, soil enrichment, seed dispersal and replanting parts of tubers, all of which eventually facilitate the growth and regeneration of resources, though these interventions do not always take place intentionally.

In our recent international cooperative project in Cameroon (described in more detail in Chapter 4), we investigated the distribution and abundance of the major wild food species in the forest of southeastern Cameroon. Hirai (2014) surveyed a total of about 4,000 plots in current and abandoned fields, and the vegetation of these plots around the village of Gribe, inhabited mainly by Kounabembe (Bantu-speaking) cultivators and Baka hunter-gatherers. In the season of 2012, a total of 47 hectares, comprised of 450 plots, were cleared for cultivation. In the cleared fields, a total of 3142 tree individuals (belonging to 240 species) with 10 cm DBH and over were left uncut, i.e., 66–67 individuals per ha of cleared fields. The villagers were asked about the reasons for leaving these trees. Some said they provide shade to protect the fields from intense sunshine, especially in the fields of cacao. Others said these trees are too hard to cut with the small axes they usually use. The wood of *Irvingia gabonensis* (called *peke* by the Baka) in particular, is extremely hard, and trees of this species are often left uncut in the crop fields. *Irvingia gabonensis* produces a quantity of oily nuts, which are used for cooking, and is an important source of cash income (Ichikawa, 2020; Toda and Yasuoka, 2020; Hirai and Yasuoka, 2020). Thus there are economic benefits to leaving them in the fields, as well. Another food tree species often found in the fields is *Ricinodendron heudelotti* (called *gobo* by the Baka), which also produces edible nuts (used for making "*sauce jaune*," yellow-colored sauce) for sale. They were probably left deliberately because their wood is not hard but easy to cut down. As mentioned in Chapter 4, Fongzossie et al. (2014) found in a preliminary study on the distribution of wild food plants that some food plants were more abundant in the secondary forests than in the mature forest. These facts suggest that there may be relatively more edible fruit tree species in the secondary forest grown in abandoned fields than in the uncut forest.

2.5.3. Further examples of human impacts on vegetation

There have been new discoveries about the impacts of both intentional and unintentional human activities on the landscape through a series of studies of historical ecology on local landscapes. The "forest islands" distributed along the boundary between forest and savanna in west Africa have already been introduced in this chapter. I would like to introduce some other examples here.

In the rainforest zone of central Africa, there are places where the forest floor is covered with dense herbaceous vegetation of the Marantaceae family. Marantaceae plants are monocotyledonous plants with large leaves on slender stems that can be 1–2 meters long. In forests with dense cover of Marantaceae plants, the middle layer of the forest is relatively open with low tree density, and these plants receive sufficient sunlight to grow densely on the rainforest floor, along with plants of the Zingiberaceae and others that prefer similar bright environments. These abundant herbaceous plants are important foods for great apes, in particular gorillas, and appear to have supported the lives and promoted the development of complex social organization in great apes such as gorillas (Wrangham, 1986, cited in White, 2001). Marantaceae plants are also used for a variety of purposes by humans. In some species, the seeds and young shoots are eaten. The large leaves are used for roofing, matting, wrapping, plates, pot lids, cups, and cigarette rolls and in many other ways. The leaves, which have a faint aroma, are used to wrap fish, mushrooms, animal meat, and other foodstuffs with palm oil, salt, chili peppers, and then steamed over embers from a bonfire, a dish worthy of the name "forest gourmet." The skins of the stalks are used for weaving baskets. It is also useful as an all-purpose household material (Tanno, 1981; Ichikawa, 1992; Hattori, 2006).

Forests densely vegetated with herbaceous plants are typically found in poorly drained areas and riversides in tropical rainforests. Marantaceae forests, however, are also found throughout the forest in various sizes, often in areas of natural or human-induced vegetation disturbance such as wildfires, gaps caused by fallen trees, elephant roaming, and areas of habitation, logging, and cultivation (Aubreville, 1967). In Ghana in particular, approximately 30% (1,400 km^2) of the forest area is covered with this vegetation (Marantaceae forest), which is believed to have been formed by wildfires spreading from fires caused by slash-

Chapter 2

and-burn agriculture (Swaine, 1992). The fires burn the vegetation on the forest floor but have little effect on the canopy. Fast-growing herbaceous vegetation quickly invade into the burned forest floor and thrive, suppressing the growth of other vegetation. Based on these observations, Swaine argued that many of the African Marantaceae forests were formed by wildfire. If this theory is correct, it means that the vegetation on which great apes (gorillas in particular) depend may have been expanded by fires and other anthropogenic effects associated with slash-and-burn agriculture.

In the forests near the ecotone zone with savanna in the western part of the Congo Basin, there are periods when monthly precipitation averages less than 50 mm. The trees there are stressed, and semi-deciduous forests spread, which are different from the usual tropical rainforests dominated by evergreen trees. The major tree species in these forests are *Triplochiton scleroxylon* of the Sterculiaceae family and *Terminalia superba* of the Combretaceae family (Letouzey, 1968; 1984). These trees can be large, reaching more than one meter in diameter, and are a major target of large-scale logging in southeastern Cameroon. *Triplochiton scleroxylon*, known as "*bado*" in Baka language and *ayos* in the common name of the region, also hosts a large number of edible caterpillars in their season. These are the so-called sun trees, which require open spaces with sufficient light for germination and growth. Moreover, when one enters a forest dominated by these trees, there are few young trees, which are supposed to carry on the next generation. Based on these facts, Chujo (1992) and Shikata (2006) pointed out that the environment in which these tree species had grown most likely had been a fairly large open space, rather than a closed forest as we see it today. If there was human involvement in the formation of such a space, such as clearing for slash-and-burn agriculture, we must reconsider the concept of "intact forests" in this region.

2.5.4. Long-term vegetation change in the Ituri Forest

Vegetation in the northeastern part of the Congo Basin suggests human involvement over a long period. Although the forests in this region are comprised of many tree species, a few species of the subfamily Caesalpinioideae (Fabaceae) dominate the forests. In the Ituri Forest, three species of the Caesalpinioideae, *mbau (Gilbertiodendron dewevrei)*, *eko*

(Julbernardia seretii) and *tembu (Cynometra alexandri)* are dominant (Itani, 1974). In particular, the *mbau* form single-species-dominant forests, with this species alone accounting for more than 75% of all trees with a DBH (diameter at breast height) greater than 10 cm, and more than 90% of all canopy species with a DBH greater than 30 cm (Hart et al. 1989). The floor in *mbau* forest is dark with large overlapping leaves and little undergrowth. Forests dominated by *eko* and *tembu* are often found not far from the *mbau* forest. Although these two species are dominant, they account for only 20–40% of the total number of trees, forming a mixed forest that includes a wide variety of other tree species (Hart et al. 1989). The forests are relatively bright, with herbaceous plants such as Marantaceae and Zingiberaceae growing on the forest floor in many areas. The Ituri Forest is composed of a mosaic of *mbau* forests (single-species-dominant forests) and mixed forests (*eko* and *tembu* forests), distributed in blocks ranging from a few square kilometers to several dozen square kilometers in some areas.

So how do we explain the mosaic vegetation of the Ituri Forest? One possible factor could be differences in environmental conditions, such as topography, soil, and moisture conditions, but this does not explain the distribution of *mbau*, *Gilbertiodendron dewevrei* forests. Mbau forests are widely distributed in the lowlands of the Congo Basin, from the eastern Congo Basin in DRC to the western parts, such as Cameroon and Congo-Brazzaville. The areas of *mbau* distribution varies climatically in terms of the length of the dry season and other factors. The *mbau* forests in the western Congo Basin are commonly found in lowlands along river systems and where the groundwater table is shallow. The Aka hunter-gatherers in the Likouala Region of Congo-Brazaville sometimes get water from holes dug in the *mbau* forest.

However, Hart et al.'s (1989) detailed study of the distribution of vegetation types in the Ituri forest found that their distribution was not related to specific topographic, soil, or climatic conditions. Instead, Hart (2001) noted that *mbau* and *eko* have quite different reproductive and growth characteristics. Mbau trees grow much more slowly, at a 3.3% diameter growth rate in 10 years, than *eko* trees which show a 12.5% increase. But *mbau* trees survive well on the light-poor forest floor (they are shade tolerant) and have a lower mortality rate (3.4%/10 years for trees with DBH≥10 cm) after growing into trees, compared with 16.9%

Chapter 2

for *eko* trees. Moreover, the *mbau* seeds are larger (30g on average) and have a narrower dispersal area (6–10 m from the tree) than that of *eko*, with smaller seeds (4g) and wider dispersal area (30–40 m). The survival rate of *mbau* seedlings is also higher (50%/10 years) than that of *eko* (35%/10years) (Hart, 2001; see, Table 2.2). These characteristics show that the *mbau* is stress tolerant, surviving adverse conditions in the forest understory until its turn to grow, whereas the *eko* is a relatively fast-growing, competitively dominant species. This suggests that *mbau* forests come after *eko* forests and replace them.

Hart et al. (1996) and Hart (2001) proposed the following hypothesis of the vegetation change, combining the reproductive characteristics of the two species with the analyses of phytoliths and charcoal in the ground that indicates the effects of wildfire. Namely, the younger (but mature) forests that have recently been regenerated become mixed forests dominated by faster growing *eko* species. Once the dominance of *mbau* is established, it becomes difficult for other species such as *eko* to grow in the forest, and the forest gradually approaches a pure *mbau* forest. The *eko* forest, which at first glance appears to be a mature forest, may be gradually transformed into a *mbau* forest over a time scale of several hundred to a thousand years. However, if there is a disturbance in the vegetation during that time, another secondary forest will emerge, gradually turning into a mixed forest such as *eko* forest. The fact that both types of vegetation are distributed in a mosaic of small and large blocks in the Ituri Forest may indicate that the forest has been repeatedly experienced both large and small disturbances. Hart points out that human influence has been a major factor in such disturbances, especially during the past 2,000–3,000 years. Notably, it was around this time that the Bantu-speaking slash-and-burn cultivators began to migrate into the forests from the western side of the Congo Basin (Vansina, 1990).

The traces of human activities in the Congo Basin were found in quite old time; some of the prehistoric site date back to about 1,000 years BC (Vansina, 1990; see also Roberts, 2019). During the research on the Aka hunter-gatherers and Bantu cultivators in the densely forested area of upper Motaba River in Likouala Region of Congo-Brazaville, our colleagues found several charcoal layers when they dug pits to examine the soils. The charcoal from the deepest layer dated to 2,600 BP (Hanawa and Komatsu, 1993). This charcoal probably indicates the

Where Humans Coexist with Forests

Table 2.2 Comparison of reproduction and growth between *mbau* (*Gilbertiodendron dewevrei*) and *eko* (*Julbernardia seretii*)

mbau (Gilbertiodendron and eko (Julbernardia seretii)	Diameter Increment rate	Mortality rate*	Seed weight	Dispersal range	Seedling survival
mbau	low (3.3%/10y)	low (3.4%/10y)	heavy (30g)	small (6–10m)	high (50%/10y)
eko	high (12.5%/10y)	high (16.9%/10y)	light (4g)	large (30–40m)	low (35%/10y)

*: Over 10 cm DBH. (All the data from Hart, 2001)

presence of early slash-and-burn agriculture. We were impressed by the evidence of agriculture in this area in such an old time.

When the Congo Basin forests are viewed from the sky, there seem be vast stretches of intact forests. However, the current forest landscape of the Congo Basin, even those that appear to be pristine, have in fact been impacted by centuries of human influence. Bantu-speaking slash-and-burn cultivators migrated to the Congo Basin from the savannas of West Africa nearly 3,000 years ago, and more than 1,000 years ago their distribution spread over most of the forests except for some swampy areas (Vansina, 1990). Of course, their population density has been low, but a thousand years may be enough for them to have left their footprints here and there in the forest through frequent migrations. Richards (1952), the plant ecologist who wrote *Tropical Rainforests*, also noted that African forests often look like primary forests but are in fact old secondary forests. In the future, it will be necessary to read the forest landscapes in the context of "environmental revisionism" (Headland, 1997), i.e., the history of interaction between and forest environment.

These examples suggest that many of the forest landscapes we see today may be historical products formed through the long history of interaction between forests and people. If this is the case, it requires rethinking conventional approaches to nature conservation, which has been based on the idea that humans and nature are in opposition and that human impacts on the natural environment are invariably adverse.

Chapter 2

2.6. Nature conservation and the dualistic view of humans and nature

What are the problems with nature conservation practices to date? What is the Western view of nature that has supported conventional conservation schemes? A simple expression of modern conservation can be seen, for example, in the national parks in Africa. A herd of ungulates grazing peacefully in a vast savanna. Predatory animals such as lions and cheetahs stalk them from the bushes. Hyenas and vultures swarm around the carrion they leave behind. These are familiar from TV scenes and tourist posters, but they represent a rather stereotyped image of Africa. In the savanna, everything seems to be occurring as a natural process. This is the image of the "ideal state of African nature" that the Western world sought for Africa. However, there are no human figures in that picture, and the fact that the vast savanna was once the grazing grounds for pastoralists is covered up. This nature conservation plan has been directed towards maintaining a "wildlife sanctuary" devoid of human activity.

A Western view of nature, an aesthetic sense that holds "pristine nature" to be supreme, underlies conventional conservation schemes. Crandell (1993) and Neumann (1998) have published interesting discussions on this perspective. With reference to them, I will examine the problems with the Western view of nature and the conception of "national parks" or "wildlife sanctuaries" that is based on this view. According to Crandell, Western European aesthetics of nature, which posit national parks as the ideal nature, originated in landscape painting, which became popular from the 17th century. The aristocrats and the rising middle class of the time considered the landscapes depicted in paintings to represent ideal nature and set out in search of them. They set a "frame" (boundary) on nature, just like a painting, and appreciated it as an external spectator. Nature was experienced as a beautiful view seen from the comfort of a passing car window; an object to be appreciated from the "outside." For them, nature was "landscape," and landscape was an object of "separation" and "observation." As Williams (1973) pointed out, "the very idea of landscape implies separation and observation." With the landscape reduced to an object of aesthetic appreciation, "aesthetic" nature and "practical" nature (as a place of production) diverged, and "untouched" or pristine nature was identified with the ideal nature.

For the aristocracy (and later the middle class) of the time, the appreciation and praise of sublime nature was an means to establish their class identity. As Neumann (1998) points out, the "grand tour" of the aristocracy in search of picturesque landscapes was eventually succeeded by the "consumption of nature" represented by the popular national park tours in the late 19th century. Against the backdrop of this Western aesthetic of nature, the world's first national park was established in Yellowstone, USA, in 1872. Subsequently, national parks were established in Europe, Africa, and other parts of the world following this model.

Western colonizers, who began to expand into Africa in the 19th century, saw "wild nature" there and tried to make sense of this new landscape in terms of their preexisting aesthetic. They saw in Africa a "wild landscape" that had long been lost in their homelands. This reflects the dualistic perception of the colonizers, who saw themselves on the side of "culture" and the colonies on the side of "nature." They paid no attention to the local inhabitants who had left their mark on the "pristine nature" of the landscape over the centuries. For the establishment of the ideal park as "pristine nature," it was not enough to exclude human activity taking place at the time from the park. It was also necessary to erase their presence from the history of the land. This was made possible by the historical perspective that Africa had been originally a wild land, untouched by humans, and that the colonizers' cultural and economic domination of the land transformed it into a cultural and productive space. National parks were seen as heritage sites that commemorate the primordial landscapes or wild states that colonizers encountered in the past.

However, the elimination of human activities can impact nature in the "wrong" direction from originally envisioned (Neumann 1998). The "favorable" natural landscape often requires intentional and unintentional human intervention. In Yellowstone Park, a certain number of wildfires were necessary to maintain a beautiful forest landscape. However, wildfires leave behind large numbers of blackened trees. The sight of rows of blackened trees does not conform to the ideal image of picturesque nature. The park authorities, therefore, took measures

Chapter 2

to suppress the outbreak of wildfires. The suppression of wildfires led to the accumulation of enormous amounts of dead trees, which in turn ignited spontaneously and caused a huge fire (Chase, 1987; Neumann, 1998). Similar phenomena have been reported in Tanzania. In Serengeti National Park, where livestock and pastoralists had been removed from grasslands with magnificent views, trees that had been suppressed by the livestock had grown so thick in places that they obstructed the view. These cases illustrate that maintaining "ideal nature" often requires human intervention rather than total neglect. This is precisely what the contradictory concept of wildlife management suggests – "managing" what is "wild" or "unmanaged."

Similar examples of human exclusion from protected areas have been found in the Congo Basin. For a long time, the dominant scheme was to create strict nature reserves that excluded human activities, which imposed hardship on the people who had originally lived there. One of the many cases is the Batwa people in the Virunga volcanoes and Kafuji-Biega mountains in DRC and Rwanda. The forests in these areas, the western ridge of the Great Rift Valley, are home to mountain gorillas and other rare animals. To protect these wild animals and develop tourism, national parks were established in the region: Virunga National Park in 1925 and Kafuji-Biega National Park in 1970. Following the establishment of the Parks, the Batwa (Pygmy) people who had long lived in these forests were forced to leave. Outside the parks is fertile agricultural land blessed with mineral-rich volcanic soils, but it was difficult for the Batwa people to find new homes there, because the area was already densely populated by agriculturalists who were themselves suffering from land shortages. The plight of the Batwa people, forced out of the forest and without access to sufficient arable land, continues to this day (see Lewis and Knight, 1995; Lewis, 2000; Barume, 2000; Lewis et al., 2019).

We must find another way to solve the problem and, based on our research experience, are seeking an alternative framework for nature conservation schemes to replace the Western dualistic opposition between man and nature, by situating human activities within the forest ecosystem.

2.7. Crisis in forest-human coexistence: Political ecology

In the forests inhabited by indigenous people, human culture and life are strongly dependent on the forest, as mentioned earlier. At the same time, the people have been effecting the maintenance of the forest ecosystem through their habitation and various activities. In other words, forests and humans coexist in mutual dependence. So, for example, the Mbuti do not think of the forest or the animals who dwell there as "nature against humans." British anthropologist Colin Turnbull, who studied the Mbuti in the 1950s and '60s, wrote that the Mbuti consider the forest to be their "father" or "mother." The forest protects them and provides them with food, medicine, and other necessities. They are, therefore, "children of the forest" (*bamiki na ndura*) (Turnbull, 1965). Mbuti imagine the thick canopy of the forest as a "womb" (Ichikawa, 1992). The womb is the space from which humans are born, an ideal environment for the fetus. I once asked them what happens to humans when they die. They replied, "The dead bodies remain in the ground. But the dead persons 'themselves' go deep into the forest and live in the same fashion as we do." They sometimes encounter their ancestors in the forest (in dreams?). They say that they learn new songs and dances by watching their ancestors' performances (Sawada, 1998). The forest for them is the place from which humans are born (the womb) and the world to which they return after death. In other words, human life circulates in the forest, just as soil nutrients circulate in the forest.[2] The forest is also a source of their vitality in that they learn new ritual performances with intensive singing and dancing from their ancestors who live deep in the forest.

Such a world can only exist in a closed system in which materials generally circulate within the forest. But the forest world is not such a closed system – forest materials and products are carried out or flow out in various ways. Where forest products have been commercialized, large quantities of materials are being removed from the forests. Particularly, where recent policies have encouraged development of forest areas,

---

2 It is Mbuti custom to give newborn babies the names of their dead father or other ancestors. They explain such a custom as a response to their ancestors who want to appear again in the living world.

Chapter 2

Photo 2.9 Forest viewed as a "womb"

Photo 2.10 "Children of the forest"

large scale logging and clearing of land for crop fields has destroyed vast amounts of timber resources. The corresponding degradation of water retention capacity has led to erosion and the loss of large quantities of soil nutrients. Circulation within forests cannot be maintained in such places. The survival of healthy forests and their resources demands sustainable management practices.

The degradation of these forest ecosystems has led to a growing movement for nature conservation. In the forested areas of central Africa, international pressure has led to the creation of nature reserves since the late 20th century. In these protected areas, the activities of local people who have inhabited the forests for centuries have been eliminated or severely restricted. How these developments and nature conservation and other international movements and activities have affected the relationship between local people and the forests will be outlined in subsequent chapters.

We believe that an effective way to promote the conservation and sustainable use of forests in an integrated way is to create a social system in which the indigenous people themselves are the main actors in forest management. Forests subject to protection usually cover hundreds of thousands of hectares or more. Protecting and managing these large areas through coercion demands enormous costs (manpower and expenses). A system in which the local people, who know the area well, could take the initiative in managing the area, the cost would be much less. For a management system with indigenous people's initiative, it is essential that their customary rights of use be established. According to the laws of central African countries, forest lands belong to the state and most of the governments in the region had not recognized the rights of the people in the statutory law.

This recent history of forest reserves and commercialization has clearly demonstrated that when outsiders flood in seeking forest products with commercial value, when resources can be extracted by anyone, people pursue short-term profits with no regard for sustainability, leading to resource depletion. In fact, the "empty forest syndrome" (Redford, 1992) was caused by the uncontrolled resource extraction by outsiders and their direct and indirect influences. The problem of resource depletion due to overharvesting is known as the "tragedy of the commons" (Hardin, 1968). To avoid this "tragedy," it is necessary to consider resource sustainability from a long-term perspective. To this end, we believe that the first step is to establish "local people's rights" to the resources. If the resources are used exclusively by locals, they will have the opportunity and leeway to think about their sustainability from a long-term perspective. In particular, consideration should be given to indigenous peoples, who are politically vulnerable and have few opportunities to be heard with regard to their customary use of forests.

Chapter 3

Bushmeat and the New Forest Law in Central Africa

Chapter 3

Photo on the previous page: Meat trader visiting a hunting camp

3.1. Expansion of bushmeat trade

Several million tons of bushmeat are harvested annually in western and central Africa, some of which is smuggled into Europe and the United States, leading to public health concerns about bushmeat, especially in the European Union (UK Parliamentary Office, 2005). On June 15, 2001, a news item on the BBC pointed to the global implications of bushmeat hunting in African countries (BBC, 2001). According to this news report, two shopkeepers were sentenced to four months in prison for their involvement in the illegal bushmeat trade in downtown London. The two people were said to have made large profits from selling various kinds of bushmeat, including snakes and lizards used as magical medicine, to African residents in and around London. The judge who handed down the sentence stated that "the animals they sold are endangered. Cracking down on such trade may be against local customs, but it is inevitable for the benefit of human society" (BBC, 2001).

According to the BBC, this was the first case of bushmeat (from African forests) to come before the English courts (BBC, 2001). This case raised the issue of the conservation of endangered animals in UK. Reports on the illegal bushmeat trade continued in subsequent years. The following year, the BBC reported that 10 tons of bushmeat entered London every day (which is only a small fraction of the animal meat hunted in the African forests, but indicative of the spread of the wild meat trade) and noted that harvesting bushmeat for local consumption would not be a problem, but now wild animals were hunted in huge numbers for cash, leading to a dramatic decline in their numbers. It pointed out that large animals such as elephants and buffalo tend to disappear first, then rare animals such as chimpanzees are targeted (Kirby, 2002).

Researchers who investigated illegal imports of wild game meat in 2002 reported that a total of 200 cases of bushmeat smuggling were uncovered at Heathrow Airport over a five-week period. A total of 1.5 tons of bushmeat was seized from arriving flights on a single day (Bowen-Jones and Pendry, 2003). On January 6, 2004, BBC News reported that a man who sold bushmeat "unfit for human consumption" on 23 separate occasions was sentenced to three months in prison for violating the Food Security Act, and commented that this was only the tip of the iceberg, with much more bushmeat being illegally imported

Chapter 3

into London. A similar situation has been reported in France. Chaber et al. (2010) reported that an average of 5 tons of bushmeat was estimated to be smuggled each week from the data collected from baggage checks of arriving passengers at Charles de Gaulle airport. Across the Atlantic in the United States, bushmeat has also spread on an unexpected scale, with smoked monkey, small antelope, and rodent bushmeat being sold semi-openly in New York City in 2005 at higher prices than beef and other meat (Milius, 2005).

In Europe and the United States, bushmeat is relatively expensive because it is difficult to obtain through formal channels. When ordinary livestock meat was sold for around 15 euros per kilogram in Paris supermarkets, bushmeat was sold for 20–30 euros (Chaber et al., 2010). Four kilograms of smoked monkey meat costs 100 euros, 20 times the selling price in Cameroon (5 euros), the country of origin. In New York, African bushmeat was selling for as much as USD 5–8 US per pound (Milius, 2005). The bushmeat trade has become a lucrative business.

The BBC (2004), citing American virus researchers (Wolfe et al., 2004), reported that a virus (Simian Foamy Virus) of the same strain as HIV that causes AIDS has been found in bushmeat. He warned that it could be brought to humans through bushmeat and that it could mutate into a virus dangerous to humans. The virus that causes Ebola fever is also suspected to be carried by wild animals, especially fruit-eating bats. Bats are not frequently eaten by people in central Africa, but antelopes and rodents, major sources of bushmeat, are believed to be infected with Ebola virus through consumption of fruits that bats have gnawed (Hogenboom, 2014). In addition, as reported in recent news, new pathogens of wild animal origin, such as SARS (Severe Acute Respiratory Syndrome), which broke out more than a decade ago, and COVID-19 (novel coronavirus disease) which became a pandemic in 2020, are posing major threats. Incidentally, according to the U.S. Centers for Disease Control and Prevention, three out of four new infectious diseases are zoonoses, transmitted from animals to humans (Nasi and Fa, 2020).

These reports demonstrate that the bushmeat trade is not limited to Africa, but is widespread on a significant scale. The problems of bushmeat are therefore not limited to Africa but have become a global problem. In particular, the consumption of bushmeat may lead to a loss of biodiversity, including a decrease in the number of wild animals, particularly rare and endangered animals. It may also lead to the spread of various infectious diseases such as AIDS, Ebola, and corona viruses. The concern is that pathogens that have been confined to the natural environment may be introduced into the human world through ecological disturbances caused by forest destruction for development, which have become pathways for the spread of disease.

Bushmeat consumers in the Western countries are mainly peoples of so-called African and Asian origins living in cities such as London, Paris and Brussels. In recent years, an increasing number of Africans have migrated to large cities in Western countries in search of work opportunities or to escape civil war and persecution in their home countries. This global migration reflects the progress of globalization, and in the process, the preference for bushmeat is also spreading. This growing preference for and consumption of bushmeat is creating additional demand for bushmeat in the region of origin.

These various problems with bushmeat, however, do not necessarily mean that its use should be simply banned. There are numerous reasons to continue to permit small-scale harvesting by African people who need bushmeat for various reasons.

3.2. Bushmeat use in central Africa

3.2.1. Important source of protein

In tropical Africa, wild game (bushmeat) has long been a valuable food source. Especially in the central African forest areas where other protein sources such as fish, livestock, and poultry are scarce, wild animal meat has been an important source of protein. Cassava and other tubers and plantain bananas, the main crops of the African rainforest zone, are all excellent sources of starchy food (calories), but their protein content is extremely low compared with sorghum, millet, and beans grown in the savanna areas. For this reason, forest dwelling people are more likely to suffer from nutritional disorders (for example, kwashiorkor) due to protein deficiency than in other regions. However, forested areas are not suitable for raising cattle and other livestock due to ecological constraints, such as the abundance of tsetse flies, which carry sleeping

Chapter 3

sickness, and the lack of grass and other plants used as livestock food. Therefore, it was necessary to use wild animals as a source of protein.

It is difficult to calculate exactly how much wild game meat is used in Africa, because there are considerable differences in the estimated amount consumed, depending on the time and duration of survey, weighing methods, and societies surveyed (Ichikawa, 2008, 2013). Previous studies have estimated that central African hunter-gatherers utilize on average 50–100 grams (of raw meat) per person per day, while agriculturalists in the same region utilize about 20–185 grams per person per day.

The problem is that in recent years, the meat is not merely consumed by the local people, but is sold in cities both in Africa and internationally, as we have seen. According to a survey of urban residents in Africa, the average daily consumption of bushmeat in cities (not far from forests) is 13 grams per person, one-tenth of the amount consumed in rural areas. However, given the size of the urban population, overall bushmeat consumption is substantial, with an average of 13,000 kilograms of bushmeat consumed daily in a city of one million people (Ichikawa, 2008; Wilkie and Carpenter, 1999). In the DRC, approximately 60 million people use wild game meat (Debroux et al., 2007). If they consume 100g of bushmeat per day, more than two million tons are consumed annually in the DRC. The amount consumed by the people of central African countries may reach several million tons. This large and expanding demand for wild game meat has come to be widely discussed as a "bushmeat problem."

The increased demand for bushmeat may threaten wildlife in the region (Ichikawa, 2008; Ichikawa et al. 2016). In particular, rare animals such as elephants, leopards and great apes, which reproduce at a slower rate, are particularly vulnerable. To conservationists, the trade and consumption of bushmeat is seen as a threat to healthy rainforest ecosystems, which is a rich reservoir of biodiversity. But a strict ban on hunting would impoverish local people who depend on the bushmeat. Furthermore, unregulated poaching by the people who have been excluded from their former livelihood may paradoxically accelerate the deterioration of the fauna. The bushmeat problem is not only a danger to wildlife, but also to the livelihood and food security of the local people.

According to Robert Nasi who has studied the bushmeat problem in global scale at the Center for International Forestry Research (CIFOR), about 4–5 million metric tons of wild game are harvested annually in central Africa. That is comparable to the amount of beef produced in Brazil or the EU, suggesting that an area as large as 20–25 million hectares might have to be converted to pastures in the Congo Basin to produce that much beef (Nasi et al. 2011; CIFOR 2014). For producing meat as protein source, it would be more efficient to raise pigs or chickens rather than to keep cattle, as Nasi et al. (2011) pointed out. However, for the people of the central African forest region, wildlife meat is not just a source of protein; it also has social and cultural significance, as described below. Managing wildlife resources will, therefore, remain a necessity.

3.2.2. Cultural significance of bushmeat

3.2.2.1. Two kinds of "hunger": Strong preference for bushmeat

The preferred diet among the people of central Africa consists of a starchy "staple" food such as cassava or plantain banana, with an accompanying side dish. The most popular side dish is a stew of meat, chicken, or fish cooked with palm oil, chili peppers, and salt. Among these, wild game meat is frequently used as a cheaper and more easily available source of protein than chicken or fish.

The people of central Africa distinguish between two types of "hunger." One is hunger for carbohydrates (starchy food) as a source of energy (energy hunger), called *nja* or *njala* in Bantu languages. The other is meat hunger, called *kpelu* among Bantu farmers and hunter-gatherers in the Ituri Forest and *pene* among the Baka hunter-gatherers in southeastern Cameroon. They are not satisfied if either is lacking in the diet. Especially, the deficiency of protein is often talked about in daily life. The Mbuti say they feel an uncontrollable hunger for meat (*kpelu, or ham ya nyama* in Swahili dialect) when they stay near the agriculturalists' village for a long period, eating only starchy food without meat, which drives them to move to a forest camp to hunt animals. Conversely, if the diet in the forest is dominated by bushmeat, they become "tired" of eating meat, and will come to the vicinity of

Chapter 3

the agricultural village where starchy food (crops) is more abundant to satisfy their hunger (*nja*).

Hunter-gatherers such as the Mbuti, Aka, and Baka have a strong appetite for meat. When an animal is caught, they first cut out its internal organs, such as the liver and heart, and roast them over an open fire or wrap them in the large leaves of Marantaceae plant and steam them. The fatty ribs are especially favored. The skin is also boiled or grilled. Smaller animals are roasted over a bonfire and eaten. After the hunger for meat is appeased, the meat is chopped up, bone by bone, and boiled in a pot to make a stew, which is then eaten with starchy foods such as cassava, plantain bananas or wild yams. The meat is also often smoked over a fire to preserve it for later use or to exchange with agriculturalists for crops. The smoked meat, blackened and hardened by the fire and smoke, is scraped off the surface with a knife, carefully washed with water, and stewed for a long time with palm oil, salt and chili peppers until it becomes soft, and a unique flavor is added. Wild game meat from forest areas is generally low in fat and often dry and tough, and much of it gives off the so-called wild animal smell. They value such meat as "meat of forest." Especially for those who have moved from the countryside to the city, such meat reminds them of their homeland and gives them a "wild power" that they cannot get from fish or chicken sold in town. As discussed above, bushmeat is sometimes sold in large cities at a higher price than beef or other meat. As noted, the market for bushmeat is flourishing in towns, where there is no shortage of alternative protein sources, because of people's deep-rooted preferences for it.

Supported by strong preferences, animal meat plays an important role in their society. In the Mbuti society, after the hunted animal is dismantled into several parts, such as the head, limbs, breastbone, and internal organs, the parts are distributed to the hunt's participants according to the role they played on the day. For example, the woman who transported the animal receives one of the fore legs, the one who assisted in its capture is given the breast, the one who use other's net is given one of the hind legs. Other people who were not blessed with a catch, as well as those who did not participate in the hunt are also given portions of meat by those who already have. It is then cooked by each family and distributed again among family and other camp members for the meal. Through this repeated distribution, the meat is

Photo 3.1 Using a child to distribute the meat

widely distributed to the members of the same camp (Ichikawa, 1982; 2005; Kitanishi, 2001). It is supported by an ethic that discourages the monopolization of valuable meat and encourages sharing. The sharing of meat has not only the subsistence function of equalizing food consumption, but also confirms and strengthens social relations within the group. In this respect, meat is an integral part of communal meals at weddings, funerals, and other ceremonial events. The consumption and distribution of this precious food has deep social meanings that are supported by ethical values.

3.2.2.2. Avoidance of dangerous animals

Of more than 200 species of wild animals that Mbuti hunter-gatherers consider as food, three to four species of forest antelopes (duikers) account for most of the captures, with more than 80% (in numbers) of the catch by hunting with nets or bows and arrows (Ichikawa, 1983; 1993). One effect of this high dependence on a few species is that it allows for a large number of other species which are each few in number to carry a heavy cultural load. Thus, these minor animal species are used for expressing people's identity, or their belonging to specific categories of sex, generation, descent group, etc., thereby regulating social behavior.

Chapter 3

Diseases and other misfortunes that can not be explained otherwise are also attributed to such animals. Because they are only a minor food source, the prohibition of eating them does not have a significant impact on the people's nutritional status.

While the Mbuti people use a total of 230 diverse animal species as food, including 57 large and medium-sized species of mammals, 108 species of birds, and 9 species of reptiles, about half of them are avoided by people belonging to particular descent groups or social categories (Ichikawa, 1987). These species are "marked" with cultural meanings in addition to their nutritional value. Of the 57 species of medium- and large-sized mammals that are considered as food, 84%, or 48 species, are avoided by certain people for one reason or another. For example, there are totemic animals that are closely related to the ancestors of a particular descent group (clan or lineage) and are not eaten by members of that group. Eating forbidden animals, called *nginiso* (meaning "forbidden"), is believed to incur the wrath of their ancestors and the loss of teeth. Some foods are prohibited in relation to certain livelihood activities. For example, women are not allowed to eat Bates antelopes caught by net hunting, and the heads, livers, or hearts of other duiker species. These prohibitions are called *musilo ya nkuya* (prohibitions of net hunting) and violating them is said to incur the wrath of the master of the forest (Apakumandura), who will close the forest, making it impossible to catch game. These prohibitions are established as social norms and violations are believed to bring misfortune to the entire group.

Other animals are avoided among the Mbuti of Ituri, depending on an individual's life-stages. For example, pregnant women and their husbands, parents with infants, and young people during rites of passage each have particular animals that must be avoided. Eating these prohibited animals is believed to cause serious disorders such as disease or deformity in the person or their children. These are considered "bad" or "dangerous" animals and are collectively referred to as *kuweri* among the Mbuti. For example, parents with a newborn infant do not eat Gabon duiker (*seke*), Bates antelope (*anbilo*), or Victoria genet (*pita*), which are believed to cause severe febrile illnesses in their children. Nile crocodiles (*ngwende*) and dwarf crocodiles (*amanato*) are believed to cause severe diarrhea with bloody stools, and brush-tailed porcupines (*njiko*) and Guinea-fowls (*kanga*) are believed to cause severe skin diseases. To protect the children from these "bad animals," Mbuti children often wear an "amulet" called *anbe la bakuweri* (literally, a small piece of *kuweri*) on their waist or wrist (see photo 3.2). These small pieces are made from the bones or fur of disease-causing animals, the wood or seeds of trees they feed on, or other items closely related to such animals. The Mbuti hope that they will have a "sympathetic" effect for preventing disease.[1]

Mbuti believe that all forest animals have the "power" to inflict disease. Newborns are highly vulnerable, and for the first several days after birth, parents maintain an aversion to all animal (mammals and reptiles) flesh. When the newborn's umbilical cord begins to dry, the father rubs ashes or charcoal of burned duiker's hair and certain forest plants into small cuts on the child's body. Only after the child has been treated in this way to bolster resistance to the diseases caused by forest animals can the parents eat wild animal meat. However, they continue to avoid certain *kuweri* animals which are credited with a particularly strong disease-causing "power." As the child begins to walk, and gradually its resistance to the diseases inflicted by animals strengthens, fewer animal species must be avoided. It is up to the parents to decide which animals to avoid and for how long, but a general rule of thumb is to wean a child after the next pregnancy. After that the parents no longer need to avoid "bad animals" for the sake of their children, and the children themselves must observe their own avoidance. This avoidance is loosened as they grow older, but strengthened again during the rites of passage: circumcision rite (*nganja or nkumbi* in Swahili dialect) for boys and puberty rite (*elima*) for girls. Because these periods mark the social birth of the adult, they must observe strict avoidance like that of early infancy. By the time they have completed their rite of passage, they are able to eat all animals except for the "meat for the old," such as black Guinea-fowls, which are considered particularly dangerous.

The folk belief that wild animals bring diseases is widespread among hunter-gatherer societies in the central African rainforests. The Efe,

---

1   Other measures are also taken to protect children from animal venom, such as the roasted powders of poisonous snakes, centipedes, or other poisonous substances rubbed into incisions on the body.

Chapter 3

3.2.1 Victoria genet (fever)

3.2.2 Black Guinea-fowl (fever)

3.2.3 Dwarf crocodile

3.2.4 Porcupine

3.2.5 *Angbe la bakueri*

Photo 3.2 Examples of *kuweri* animals

who live next to the Mbuti in the northern Ituri Forest and speak a Sudanese language, call the "bad animals" that bring diseases "*eke*" and avoid them as the Mbuti do *kuweri* (Terashima, 2001). The Aka in the northern Republic of Congo (Lewis, 2008) and the Baka in southeastern Cameroon (Ichikawa, 2007) also have similar practices. Such practices and the animals avoided are called *ekila* among the Aka, *kila* or *pondi* among the Baka in Cameroon (Brisson and Broursier, 1979). Among the Baka living in the northwestern part of the Republic of Congo, all forest animals are believed to have the potential to cause disease in children, and 30 diseases are named after the animals believed to cause them. Like the Mbuti, most of these diseases are inflicted on infants and fetuses through the parents eating those animals (Sato, 2001b).

Such beliefs that forest animals bring mysterious diseases is widespread throughout central Africa. Indeed, in recent years, as rural

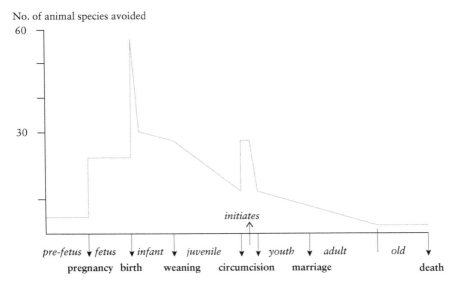

Fig. 3.1 Life stage and number of animal species avoided among the Mbuti

development and forest destruction have progressed, new viruses, such as HIV and Ebola and other pathogens that had previously been isolated in the wild have been introduced to the human world through contact with wildlife. The local people in the central African forests, have long shared the perception that forest animals are dangerous creatures that require careful handling.

In any case, wild animal meat (bushmeat) is important to forest people not only in its positive aspect as a source of nutrition and a lubricant for their social life, but also in its negative aspect of bringing diseases and other misfortunes. The African people's desire for wild animal meat is not merely due to a lack of alternative sources of protein. Wild game also provides the "power of the forest," which cannot be obtained from livestock meat or fish. This is the cultural background underpinning the expanding of the bushmeat market. African people do not depend on bushmeat simply because they are poor. In fact, as the people become wealthier, the demand for bushmeat may increase. The migration of Africans and the proliferation of their food culture has further spurred demand for bushmeat. Bushmeat is already becoming a "luxury food" or "food of nostalgia" (a reminder of distant homeland) in major cities in Africa and the West. The bushmeat problem cannot be

Chapter 3

resolved by simply giving Africans alternative sources of protein because desire for it is deeply rooted in their culture.

To date, the forest peoples (including hunter-gatherers) in central Africa are not directly involved in the large scale bushmeat trade. However, increased demand from outside societies will sooner or later lead to a decline in wildlife. And international pressure to protect wildlife will lead national governments to pursue policies that restrict hunting by local peoples. Furthermore, recent epidemics of zoonotic diseases have spurred protection policies. It is not difficult to imagine the difficulties these situations will pose to the food security of the indigenous forest people and the maintenance of their culture.

3.3. Expansion of bushmeat trade and its impact

3.3.1. Commercialization of forest products

The hunting and use of wild animal meat in Africa is today regarded as a "bushmeat problem" from the standpoint of wildlife protection and new zoonotic diseases. The problem is no longer confined to the interior of Africa. Globalization has penetrated deep into the forests and brought the inhabitants of the African forests into contact with the global economic system. Let us look at the Ituri Forest in the DRC as an example of the "bushmeat problem" within the context of the changing conditions affecting Africa.

The Mbuti of the Ituri Forest first came into contact with the world economy through the ivory trade that flourished in the late 19th and 20th centuries. After the Berlin Conference in 1884–85, Leopold II of Belgium, who acquired the Congo as his "private territory," and named it "Congo Free State," began to exploit the abundant forest products. Initially, the major products were wild rubber and ivory, which together accounted for 95% of all exports from the Congo Free State (Jewsiewicki, 1983; Nelson, 1994). Wild rubber was extracted by the local people under harsh quotas (see Chapter 5). Ivory depended on hunting by the local people who were paid low prices by concession companies or government agents. The Bantu and Sudanic speaking agriculturalists were the major suppliers of ivory in the Ituri Forest and elsewhere in the Congo. The Mbuti and other Efe hunter-gatherers were also involved in these activities through their agricultural "patrons" (see also Grinker, 1994, and Chapter 5). While agriculturalists also tried to hunt elephants with traps with falling spears and pitfalls (Schebesta, 1936a), the acquisition of ivory owed much to the spear hunting by the Mbuti and Efe hunter-gatherers in the Ituri Forest. An old photograph (stored at Powell-Cotton Museum in Kent, UK) taken at Mawambi trading post (now deserted) on the right bank of Ituri River depicts a scene of weighing the wild rubber and ivory brought by the villagers, and suggests the importance of these products at the time. The photograph was taken by a British explorer, Captain Powell-Cotton, on his honeymoon journey to the Ituri Forest in the early 20th century (Powell-Cotton, 1907).

We do not know precisely when the hunter-gatherers in central Africa started elephant hunting. There is some evidence that elephant hunting had already been practiced by the hunter-gatherers in the present-day Gabon in the 1600s (Schlichter, 1892; Kitanishi, 2012; see Chapter 5 for details). In a study of central African history, Klieman (2003) wrote that elephant ivory had been an important component of the Atlantic trade since first contact with Europeans in the 17th century. In the Ituri Forest of DRC, which is far from the Atlantic coast, elephant hunting was probably not a major hunting practice until relatively recently. An old Mbuti man in Teturi area (my study area in the 1970s and '80s) once told me that they had mainly hunted bush pigs and other smaller mammals with spears (Ichikawa, 2021). It is understandable that they had not engaged in elephant hunting frequently, because it was a dangerous work, whereas there were plentiful smaller animals, which could be easily hunted in the forest. Thus, it was probably around the time that Arab traders arrived in the late 19th century that the Mbuti started actively hunting elephant. Arab traders had reached the eastern part of the Congo Basin Forest by the middle of 19th century (Forbath, 1977; Mandjumba, 1985). When Henry Morton Stanley passed through the Ituri Forest in the 1880s, the area had already been under the influence of Arab traders who came from the East African coast (Stanley, 1890). Travelers to this region in the late 19th century also briefly mentioned elephant hunting by various Pygmy groups (Stanley, 1890; Casati, 1891; Parke, 1891; see Chapter 5). The area was gradually brought under Belgian rule, through "*la campagne contre Arab*" (anti-Arab Campaign) from 1892 to 1894.

Chapter 3

Photo 3.3
Mbuti hunter polishing a spear

Photo 3.4
A young elephant killed with a spear

According to Mbuti elders, they lived in the forest near their patron villagers and trading posts and actively hunted elephants. When they killed an elephant, they brought the tusks to their patron villagers, who sold them to the traders. The Mbuti were given salt, tobacco, clothes, and agricultural food by the villagers. As elephant hunting became more common, the motivation for it was gradually internalized by the Mbuti. Elephant hunting was high risk, but it provided a huge quantity of meat when successful. As such, elephant hunting became invested with rich ritual performances and social significance, as described by various authors (e.g., Trilles, 1932; Schebesta, 1936a; Putnam, 1948; Turnbull, 1965; Harako, 1976; Joiris, 1998; Lewis, 2002). Before an elephant hunt, ceremonial song and dance were performed to pray for success, and after a successful hunt, feasting would continue for days. Large-tipped spears were made especially for elephant hunting, and those who killed many elephants became "master hunters" (*mtuma*, or *batuma* for plural) who were famous in the local community, especially among the agriculturalists who profited from the ivory trade. Meanwhile, the Mbuti became known to Western society as brave elephant hunters, who hunt the largest terrestrial mammals with spears, sometimes a single hunter by himself (Ichikawa, 2021). Elephant hunting thus came to have deep cultural significance in Mbuti society, despite the harsh deprivations of Leopold II and the Belgian colonial government that followed. This situation continued until recently when elephant hunting was prohibited for the people without permit.

3.3.2. Expansion of bushmeat trade

The second major change in the Mbuti hunting lifestyle was the trade in duikers (forest antelope). After Belgian colonization in the early 20th century, and especially after World War II when Belgium began to implement various development programs, the Ituri Forest was developed for gold mines as well as plantations of coffee, cotton, papaya (for extracting latex) and other crops. This regional development attracted an influx of migrants, and several cities formed in the hills east of the Ituri Forest. The inhabitants were attracted by bushmeat, especially the duikers hunted by the Mbuti as a source of protein. Duikers were relatively abundant in the forest and could be readily captured by net hunting. They provided an inexpensive and valuable source of protein in this region where cattle and other livestock were scarce. As mentioned earlier, they were also valued by city dwellers as a source of "wild power" that could not be obtained from livestock. Thus, in the 1950s, commercial trading of bushmeat began in the Ituri Forest. Traders bartered for the meat captured by the Mbuti and transported it to the towns in the east where they sold it for as much as five to six times the price they had paid the Mbuti. They also carried rice, cassava flour, and other Mbuti favorites, as well as tobacco and clothes, to the Mbuti

Chapter 3

Photo 3.5 A Blue duiker in the net

Photo 3.6 Brush-tailed porcupine

Photo 3.7 Meat trader visiting a Mbuti forest camp

camps deep in the forest, where they set a fixed rate and exchanged these goods for bushmeat. Through this kind of bushmeat trade, the Mbuti became directly involved in commercial exchange for the first time.

In the DRC, civil war and political instability have been continuous since the 1990s. During the civil war, roads, rivers, and other transportation infrastructure were devastated, and it was difficult to ship coffee and other agricultural products which had been the main source of cash income in rural areas. Under these conditions, bushmeat provided an accessible source of cash income, because it does not require a large investment, is not as bulky as agricultural products and is easier to transport, and was in high demand in local markets. In the forest of Equateur region, the local people smoked bushmeat and transported it on foot or by bicycle for trading in provincial cities 100–200 kilometers away, sometimes further (Kimura, 2017). With the cash they earned, they purchased necessities such as soap, salt, clothes, plates, pots and other manufactured goods, and then returned to their villages. Some of these goods were exchanged for bushmeat to sell on their next trip to the city.

3.3.3. Influences of economic crisis: The Cameroon case

As we have seen, the commercialization and exportation of forest animal meat has been long established in the central African region, albeit to varying degrees, and more recently, it has rapidly accelerated, creating what has come to be known as the "bushmeat problem." As discussed above, this problem is in fact multiple, including loss of biodiversity, threats to rare species, and health and sanitation problems, such as zoonotic diseases. But why did the bushmeat trade expand so rapidly? I would like to examine the case of Cameroon, where an economic crisis in the late 1980s and 1990s and subsequent structural adjustments were important factors affecting bushmeat hunting. The expansion of logging operations during this period provided access to the interior forest of the country and stimulated a consumption economy, which in turn increased demand for bushmeat. Let us see how these changes encouraged the expansion of the bushmeat trade.

Cameroon, located in midwestern Africa, has a total of 20 million hectares of tropical rainforest, and as discussed in Chapter 4, logging has rapidly increased in recent years. Logging workers gathered at a

Chapter 3

logging base deep in the forest, and a small town consisting of stores, restaurants, and taverns selling daily necessities and miscellaneous goods was established around the logging base. Meat from the nearby forests was sold to these residents, and local restaurants served bushmeat from the forests. As logging roads provided easier access to the deeper forests, the meat trade expanded to distant towns and where it sold for high prices.

The economic crisis and structural adjustment programs of the 1990s influenced the bushmeat trade in the various ways. According to Sunderlin et al. (2000), Cameroon's public sector was reduced in 1991–1992 under pressure from the IMF and the World Bank, and wages were drastically cut in 1993. As a result, urban unemployment rose from 7% in 1983 to 24% in 1994, and the poverty rate rose to 20% of the population. As living conditions deteriorated in the cities, the population that had previously flowed into the cities began to return to rural areas. Especially in the five years after 1993, the rural inflow exceeded the rural outflow in some areas (Sunderlin et al., 2000).

While many migrants to rural areas cleared forests and began farming, some took up bushmeat trading as a quick means of earning cash. They began to enter the forest, carrying with them food such as wheat flour for making *beignets* (donuts) and cassava flour, alcoholic beverages (especially a cassava-based spirit called *"ha"*), as well as steel wire used for trapping. Many of these items were given as advances, and the Baka hunter-gatherers paid for them with the bushmeat they captured in the forest. Thus, the Baka who had received large advance payment (in the form of food, wires, and other goods) were forced to hunt intensively, as they needed large quantities of meat to repay their debts. As discussed below, in a small village with a population of about 200 Baka people in the East Region of Cameroon, after the opening of a road in 2001, hunting pressure rose to 15–20 times the previous level in a short period of time, far exceeding sustainable levels of hunting (Yasuoka, 2014; Bobo et al., 2015). The arrival of large numbers of traders led to the removal of large amounts of bushmeat from the forest. Thus, the bushmeat problem is intricately linked to the impacts of development projects and alternative sources of cash income in the region, as well as to political and economic conditions such as conflicts and poverty issues.

3.4. Policy for wildlife conservation: The Cameroon case

3.4.1. Crisis of tropical rainforests and a new approach to wildlife conservation

Increased commercial hunting has raised concerns about the threats to biodiversity, especially in the Western world. According to the International Union for Conservation of Nature (IUCN), 34 animal species, including 17 primate species, are threatened with extinction in central and western Africa (IUCN, 2006). In particular, great apes such as gorillas and chimpanzees, and large mammals such as elephants are threatened with extinction. In addition to their small populations, these animals reproduce at a slow rate and are therefore at greater risk from hunting. In addition, the ecological conditions of tropical rainforests, i.e., their biodiversity, adversely affect these rare species. When specific species are being hunted, a substantial reduction in size of the target population and decline in hunting efficiency will curtail further hunting. But in tropical rainforests, where many species coexist, providing a diverse target population, hunting continues as long as enough species are present at sufficient densities. If rare species are then encountered, they are of course targeted as well. Large mammals bring in large amounts of meat, so they are likely to be targeted if encountered. Thus, large animals such as elephants and great apes, which reproduce slowly, disappear first, followed by larger types of duikers and monkeys. In the Congo Basin, it is estimated that the duikers population has already been reduced by half by hunting (Hart, 2000). In some areas, excessive hunting pressure has led to the so-called "empty forest syndrome" (Redford, 1992), in which game animals almost disappear from forests, even if the forest vegetation appears to be in good condition. A recent study summarizing the impacts of hunting on fauna in the tropics (Benitez-Lopez et al., 2019) found that 27% of medium-sized mammals and 40% of large mammals have so far been lost due to hunting, and if this trend continues, it is expected that 50% of tropical forests (70 % in Western Africa) will be missing game animals. In 50% of the forests that are considered intact, the "empty forest syndrome" appears to be progressing.

In response, conservation activities have intensified. Recent trends have, however, pointed to a need for a different approach to protection.

Chapter 3

Traditionally, the destruction of tropical rainforest ecosystems has often been viewed from a global perspective as a problem of adverse effects on the earth's atmosphere, such as greenhouse gas emissions, and loss of biodiversity (especially rare animals and genetic resources). That is why they have been called "global environmental problems." To protect this "common property of humankind," it was long believed to be necessary to create "wildlife sanctuaries" where all human activities were excluded.

Among the myriad problems with this approach is the fact that global issues are not directly recognized as such by local people. If access to forest resources is prohibited, the local people's primary concern is their own livelihood. At the same time, however, the rapid deterioration of forest fauna due to excessive hunting is also threatening the livelihood of the local people. For the local people, the degradation of forest ecosystems, including wildlife, is not so much a "global environmental problem" as a "local environmental problem." For people who depend on the forests for their livelihoods, the creation of a "wildlife sanctuary" deprives them of their livelihoods, and in this sense, it is no different from destruction of forest ecosystems. Therefore, it is necessary to construct a new model of conservation that replaces the conventional paradigm of a "wildlife sanctuary." The new model will be of environmental conservation that does not exclude humans from forests, but rather allows forests and humans to coexist in harmony. To achieve this, it is essential to use forest resources sustainably.

3.4.2. Forest zoning

In 1994, the Cameroon government enacted a new forest law to control the use of forest resources, including wildlife. This law established zoning (forest classification by use) for forest protection and resource management. First, forests were classified into permanent and non-permanent forests, and the former were further divided into protected forests and timber production forests. The latter could be used for cultivation, and hunting by "traditional methods" (as described below) was permitted. This zoning divided the permanent forests of south-eastern Cameroon (belonging to Boumba-Ngoko Department, East Region) into three national parks and 22 logging units (classified as permanent forests). Furthermore, the permanent forests were divided into 9 general hunting areas (*zone d'intérêt cynégétique* in French) in the logging areas, and 14 community hunting areas (*zone d'intérêt cynégétique à gestion communautaire*) were set mainly in non-permanent forests (areas where agriculture is possible). While these community hunting areas are open to local people for hunting, they comprise only about one-tenth of the land that was previously available to them. Thus the forest zoning has greatly restricted local people's access to forest resources (see Figure 4.4 in Chapter 4). Moreover, most of the forests where local people could hunt overlapped with agricultural areas along roads, where animals were already scarce due to years of hunting pressure. In contrast, the "general hunting areas" in permanent forests are still home to many animals, but these areas are now being used for sport hunting for wealthy Western people who hunt large game for pleasure (Ichikawa et al., 2016).

While the demand for bushmeat is increasing, the sustainability of hunting is further jeopardized by this restriction of the area that can be hunted by the local people. Prior to large-scale logging and the associated road network, hunting in the area was primarily limited to subsistence hunting and hunting pressure was within a sustainable range (Yasuoka, 2006a). However, once logging roads were opened and large numbers of traders entered the deep forest in search of bushmeat, hunting pressure quickly skyrocketed, far exceeding sustainable levels (Yasuoka, 2014; see also Bobo et al., 2015 and Chapter 4). If this hunting pressure is left unchecked, the animals will quickly decline, threatening the local fauna and the livelihood of the people who depend on them.

3.4.3. Hunting regulations and people's livelihood

3.4.3.1. *Two types of hunting zone*

In response to rising hunting pressure, the Cameroon government took measures to control hunting and protect wildlife, incorporating wildlife regulations into the forest law system. I will examine how Cameroon's new forest law affects the local people.

Article 27.4 of the Forest Law and Article 27 of the Presidential Decree of 1995 contain provisions on community forests. However, the main purpose of community forests in Cameroon is to give local people the right to harvest timber in non-permanent forests (areas available for agriculture). They can also hunt there, but the number of game animals in those areas is in decline due to years of hunting. Moreover,

Chapter 3

a community forest covers less than 5,000 hectares each, which is too small to provide for the local people accustomed to hunting in forests several times that size. Therefore, in 2001, the Cameroon government decided to create two types of hunting areas. One is the "general hunting zone" (*Zone d'Intérêt Cynégétique* = *ZIC*), which is to be used mainly for sport hunting by wealthy foreigners. The local community will receive a portion of the license fees. The other is a "community hunting area" (*ZIC á Gestion Communautaire* = *ZICGC*), which can be up to 100,000 hectares in size. It is entrusted to *COVAREF* (*Comités de Valorisation des Ressources Fauniques*), a "Commission for the Development of Animal Resources," made up of representatives from both Bantu agriculturalists and Baka hunter-gatherers. The *ZICGC* can also be rented out for sport hunting for a fee, instead of being hunted by its residents. In this case, the residents will receive the lease fee and 10 percent of the hunting tax paid by the sport hunting operator.

However, it is unreasonable that most of the community hunting zones (*ZICGC*) are in the non-permanent forests (areas close to villages) where the game animals have decreased, while major parts of the permanent forests where animals are abundant are designated as sport hunting zones for wealthy foreigners. According to conservationists, sport hunting allows for the sustainable management of animal population because the species and numbers of animals to be hunted can be predetermined and regulated. Moreover, they argue that it is beneficial to wildlife conservation and management because the fees paid by sport hunters can be used for wildlife conservation. In contrast, they argue that it would be difficult for the local people to manage hunting and animal resources would likely be depleted by excessive hunting by people seeking immediate cash income without caring about long-term sustainability. However, this is a policy that reject the possibility of local people's capacity of managing their own resources.

3.4.3.2. Regulation of hunting methods and target animals

Under pressure from international conservation groups, the Cameroon government has tightened hunting regulations. First, it decided that local people without hunting licenses would only be allowed to use "traditional hunting methods." A "traditional hunting method" is "hunting with tools made of plant materials" (Decree 1995, Article 2-20). In the case of the

Baka, however, nearly 90% of their daily catch is caught in snares with iron wire (Hattori, 2012), which means that this hunting method is illegal. Bantu agriculturalists often hunt with shotguns, but 40–50% of their catch is made with iron wire (Bobo et al., 2015). In our study area in the East Region (see Chapter 4), gun hunting is sometimes done at night with flashlights, which is also illegal (Article 80 of 1994 Forest Law).

Regulations also stipulate the target animals to be hunted. The 1994 Forest Law, the 1995 Presidential Decree, and the 2006 ordinance of Ministry of Forests and Animal resources classified the animals that may be hunted in the forest into three categories. The first category, animals of Class A, are species that are threatened with extinction and are strictly protected. This includes 32 species, including great apes and leopards, 16 of which are found in the rainforests of southeastern Cameroon. Species in Class B are also subject to protection but can be hunted with a government permit. There are 16 species in Class B, 11 of which are distributed in the study area (in the East Region). Those who hunt or hold any of these protected species without a permit incur a fine (50,000–200,000 CFA francs, approximately 75–300 euros) or imprisonment (20–60 days) (Forest Law, Article 155). Species that are not subject to protection are Class C, which allows hunting with "traditional methods" (Djeukam, 2012). These protected categories are supposed to be periodically reviewed by the Ministry (Djeukam, 2012), but that did not happen until recently.[2]

Previous studies on the species composition of the catch demonstrate that the major targets differ slightly from area to area (Yasuoka, 2014). However, these differences were probably not considered when determining conservation classes. The major species caught in the forests of southeastern Cameroon are medium-sized forest antelopes called red duikers, among which Peter's duikers (*Cephalophus callipygus*), weighing 15–20 kg, are the most caught, accounting for 60% total head of catch (Yasuoka, 2014). This shows they are relatively abundant in the forest, but this species belongs to Class B and is subject to protection.

---

2   The hunting regulations were revised by the Ministry of Forests and Fauna decree dated April 1, 2020, adding to the protected species (especially those in Class B). (*Arrêté No 53/ MINFOF du 01 Apr, 2020 fixante de modalités de repartition des espèces animales en classes de protection*).

Chapter 3

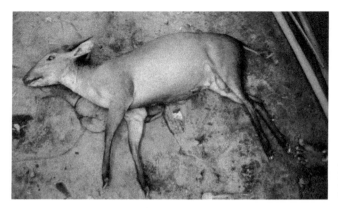

Photo 3.8
Red duiker
weighing 15–25 kg

Photo 3.9
Blue duiker
weighing 4–6 kg

In the villages (Zoulabot and Malea) surveyed by Yasuoka and Hattori, Class A and B species accounted for 70–90% of the animals captured (see Table 3.1). Furthermore, the Forest Law and regulations prohibit local people from hunting for commercial purposes (Decree, 1995, Article 24-(3)). The law states that the sale of game meat is allowed only if a permit (*Permis de collect*) is obtained from the government, but this applies mainly to sport hunting, and it is illegal to buy or sell game meat caught by local people without a permit.

3.5. Toward sustainable hunting for bushmeat: Cameroon

Bushmeat is a valuable food source for the local African peoples. Especially in the humid tropics of Africa, many people suffer from protein deficiency compared with drier regions, and the use of bushmeat

Bushmeat and the New Forest Law in Central Africa

Table 3.1 Composition of the catches by protection class

Protection Class	Zoulabot Head (%)	Malea Head (%)	Gribe Head (%)	Total weight kg (%)
A	71 (10.7)	11 (4.8)	32 (5.7)	317.07 (9.4)
B	519 (78.4)	147 (64.2)	60 (10.7)	1096.71 (32.4)
C	72 (10.9)	71 (31.0)	470 (83.6)	1971.72 (58.2)
Total	662 (100.0)	229 (100.0)	562 (100.0)	3385.5 (100.0)

(Data derived from Hattori, 2012; Yasuoka, 2006a; Bobo et al, 2015)

is indispensable to the healthy life of these people. Bushmeat is also a medium for identifying an individual's gender, age, descent group affiliation, and place in the life history of the forest people. The government restrictions on hunting ignore such local realities, and if they are strictly applied, they would threaten the livelihood and culture of local people who are highly dependent on forest wildlife.

In Africa, wild game is important both nutritionally and in terms of household income. According to Davies and Whitten (2007), protein deficiencies account for about 15–20% of the population in Latin America and Southeast Asia, both of which show a declining trend, whereas in the humid regions of Africa, it reaches 30–35% and in some places more than 40%. In recent years, this percentage has been even increasing. The supply of livestock meat as a source of protein has increased rapidly in South America from 30 kilograms per person per year in 1970 to 70 kilograms in 2000, while in Africa it has remained almost unchanged at around 10–20 kilograms. The supply of meat to poor people is even less, since it is not equally consumed among the people. In other words, many African people are chronically undernourished, especially in terms of animal protein from livestock and other sources. In many parts of Africa, the shortage is supplemented by wild animals. Of course, there are other sources of protein in the wild, such as fish and wild birds, but bushmeat is the main source of protein except in areas where a stable fish supply can be expected, such as near the coasts and major rivers.

Furthermore, bushmeat is one of the few sources of cash income for rural people. Very rough estimates suggest that in central Africa, about 20–50% of the catch is used for household or intra-village consumption, and about half or more is taken out of the village for sale (Nasi et al., 2008). For example, in the 1980s and early 1990s, local hunters in the vicinity of the Dzanga-Sangha National Park in Central Africa Republic

Chapter 3

earned an average of USD 400–700 per year from hunting (Noss, 1998), which was equal to or greater than the wage of a park guard. Near the Dja reserve in Cameroon, hunting has been reported to bring in as much as USD 650 per hunter per year (Ngegues and Fotso, 1996). These figures suggest that hunting and trading of bushmeat is a substantial source of income, at least in the short term. Estimates for the wider region suggest that in the midwestern Africa region, roughly USD 40–200 million of bushmeat is harvested for sale annually (Fa, 2007). If half of the catch was sold, this would mean that an average of USD 80–400 million worth of bushmeat was captured and used each year. In Gabon, it has been reported that USD 25 million worth of bushmeat is sold annually (Nasi et al., 2008). The amount sold there was estimated to be 20% of the total catch (Fa, 2007), so if actual catch was converted to cash, it is calculated that USD 125 million worth of bushmeat was captured annually. In the DRC, it was reported in 2007 that 1.1–1.7 million tons of bushmeat was used annually, an amount equivalent to at least USD 1 billion, even taking into account the low cost of bushmeat in the Congo (Debroux et al., 2007). By comparison, logging revenues in the DRC for the same period were estimated at USD 150 million per year, which illustrates the economic value of bushmeat. Moreover, an indiscriminate ban on bushmeat trade would have a tremendous impact on the livelihoods of the local poor people, who are more dependent on bushmeat (Nasi et al., 2008). In the central African region, hunting by local people for subsistence has been sometimes tolerated, as long as it does not conflict with the protection of rare species, because a total ban on hunting by the local people would require economic compensation that would be impossible to pay.

To plan animal conservation compatible with the livelihoods of local people, it is first necessary to have information on the local needs for bushmeat and the level of sustainable hunting. This kind of information has been sporadic to date, and it has only been obtained from short-term studies conducted in specific areas, which is by no means sufficient. Data on animal densities and growth rates are essential for estimating sustainable hunting levels, but reliable data on these are limited. With these points in mind, rough attempts are made here based on data collected by previous surveys. In an example from South America, Robinson and Bennett (2000) found for the Peruvian forests that hunting pressure (harvest rate) exceeding 150–200 kg per square kilometer per year is not sustainable. For Africa, Koster and Hart (1988) estimated the biomass of duikers in the forest at 174 kg per square kilometer from direct visual observation. But in a similar area, Wilkie and Finn (1990) estimated 8–9 times this figure (biomass of 1,497 kg per square kilometer) from the density of dung distribution. Another report from Ekom, Cameroon, found a value as high as 1,326 kg per square kilometer while luring the duikers by imitating their chirps, in the same site where a value of 184 kg was obtained from simple visual observation (Nasi et al., 2008). Considering these observations, it might be possible to sustain hunting to higher levels than those estimated for South America by Robinson et al. In the Lobaye region of the Central African Republic, where as many as 800,000 duikers were harvested for the skin trade between 1925 and 1950 during French colonial rule, hunting continued in the early 21st century, and the area was a major source of duiker bushmeat (Nasi et al., 2008).

Thus, while the sustainability of hunting can be evaluated from the data of biomass, growth rate and other variables of the target animals, the data on biomass varies considerably depending on which figures are adopted, and it is also not certain to what extent the figures on which they are based can be generalized. The level of sustainable hunting needs to be further examined in light of long-term observations on the ecology and demography of animal populations and reliable data on different research sites.

As discussed in Chapter 4, new methods such as nighttime census surveys and camera-trap (with sensor camera) surveys have been tried and results published one after another regarding the fauna and its abundance. Ingram et al. (2015) proposed an indicator to assess the sustainability of hunting in the absence of animal abundance data. This indicator, inspired by the sustainability assessment of fishery resources, attempts to assess hunting pressure based on "changes in the average weight of captured animals" and "temporal and spatial changes in the number of animals captured." However, these methods require data to be collected over a long period of time from a wide range of study sites. There may be other ways to monitor hunting pressure that can be easily employed by local people.

Chapter 3

We began a five-year research project in 2011 that aimed to establish sustainable use of forest resources, including hunting. The details of this project are presented in the next chapter, and here I would like to look briefly at the survey on animals and hunting by local people.

Cameroonian ecologists surveyed the mammal population and the hunting activities of local people. The results showed that the catch of red duikers (weighing 15–25 kg) and blue duikers (4-6 kg), the main species in the area, was already far beyond the sustainable range at the time of research (Bobo et al., 2014; 2015). Yasuoka also found that when the logging roads opened, a number of traders began to visit the area seeking bushmeat. The average catch in the area jumped from 0.9 animals per hectare to 13–16 animals per hectare, far exceeding sustainable levels, which is estimated at 0.5–6.0 head/ha (Yasuoka, 2006a; 2014; see Table 3.2). This excessive hunting pressure is due to hunting for a commercial purposes, with more than 90% of medium-sized red duikers and 70% of blue duikers used for trade (Kamgaing et al., 2019).

Yasuoka observed that the composition of prey changes as hunting pressure increases. In southeastern Cameroon, duikers comprise major catch, accounting for more than 80% (in number of head) of the total catch (Yasuoka, 2006a, b). Peters' duiker, a medium-sized duiker weighing 15–20 kg, is particularly common in his study area, Zoulabot ancien. However, in the Lobeke area, situated along the major road connecting Yokadouma and Moloundou on the border of Congo-Brazaville, the main catch is comprised of smaller blue duikers (4–6 kg), despite being caught with a similar snare trapping method. According to Yasuoka (2014), this difference is due to the stronger hunting pressure in Lobeke area with a higher human population density. In other words, the medium-sized red duikers (Peters' duikers), which reproduce relatively slowly, decline quicker because they cannot withstand high hunting pressure, while the smaller blue duikers, which reproduce at a faster rate, remain more abundant. Based on these results, Yasuoka et al. (2015) proposed an indicator for the local people to monitor hunting pressure. It is the B/R (or B/M) ratio, or the ratio of blue duikers (B) to medium-sized (M), or red (R), duikers in the capture. The indicator increases as hunting pressure becomes stronger, because medium-sized duikers become less abundant relative to blue duikers. Yasuoka emphasized that using such an easy-to-understand indicator will allow local people to

Table 3.2 Maximum sustainable catch (MSC) and actual catch before and after construction of the logging roads

	MSC (head/km²/yr)	Actual catch (head/km²/yr)	Source	remarks
Red duikers	0.5–6.0	0.9	Yasuoka 2014	before
Red duikers	0.5–6.0	13–16	Yasuoka 2014	after
Red duikers	0.89–2.5	2.93	Bobo et al. 2015	after
Blue duikers	1.28–3.91	12.17	Bobo et al. 2015	after

manage animal resources. The validity of this indicator will be examined in a project currently underway by Yasuoka and his team.

Achieving sustainable levels hunting of wildlife is difficult, but it is only through such efforts that both the global issue of conservation and local interests in improving the livelihoods and maintaining the culture of the forest-dependent people can be satisfied.

Chapter 4

Toward a Sustainable Use of Non-Timber Forest Products: Attempts in Southeastern Cameroon Forest

Chapter 4

Photo on the previous page: Workshop held at the field station in southeastern Cameroon

Toward a Sustainable Use of Non-Timber Forest Products

4.1. Research in Cameroon

The political situation in the former Zaire, which had been under the dictatorship of President Mobutu since the 1960s, began to deteriorate rapidly in the 1990s. The inflation of the Zairean currency, which had continued since the late 1970s, had become increasingly severe. Its value had steadily fallen from 0.5 Zaire for 1 USD at the time of my first research in 1974, to 50 Zaire for 1 USD in 1985, and to 700 Zaire in August, 1990.[1] Consumer prices rose accordingly at tremendous rates. People in the towns lost confidence in their currency and preferred to be paid in US dollars rather than Zairean currency. Loss of confidence in currency means the loss of confidence in the state that issues it. When we passed town on the way back from the Ituri Forest at the end of 1990, people anxiously asked us, "*Nchi yetu iko na kufa?* (Is our country dying?)."

In the summer of 1991, insurrections in the capital Kinshasa and other parts of the country sparked an emergency and foreigners fled the country. I was in Brazzaville with Koichi Kitanishi (then a graduate student) preparing for research on the Aka hunter-gatherers, and was not greatly affected. Other Japanese researchers in Kinshasa at the time, together with the embassy staff and other Japanese residents, escaped to Brazzaville by crossing the Congo River. When we saw the smoke rising on the other side of the river, we realized that Kinshasa was in a state of emergency. At the Center for Research in Natural Science (*CRSN*), former *IRSAC* (*Institut pour la Recherche Scientifique en Afrique Centrale*), situated on the outskirts of Bukavu in eastern Zaire, fellow research team members Hideaki Terashima and graduate students Rosei Hanawa and Kaori Komatsu were preparing for field research in the interior forest. I suggested that they should leave Zaire and come to investigate the Aka hunter-gatherers and Bantu agriculturalists in the northern part of Brazzaville Congo.

Two weeks later, I met the three researchers who had moved from eastern Zaire, at the port of Dongo on the Ubangi River in Likouala

---

1   The rapid decline in Zairean currency continued thereafter. The exchange rate abruptly fell from 65,250 Zaire for 1 USD in December, 1991, to more than 2 million Zaire at the end of 1992, to 117 million Zaire at the end of 1993. The annual increase in consumer prices rose to 256% in 1990, 2500–4500% during 1991–1993, and almost 10,000% in 1994 (Beaugrand, 1997).

Chapter 4

Region, northern Republic of Congo. We decided to study the Aka hunter-gatherers and Bantu-speaking slash-and-burn agriculturalists in the Motaba River region. Previously, the late Tadashi Tanno and Kiyoshi Takeuchi had begun researching the Aka in the Ibenga River, north of the Motaba River. I had conducted a preliminary survey in 1990 with Takeuchi in the upper reaches of the Motaba River. Kitanishi had already started researching the Aka hunter-gatherers living in the upper Motaba River, and Hanawa and Komatsu, together with Terashima, began researching the Bobanda, Bantu-speaking slash-and-burn agriculturalists in the middle reaches of the Motaba River.

In the late-1980s and '90s, the central African region experienced a growing wave of "democratization" and constant conflicts with the old powers. When I left three graduate students on the Motaba River in late-1991 and returned to the country in 1992, the Republic of Congo was politically unstable. The Congo had been governed by a one-party dictatorship since independence, but a multi-party system was introduced in 1990 and a new president had been elected. The former president's faction, which had revolted against the new president, tried to regain power. By mid-November 1992, when I returned to Brazzaville with the students, who had been conducting research in the Motaba River region since the previous year, the atmosphere in Brazzaville was disturbing. Armed military police (*gendarmes*) had set up checkpoints throughout the town. A short time later, the Congo descended into a civil war between the current and former presidents and a third force in a three-way conflict. Due to these circumstances, our research in the northern part of the Congo was cut short.

Our next focus was on the Baka hunter-gatherers and Bantu slash-and-burn agriculturalists living in the forests of southeastern Cameroon. Anthropological research by Japanese in Cameroon until then had been limited to primatological research in the tropical rainforests of the Littoral Region and the arid zone of the Extreme North, and linguistic and social anthropological surveys in the Adamawa and Extreme North Regions. There has been no anthropological research in the forest areas, especially those inhabited by hunter-gatherers. It was a valuable opportunity for me to visit the society of the Baka hunter-gatherers, adding a third major group to my previous investigations of the societies of the Mbuti and the Aka. In the summer of 1993, Daiji Kimura (now professor emeritus of Kyoto University), Rosei Hanawa, Koichi Kitanishi and Kaori Komatsu, who had moved from Congo, visited Cameroon to conduct preliminary research in the forest areas of the East Region. In early 1994 I joined them and began full-scale research in the forest areas of Cameroon's East Region. Since then, we have continued researching the Baka hunter-gatherers and slash-and-burn cultivators in the region for more than a quarter of a century.

The forests of the East Region of Cameroon are situated at the western edge of the Congo Basin and extend to the Sanga River basin, a tributary of the Congo River. It is 2000 km in a straight line from the Ituri Forest. The area was inhabited by Baka hunter-gatherers. They had a similar physical appearance to the Mbuti and Aka, at least externally. Recent genetic studies suggest that the genetic divergence between the Mbuti of the eastern Congo Basin and the Baka of the west occurred some 20,000 years ago (Verdu and Destro-Bisol, 2012). Nevertheless, these forest peoples have developed several similarities, including a forest-dependent hunting-and-gathering lifestyle and material culture, song and dance characterized by polyphony and beliefs in forest spirits, despite belonging to different language systems.

4.2. State of forests and peoples in Cameroon

Extending from north to south in the middle of the African continent, Cameroon is called "Africa in miniature" because it has most African landscape types within a single triangular-shaped country. The northern part of the country is dominated by dry savanna, while the southern part is covered by tropical rainforests. The total forest area in Cameroon is estimated to be around 20 million hectares, most of which is so-called tropical moist forest (tropical rainforest including semi-deciduous forest). Between 1980 and 1995, 2 million hectares of forest were logged. Since the devaluation of the CFA franc in 1994 (to one-half of its value against the French franc) resulted in the relative decline in transportation and labor costs, logging operations have significantly increased and reached into remote forest areas where logging had previously been unprofitable. As a result, Cameroon became, for a time, the world's fourth largest timber exporter after New Guinea, Gabon, and Malaysia. In 1996–1998, when logging was at its highest, an average of 1.7 million cubic

Chapter 4

meters of timber, valued at USD 230 million, was exported each year, accounting for one-tenth of the world's timber exports at the time (Bikie et al., 2000). The area of forests subject to logging (either on-going or planned) in 1959 was only 8% of the total forest area, but by the late '90s it had expanded to 76% of Cameroon's total forest area. In contrast, only 6% of the forest were protected at that time, and much of that was only in principle.

In 1994, a short time after we began our research, I counted logging trucks passing through the vicinity of Yokadouma, the capital of the Boumba-Ngoko district in East Region. About 100 trucks daily during the dry season when road conditions were good, and as many as 50 trucks daily even during the rainy season when roads were bad, were passing through town carrying huge trees. The trucks were heading toward the port of Douala. The secondary forests on both sides of the road that runs north-south from Yokadouma to Moloundou on the border with Congo-Brazzaville, were spared from large-scale logging to provide residential and agricultural areas for the local people. However, these roadside forests were merely a screen that hid the devastation behind them. A little deeper into the forest, there were webs of logging roads running throughout the forest.

In addition to large-scale industrial logging, the economic crisis of the late 1980s and subsequent structural adjustment programs had a major impact on deforestation in Cameroon (Sunderlin et al., 2000). As described in the previous chapter, public sector employees were reduced and wages were drastically cut under pressure from the IMF and World Bank, which resulted in the rise of unemployment and poverty rate of the urban population. As living conditions deteriorated in the cities, the population that had been flowing into the cities began to return to rural areas. In the five years from 1993, the rural inflow exceeded the rural outflow in some areas (Sunderlin et al., 2000).

In rural areas with growing populations, efforts were first made to produce agricultural food for subsistence and domestic consumption, such as plantains and cassava, rather than tree crops for export, such as cacao and coffee. In addition to the need for subsistence food to support the growing population, the people themselves saw the advantage of food crops that could be sold more reliably in domestic markets than export crops, the prices of which were unstable. They maintained their existing cacao and coffee fields and cleared new land for cultivating food crops. Meanwhile, when market prices for cacao and coffee rose, their cultivation also expanded. In this way, the growing rural population also contributed to the loss of forest cover . In large-scale logging operations in Cameroon, a small number of species with high market value are selectively extracted (selective logging), leaving a considerable amount of vegetation cover on the ground surface. The forests subject to logging are classified as "permanent forests," and agricultural activities are not allowed. In contrast, agricultural activities remove more vegetation from the crop fields. In fact, analysis of aerial photographs and satellite imagery shows that the rate of deforestation in the decade following the economic crisis of 1986 was ten times that of the previous decade (Sunderlin et al., 2000), due to the expansion of agriculture into the forest areas.

The problem is not limited to the decreasing forest cover, either. In some areas the forests remain in good condition, but have been "emptied" of game animals due to excessive hunting. In the rural areas of the Congo Basin, large quantities of bushmeat are consumed (see Chapter 3), providing a major protein source to the local people (Wilkie and Carpenter, 1999). In the tropical rainforests of central Africa, cattle and other livestock husbandry is generally not viable due to the presence of the tsetse fly and lack of adequate pastureland. For the inhabitants of this region, bushmeat is an important source of protein, which is often in short supply. Moreover, for people who are losing contact with the wilderness of the forests due to urbanization and deforestation, bushmeat is highly valued as a source of "wild power" that cannot be obtained from livestock meat or fish (see Chapter 3). Although the bushmeat trade itself has been around for some time, the market expanded in the 1990s as both trade and consumption of bushmeat increased. In places where transporting important cash crops, such as cacao and coffee, had become challenging due to the disruption of transportation networks and the deterioration of infrastructure, bushmeat became an immediate source of cash income. In Cameroon in particular, people who moved to rural areas from the cities began to engage in the trade of bushmeat as an easy means for acquiring cash income.

Such commercial hunting has significantly reduced animal populations in the forest. In the Congo Basin, hunting has halved the number

Chapter 4

of forest antelopes (Hart, 2000). Rare species such as gorillas and chimpanzees, and large mammals such as elephants are threatened with extinction. As discussed in Chapter 3, these animals reproduce slowly and are therefore at greater risk from hunting. In addition, the ecological conditions of the tropical rainforest, i.e., its biodiversity loss, have contributed to the decline of these rare species.

International concern over rapid deforestation and biodiversity loss led to the expansion of the conservation movement. In Cameroon, the World Wide Fund for Nature (WWF), and the Wildlife Conservation Society (WCS) were conducting ecological surveys that would serve as the baseline for protecting the area on the western side of the Sangha River. Then, in 2001, the area of 217,800 hectares, including the swamp zone in the Lobeke river basin on the western side of the Sangha river, were designated a national park by the Cameroon government. In addition, the Nouabale-Ndoki national park and Dzanga-Sangha protected areas were established in the adjacent region of the Republic of Congo and the Central African Republic, respectively, creating a tri-national conservation area spanning Cameroon, Congo and Central Africa. Moreover, in 2005, Cameroon designated 238,200 ha of forest on the western side of the Boumba river (a tributary of the Ngoko and the Sanga), and 309,300 ha along the Nki river, which flows into the Dja river, as national parks (Boumba-Bek and Nki national parks, respectively).

To date, the protection of tropical rainforests has often been demanded from a global perspective, in response to concerns such as the impact on the earth's atmosphere (prevention of global warming) and the protection of biodiversity (and genetic resources). From this perspective, it has been viewed as a "global" environmental issue, and to protect the "global commons" (common property of humankind), it has been deemed necessary to create "wild sanctuaries" that exclude all human activities. This is an adaptation of classic protectionism to the modern age of globalization. However, the world is not so homogeneous and integrated that global issues are necessarily recognized as such from a local perspective. And thus, those in the world outside of the forests, or those in the "global North" who loudly advocate for the protection of forests, are often perceived by the locals who are directly impacted by these reserves to be "foreigners who don't live here and have no rights, interfering with other people's land."

Deforestation and defaunation (becoming empty forests) directly threaten the livelihood of the local inhabitants. The slash-and-burn agriculture and hunting activities that have supported their livelihoods and culture are at risk of becoming unsustainable in the near future. For the local people, the destruction of forest is not so much a "global" as a "local" environmental problem and strict forest conservation plans such as wildlife sanctuaries deprive them of the means of their livelihoods. For them, exclusive sanctuaries are effectively no different from deforestation.

We therefore need to develop a new model of forest conservation to replace the traditional paradigm of "wildlife sanctuaries." We need a model of forest conservation that does not exclude humans from the forest, but rather enables humans and nature to coexist in the forest. Despite many attempts at forest conservation, we do not yet have a clear picture of the optimal relationship between forest and humans in protected areas. Although classical conservationists may consider a world in which nature and humans coexist in harmony to be a postmodernist illusion (Attwell and Cotterill, 2000), it is important to be clear about the desirable relationship between forest and humans when considering forest conservation.

Some new initiatives in and around the protected areas in Cameroon have sought to restore those relationships. For example, in Lobeke national park, local residents have been granted access to the park to collect plant foods, honey, medicinal plants, etc. for some time, despite the presence of poachers from outside who hunt game animals with guns and capture grey parrots for sale (WWF Cameroon, 2001). In park management, rather than implementing a fully pre-designed master plan as in the past, new approaches such as adaptive management are being explored. These plans are intentionally flexible, adapting to feedback from each stage of implementation as appropriate. Furthermore, at least in the initial planning, the recent conservation projects in this region are unique in that they recognized local people as active players in conservation, rather than as destroyers of forests and impediments to conservation (Davenport, 1998; Cuttan and Tshombe, 2001). Among other things, the coercive exclusion of humans from a vast area with a

Chapter 4

circumference of hundreds of kilometers require an enormous amount of manpower and expense just to monitor poaching. There is some evidence that proactive protection by local people can be far more economical and effective. It has also become clear that strict human exclusion from wildlife sanctuaries is not as effective, even as means of conservation, as a multiple-use reserve that allows local people to use forest resources (Curran and Tsombe, 2001). Although many of these attempts have not been as successful as was initially hoped, and many issues remain to be resolved, this may be the only way to successfully conserve forests in the long run.

4.3. SATREPS project in Cameroon

While I was thinking about the situation of the forests and the people in central Africa, I received an invitation from a university colleague, Shigeru Araki (now professor emeritus at Kyoto University), to join him in applying for an overseas technical and scientific cooperation project. I accepted his invitation and joined the project as head of the forestry group. The project was jointly funded by the Japan Science and Technology Agency (JST) and the Japan International Cooperation Agency (JICA) and was called the Science and Technology Research Partnership for Sustainable Development (SATREPS). Our project was titled "Establishment of Sustainable Livelihood Strategies and Natural Resource Management in Tropical Rain Forest and its Surrounding Areas of Cameroon: Integrating the Global Environmental Concerns with Local Livelihood Needs." The plan was adopted in 2010, and after almost a year of repeated negotiations with local institutions regarding implementation methods and other matters, full-scale activities began in Cameroon in the summer of 2011. The project was a five-year plan that would run through 2016, in cooperation with the National Institute for Agricultural Development (*L'Institut de Recherche Agricole pour le Développement, IRAD*) as the main Cameroonian counterpart, as well as researchers and graduate students from the University of Yaounde I, Dchang Agricultural University, and the University of Douala (Woin, et al., 2012).

The project consisted of three groups: agriculture, forests, and soil. The agriculture group aimed to increase the productivity of agriculture, mainly of cassava cultivation, in the peripheral parts of tropical forests. The forest group focused on the sustainable use of "Non-Timber Forest Products" (NTFPs). The soil group analyzed the soils that support forest ecosystems and agricultural production and the effective use of soil nutrients. In conventional overseas technical cooperation projects, agricultural development and forest conservation are typically pursued through distinct projects in different sectors. This project was original in integrating the two. In other words, while the agricultural team aimed to mitigate the expansion of agricultural land into forests by improving agricultural productivity, the forestry team aimed to establish an alternative method to large-scale logging, i.e., to use NTFPs without cutting down trees, thereby achieving both forest conservation and improving people's livelihoods.

The research by the forest group consisted of the following three layers (Figure 4.1).

(1) Ecological research of forest flora and fauna: In addition to basic surveys of the flora, fauna, and vegetation around the project area, the ecological potential of NTFPs was clarified through surveys of the distribution, abundance, and fluctuation of NTFPs that might be effectively used.

(2) Research on the use and sustainability of NTFPs: The sustainability of resource use was evaluated by comparing the data of actual use with the resource potential (abundance, etc) estimated from the results of (1) above.

(3) Investigation of social relations concerning resource use: Sustainable use of forest resources requires prevention of over-exploitation due to excessive competition. We sought to identify ways for local people to mitigate competition and to explore social systems that would enable long-term sustainability based on, or derived from, local customary ways.

The ecological research in (1) above was promoted by Cameroonian researchers. Dr. Bernard Aloy Nkongmeneck, his former student Dr. Evariste Fongnzossie, and their students from the Faculty of Science,

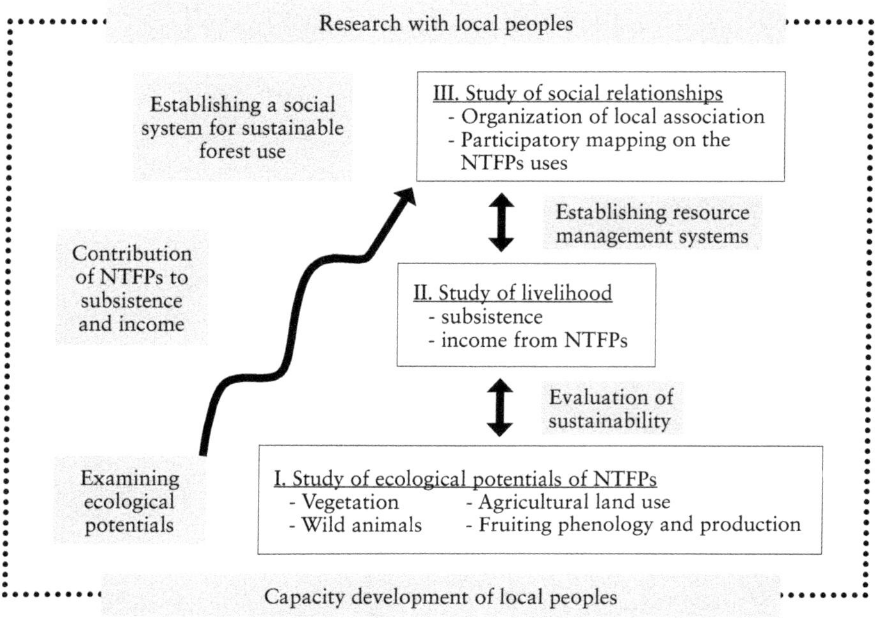

Chapter 4

Fig. 4.1 Project Design

140

University of Yaounde I, conducted the plant ecological survey. Dr. Serge Bobo Kadiri of Dchang Agricultural University conducted the fauna (mammals) survey with the assistance of his students. In our previous surveys in Africa, local researchers had participated as collaborators, but had generally played only a formal, or liaison role with the local government. In this project, however, Cameroonian researchers and graduate students conducted surveys and produced results in their respective fields. From Japan, young researchers such as Hirokazu Yasuoka, Masaaki Hirai, Koji Hayashi, and Mikako Toda conducted 1) ecological surveys, 2) livelihood surveys, and 3) social relations surveys. Hirai drew on his experience as a Japan Overseas Cooperation Volunteer (JOCV) in French-speaking Africa (Senegal) and conducted his ecological survey in cooperation with local people from both Baka hunter-gatherers and the Kounabembe (Bantu) agriculturalist groups.

These activities were conducted with the full cooperation of the local people. Through long-term collaboration between researchers and local people, the researchers learned indigenous knowledge about the forest and compared it with scientific knowledge. Conversely, they also

Toward a Sustainable Use of Non-Timber Forest Products

attempted to translate scientific knowledge into local knowledge. In the process, local people were exposed to (scientific) ecological knowledge and had opportunities to learn scientific methods and techniques. One objective of this project was to promote knowledge and capacity development through such exchanges.

4.4. Project site and research station

The project's research base was in the village of Gribe, in the Boumba-Ngoko prefecture of the East Region (see Figure 4.2). Although we had not previously conducted research on this village, there were good reasons for choosing it as our base. First, the population of Gribe village was appropriate in both size and ethnic group mix, with about 400 Bantu-speaking farmers, mainly the Kounabembe, and about the same number of Baka hunter-gatherers (Toda, 2014). At this size, most of the means of livelihood and other activities characteristic of the region could be observed, and differences between ethnic groups, households, and individuals can be identified. Second, the village was relatively easy to access because it is a large regional village connected to Yokadouma, the capital of Boumba-Ngoko district to the northeast, by a road that is accessible to cars via a *bac* (floating bridge) over the Boumba River. To the west, it can be reached from Lomie in a few hours' drive, unless the bridge over the Bek river is washed out by heavy rain and flooding. These roads were cleared or renovated from 1999 to the 2000s as logging roads. Although they are rough and can be quite challenging during the rainy season due to fallen trees and muddy conditions, they also provide evacuation routes in case of emergency.

The crucial point, however, was the location of the village. About a dozen kilometers south of the village lies the recently (in 2005) established Boumba-Bek national park, which restricted entry by the local people. In addition, there is a logging area (classified as permanent forest) behind the narrow agricultural zones (classified as non-permanent forest) on both sides of the road that runs through the village. Not only is agriculture prohibited in it, but part of the permanent forest zone had recently been designated as a sport hunting (trophy hunting) area for wealthy Westerners. The local people were not allowed to hunt in this area. According to conservation groups and the Cameroonian

Chapter 4

government, sport hunting is "sustainable" because, unlike hunting by the local people, which is difficult to control, the species to be hunted and the number of animals to be hunted are clearly defined and can be regulated. In addition, the revenue from the hunting license and other taxes can be used for wildlife conservation. However, this perspective completely disregards the interests of the local people. They have been deprived of access to most of the forests that have supported their livelihoods and culture for centuries by the large-scale logging in the name of "sustainable forestry." They have also been excluded from the forests reserved for conservation programs and "sport hunting." Thus, almost 90% of the forests previously used by the local people have been lost, and allocated to large-scale logging, conservation, and sport hunting (see Chapter 3). Today, local people have free access only to a few kilometers of secondary forests on either side of the roads. This is a typical case of "green grabbing" (Fairhead et al. 2013). Similar examples can be found around the world, especially in the Congo Basin, where people living in forests with rich biodiversity are caught between development (logging) and nature conservation. Our SATREPS project sought to address these issues.

Upon selecting a research site, it was necessary to obtain the residents' approval. We asked the village chief and some of the villagers to attend the meeting and explained our project. Fortunately, the villagers had no objection to starting the project. Perhaps the prospect of employment opportunities played a role in their approval. However, there were problems of acquiring land for the construction of our research station. By law, Cameroon's forest land belongs to the state. In practice, however, long-term residents, especially the agriculturalists, have customary rights to the land. Even if the land is legally owned by the state, once the land has been cultivated, the person who first cultivated it has the right to further use, even if it has become secondary forest after being abandoned. People and organization from outside cannot cut the forest and use the land freely. The land we wanted to build on was secondary forest along the road at the edge of the village, which had once been cultivated, and the villagers, who claimed customary rights to the land, were reluctant to allow us to build. Once we had managed to negotiate their consent, we asked a land management official from Yokadouma to conduct a site survey. In the presence of the customary right holder living next to the

Toward a Sustainable Use of Non-Timber Forest Products

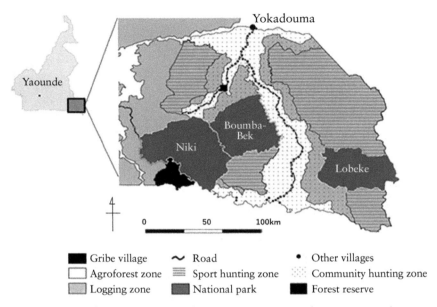

Fig. 4.2 Zoning of project area, southeastern Cameroon (The community hunting zone in the logging zone (dotted area with grey color) to the southeast of Gribe is now leased to a sport hunting company. Adapted and modified from Hirai (2014) and Ichikawa (2020).

proposed site and our project counterparts from the National Institute for Agricultural Development (IRAD), the land was surveyed and stakes were placed to mark the boundaries. Thus, the land for the station was formally authorized for use by us and our counterpart, the National Institute for Agricultural Development.

Professor Makoto Kimura of Kyoto University's Faculty of Engineering and architect Mr. Haruhumi Yasuda took responsibility for the station's construction. Professor Kimura is a civil engineering researcher who had been working with local farmers on a project called "Michibushin" (literally: road construction), in which sandbags are piled up on bad roads in rural villages in Africa to make them passable for vehicles. Mr. Yasuda was a researcher of architecture, especially interested in the construction of using soil. Mr. Yasuda designed and constructed the station using special bricks made of soil (sun-dried bricks made of red soil and 10% cement, see Yasuda, 2015). He managed all aspects of the station construction, from design to procurement of materials and supervision of construction works.

Chapter 4

Photo 4.1 Construction of research station

Photo 4.2 Research station in Gribe

The first step of the construction was to remove the trees growing on the building site and clear the bumpy site. Although it would have been easier to use bulldozers, we decided to do as much as possible with the local labor. We recruited applicants from both the Bantu agriculturalists and the Baka hunter-gatherers. Chainsaws, axes, and machetes were used for cutting trees and shrubs, and tools called *tako* ("octopuses") were made locally to manually level and compact the ground. The building's walls were made of bricks made of red soil (laterites) mixed with 10% cement and compacted with tools imported from South America. Timber for the pillars and beams was procured at a nearby logging and milling station. The roof was made of tin for durability, but the attic was covered for insulation with raffia palm leaves, which grow in nearby swamps. The project policy was to construct the station using local materials and human labor as much as possible (Yasuda, 2015). Because of this, the construction works took nearly a year, far longer than planned. The completed station turned out to be a cool and truly comfortable building. The long construction period had the benefit of facilitating communication with the villagers, and I believe that their understanding of the project deepened through this period.

4.5. Results of the project (1): Use of forest land and NTFPs

4.5.1. Sustainability of slash-and-burn agriculture in the project area

To understand the land use pattern in the project area, it was necessary to identify the distribution of crop fields (currently used and abandoned sites) around the village of Gribe. Agriculture in the area is mainly based on slash-and-burn cultivation, with plantain and cassava as the main crops for subsistence, and cacao as a cash crop. Cacao cultivation had been growing in the region since the mid-1990s, when the CFA franc was devalued, and the international market price of cacao rose. Hirai, a core researcher on the project, with the help of local people, surveyed the locations and areas of currently used and abandoned crop fields using GPS and other surveying instruments (Hirai, 2014). They found a total of about 4,000 plots in the vicinity of Gribe village that had been used

Chapter 4

as crop fields from the 1960s to the present. Around 90% (3,637 plots) of these plots were found in secondary forest, i.e., land that had been cultivated at least once in the past. This indicates that there had not been much expansion of cultivated land into primary or mature forests in recent decades. We had begun our research with a preconceived notion that cultivated land was continually expanding deeper into the forest and were concerned about the impacts of such expansion on the forest environment. But, in fact, this was not the case.

In the 2012 season, when the survey started, the cultivated fields ranged from about 0.12 to 0.24 hectares per plot, which is not very large. In the 2012 season, a total of 239 plots (47 ha) were cultivated, of which 89 plots (11 ha) were cultivated by the Baka hunter-gatherers, and 150 plots (36 ha) were cultivated by Bantu-speaking (mainly Kounabembe) farmers (Hirai, 2014). On average, a Baka cultivate only about half (0.12 ha per individual) as much land as the Konabembe and other Bantu farmers (0.24 ha per individual), but the difference in the fields that are actually harvested is much larger. This is because many of the Baka's fields are not properly managed and abandoned in the middle of cultivation, as discussed in the next chapter.

According to Cameroon's forest law, cultivation of land for agriculture is limited to the "agroforest zone," a non-permanent forest area, 3 km wide on both sides of the road. The total area of cultivable land available to the people of Gribe village is approximately 7100 ha (Hirai, 2014). If 50 ha are cultivated each year, it would take about 140 years to use all of the available land. Of course, some parts of land are not suitable for cultivation due to topography, soil, and other conditions. However, even if a sufficient fallow period is allowed, there is still a margin of 100 years or so before the land that has been cultivated can be used again for cultivation, if the available land is fully cultivated (fallow period 10–15 years). During such a long fallow period, vegetation and soil will recover, meaning that the cultivation practices in Gribe were within the range of sustainable agriculture that makes cyclical use of secondary forests. Importantly, while this was the situation at the time of the survey, if the population increased or agricultural production expanded to meet commercial demands for agricultural products, it will become necessary to expand crop fields into forest areas that have not previously been used for cultivation. However, we were nevertheless

Photo 4.3 Cacao garden   **Photo 4.4** Slash-and-burn field with mixed crops

surprised to find that, contrary to prior assumptions, the agricultural activities of the local people remained within sustainable levels.

4.5.2. Forest vegetation

How about, then, are the impacts of human activities such as agriculture on vegetational environment?

The flora and vegetation of the project area were surveyed mainly by Cameroonian researchers. Dr. Bernard Aloy Nkongmeneck of the University of Yaounde I, and his former student Dr. Evariste Fongzossie of the University of Douala, and graduate students from the University of Yaounde I, including Vice Tajeukem and Marie Ngansop, conducted the botanical research. They first established a baseline of 16 kilometers in a straight line from behind the village to the forest leading to Boumba-Bek National Park to the south. A total of 16 transects, each 20 meters wide and 5 kilometers long, were then established for vegetation surveys, intersecting perpendicular to the baseline on both sides. Four of these transects were located in agroforest zones (non-permanent forests that can be used for cultivation), eight in permanent forests (production forest subject to sustainable logging), and four in intermediate zones straddling both (Fonzossie et al., 2014; Tajeukem et al., 2014; Hirai, 2014). For each transect, the species of trees 10 cm or more in diameter at breast height (DBH, trees with DBH 5 cm or more were recorded for NTFP species), their DBHs (from which the basal area was calculated),

Chapter 4

Photo 4.5 Old secondary forest near Gribe village

and the number of individuals were recorded, for assessing the forest vegetation.

According to Fonzossie and Tajeukem, the average density of trees per unit area and the total basal area per unit area were 446.9 trees/hectare and 42.9 square meters/hectare, respectively, in the logging zone transects in permanent forests. Both density and basal area were higher than in the secondary forests in the agroforest zones (with 368.5 trees per hectare and 39 square meters per hectare). However, the diversity of tree species was slightly higher in secondary forests that had once been used as agricultural land (Tajeukem et al., 2014). These results may suggest that vegetation disturbance by small-scale agriculture does not simplify the forest species composition, but rather increases diversity. Although human activities often have destructive impacts on the forest environment, these results indicate that small-scale human disturbances have positive impacts on forest diversity. If such a trend is widely observed, we may have to reconsider the conventional view that slash-and-burn agriculture inevitably reduces the overall tree diversity of forest vegetation.

4.5.3. Distribution of NTFPs

During the survey of cultivated land, Hirai also surveyed the trees left on current and abandoned crop fields (Hirai, 2014). A total of 47 hectares of land cultivated in the 2012 season were surveyed, with a total of 3 142 individual trees with a diameter of 10 cm or more belonging to 240 species. The average number of trees was 66–67 per hectare. When the local people were asked why these trees were left uncut in the fields, the reasons given varied. Some said that the remaining trees would provide shade to protect the crop's seedlings from intense sunlight. Especially in cacao orchards, tall trees are necessary for shade. Others said that some trees are too hard to cut with the small axes they use. Indeed, the *peke* (*Irvingia gabonensis*) trees that are often left in the field are reportedly so hard that they are difficult to cut even with a chainsaw. In contrast, *gobo* (*Ricinodendron heudelotti)* trees are fast-growing softwood trees and are also often left in the fields. The *gobo* trees may have been left in the fields when the land was cleared because they produce edible nuts, which are used by the local people as food and for trade. If these useful trees have been deliberately left in the fields, the secondary forests in the former fields would a relatively large number of them.[2]

Although the results are tentative, Fongzossie (2014) reported an interesting distribution of non-timber resources in the forest. Comparing the distribution of eight species that produce major food NTFPs in the agricultural zone (non-permanent forest zone mostly composed of secondary forests) and the production forest (permanent forest zone, composed mainly of mature forests), he found that *gimba* (*Afrostyrax lepidophyllu,* Huaceae), which produces garlic-like flavored barks and fruits, was found at 52.4 plants per hectare in the former compared to only 10.8 in the latter. *Mbalaka* (*Pentaclethra macrophylla*, Caesalpinioideae-Fabaceae), whose seeds (beans) can be used as food, had 16.6 and 6.3 trees per hectare, respectively. The results are unsurprising because these are so-called "sun trees," meaning they do not germinate and grow without sufficient sunlight. A recent report by Ngansop et al. (2019), who studied the distribution of food plants in more detail, found that

---

2   Carrière (2002) also researched the selective sparing of trees in slash-and-burn fields among the Ntumu farmers in southern Cameroon and discussed its long-term impact on the rainforest.

Chapter 4

up to seven out of the eight major food species were more abundant in relatively new secondary forests than in mature forest. If these trends can be confirmed in other areas, or in a wider area, it would indicate that the impact of "moderate" human activities on the forests has improved the living environment for both humans and wild animals feeding on those plants. At least, this may be true for edible plants, many of which require light for germination and growth. If this is the case, we may find that permitting "moderate" human activities in the rainforests is a more effective form of conservation than wildlife sanctuaries that totally prohibit human activities.

We should not, however, forget the variability and diversity of the tropical rainforest vegetation. The distribution and density of NTFPs vary markedly from site to site. While the density of *Irvingia gabonensis* trees, called *peke*, is similar in all surveyed areas, the density of *gimba* (*Afrostyrax*), mentioned above, differs by as much as 10-fold depending on the surveyed area. The reasons for such differences are yet to be clarified. They may simply indicate an accidental distributional bias caused by the limited size of the survey area. It should be noted that tropical forests show remarkable variation in tree distribution within very small areas.

4.5.4. Production and harvest of NTFP

NTFPs are products of living trees, many of which are fruits and other reproductive organs. If these organs were removed, the next generation could not be secured. They are used by both humans and wild animals. For example, *peke* (*Irvingia gabonensis*) fruit are an important food source for elephants, which swallow the fruit whole, digest the pericarp, and excrete the hard shell containing the seeds[3] far from the fallen fruit. Elephants thus contribute to seed dispersal. Thus, in collecting NTFPs, it is necessary to leave enough fruit to ensure the reproduction of the resource base. To understand the impact of human extraction on the maintenance of healthy ecosystems, we must first assess how much of those resources is produced and how much is extracted by humans.

---

3   While red river hogs (bush pigs, *Potamochoerus porcus*) predate the seeds, cracking the hard endocarps (Beaune et al., 2012), elephants are important *Irvingia* seed dispersers in Africa, carrying seeds far from mother trees (Theuerkauf et al. 2000).

Hirai selected 10 major NTFP species important for the people's livelihood and household income and surveyed their fruit production (Hirai, 2014; Hirai and Yasuoka, 2020). The survey method was kept simple so that it could be employed by the local people. He selected 20–25 individuals of each species and placed 4 square (1m x 1m) frames at the base of each tree to divide the canopy into four equal sectors. The number of fruits falling in these frames was recorded, and the fruit production was calculated from the number of fruits falling into the frames, canopy areas, total canopy area per unit forest area, and forest area used by the local people (For detailed calculation methods, see Hirai and Yasuoka, 2020).

The recording continued from 2012 until the end of the project in 2016. There were several important findings. First, the fruit production of these plants was divided into two types. The first was those with a distinct fruiting season, represented by *peke* (*Irvingia gabonensis*), which reaches its peak fruiting season in July–August. *Gimba* (*Aflostyrax lepidophyllus*), used as condiments for its garlic-like flavor, and *mabe* (*Baillonella toxisperma,* Sapotaceae), which yields a high-quality edible oil and bears fruit in a similar pattern. The other group included the *gangendi* (*Irvingia excelsa*) and *kombele* (*Irivingia robur*), which belong to the same Irvingiaceae family as the *peke, kana* (*Panda oleosa*), whose walnut-like seeds are edible, and *gobo* (*Ricinodendron heudelotti,* Euphorbiaceae), which is used to make *sauce jaun* (yellow-colored sauce) which had longer fruiting seasons or bore fruit more or less year-round.

Hirai estimated annual fruit production using the method described above. For *peke*, used as oily condiment and one of the most important NTFPs, he converted fruit production into dried nut weight for trade, and calculated its monetary value and energy equivalent (Hirai and Yasuoka, 2020). There were marked annual fluctuations in *peke* production. In years when the fruit was abundant, 6–7 kg per hectare were produced per year in terms of dry weight of nuts. This corresponds to 10,000 to 12,000 CFA (approximately USD 20–24) when the nuts are sold to traders in the village. In other years, though, only 0.5 kg was obtained per year. The phenology of rainforest trees, including *peke*, is complex, and further research is needed to clarify what causes such great variation.

Chapter 4

Photo 4.6 Fruit of *Irvingia gabonensis*   Photo 4.7 Fruit drops survey

Irvingia fruit collected in the forest were cracked open with a machete or axe to extract the flat endosperm inside. Baka women would carry them back to the forest camp. Sometimes the nuts were dried over a campfire. At the camp, Bantu agriculturalists, the Kounabembe, waited to exchange fried donuts (called *beignets* in French), or other food and alcoholic beverages brought from the village for the nuts brought back from the forest by the Baka. The agriculturalists would dry the nuts, and when they had accumulated enough, would cart them to the village to sell to the traders. Hirai, with the help of the villagers, kept a daily record of the amounts and prices of nuts purchased by these traders, which revealed interesting facts.

Peke nuts are sold in large quantities in the village of Gribe in their season and can be seen everywhere spread out on mats to dry. *Peke* nuts are also sold in markets and on the streets of large cities such as Yaounde (capital of Cameroon), not to mention the market in Yokadouma, the nearby prefectural capital. Sometimes merchants from neighboring countries (Nigeria or Gabon) come to buy them. Furthermore, some are transported to European cities and sold in areas with African immigrant populations. Having seen large quantities of nuts being sold in many towns here and there, we were concerned about the sustainability of nut resources, but our research established that, at least in the study area, there was no need for concern. The forest area traditionally used by the people in Gribe is about 360 square kilometers. Hirai estimates that in a good fruiting year, the forest in this area produced as much as 250 tons dry weight of nuts. However, only a few percent (1–4%) of these nuts

Toward a Sustainable Use of Non-Timber Forest Products

Photo 4.8 Baka girl cracking *Irvingia* fruit   **Photo 4.9** Roasted nuts used as oily condiment

were sold to traders. In poor harvest years, fruit production was low, but in such years, the utilization rate of nuts was also low because there was not much gathering activity. The nuts collected include a portion that is not sold, but used for their own subsistence, which is much less than the portion that goes to trade. Even taking this into account, less than 10% of the nuts produced in the forest were harvested (Hirai and Yasuoka, 2020). According to Hirai and Yasuoka, other major NTFPs have similarly low utilization rates. In other words, non-timber forest resources such as *peke* are under-utilized, and there is currently no concern about degradation of the resource base due to over-extraction.

However, there are at least two limiting conditions that should be noted. First is the amount of the labor required to collect and process these nuts. It is a tedious and labor-intensive task to extract the nuts by cracking the shells with a machete or a stick one at a time. According to Hirai, it takes about five hours a day to extract two to three kilograms of nuts. The labor required for such work may be a bottleneck in nut utilization. If more effective nut extraction methods were developed, the amount of nuts extracted would likely increase.

Second is the issue of access to forests (Hirai and Yasuoka, 2020). As mentioned, most of the forests they have traditionally used are now designated as national parks or logging areas, and some of the logging areas have recently been designated as sport hunting areas. So far, nut collecting and other gathering activities are not strictly prohibited in the logging areas. However, there are fears that currently used nut gathering might be restricted as an obstacle to conservation programs, logging

Chapter 4

activities and sport hunting. Even though the existing resource base is superabundant, far exceeding harvest levels, sustainability would be threatened if the area available were greatly reduced.

4.5.5. Importance of NTFPs to subsistence and household income

NTFPs have often been called "minor forest products" mainly by foresters, government officers, conservationists and development workers, and their value has been underestimated. In Chapter 2, we saw rough estimates of the total value of market price of some NTFPs used in the DRC, based on a World Bank report (Debroux, et al., 2007). There are similar estimates of the market value of those products in Cameroon (Awono et al., 2016; Ingram et al., 2010), but there have been very few empirical studies on the importance of these products in the lives (their contribution to subsistence and household income) of local people. There had been no such research reported on our project area in the East Region. Therefore, our project tried to record the names, quantities and weights of all products brought to the villages, including agricultural products. The person who brought the products and the place they were obtained were also recorded. The survey in the Baka settlement was assisted by Baka men who could read and write. In addition, daily sales information (information on what was bought by whom, how much, and sold for how much) was obtained from traders (sometimes also shopkeepers) who stayed in the village to determine the cash income from the NTFPs. The survey was carried out by Hirai with the assistance of local people.

Hirai's (2014) preliminary report presents a Baka household of five members who brought in a total of 91 products belonging to 41 categories, including food, plant medicines, materials for tools and construction and fuel, from the forest or fields on a total of 293 occasions during a 63-day period from late August to mid-November in 2012. Of these, 95% of the staple starchy foods were agricultural crops. Very little starchy food (mainly wild yams) was obtained from the forests. However, animal meat and fish all came from the forests, as well as firewood, and materials for tools and building. Nuts such as *peke* (*Irvingia gabonensis*) and *kana* (*Panda oleosa*, Pandaceae) were also obtained from the forest. Thus, it is clear that, other than staple foods, the Baka are highly dependent on forest products for their livelihood.

As for cash income, Hirai (2014) showed that between August 30, 2012 and June 10, 2013, the people of Gribe village (Baka and Kounabembe) sold a total of 42 kinds of agricultural products, wild animals and plants to the traders surveyed, in a total of 2,698 sales, for about 26 million CFA francs, or just under 40,000 euros or about USD50,000 (Table 4.1). Of this amount, about 980,000 CFA (less than 1,500 euros, or about USD 1,900) was sold by the Baka, nearly 90% of which was from the sales of wild fruit, nuts and other NTFPs. In contrast, for the agricultural Kounabembe people, more than 80% of their income came from cacao and other agricultural products, with NTFPs accounting for only 15% of their total sales, though their income from NTFPs is much larger than that of the Baka. Among the NTFPs, three species were important: *peke* (*Irvingia gabonensis*) nuts mentioned earlier, *tondo* (*Aframomum* sp., Zinziberaceae) fruit used for seasoning and medicine, and *gobo* (*Ricinodendron heudelotti*) nuts used as an ingredient in sauces. They accounted for nearly 90% of the income from NTFPs. Among them, *peke* is the most important forest product, accounting for 40% of the total sales of NTFPs in this village. For the people in this area, especially the hunter-gatherer Baka, NTFPs are one of the few sources of cash income.

There was a marked difference in cash income between the Kounabembe and the Baka. During this period, the Kounabembe sold 25 million CFA, while the Baka sold less than 1 million CFA. For the NTFPs obtained from the forest, the agriculturalists sold nearly 4 million CFA, while the Baka sold only 870,000 CFA. Subsequent surveys also found that agriculturalists earned much more from forest products (NTFPs) than hunter-gatherers. For example, in 2015, agriculturalists earned an average of 122,871 CFA per person from the sales of *peke*, while those involved in sales among the Baka averaged only 7,245 CFA per person, a 17-fold difference between the amounts sold by the two groups (Hirai and Ichikawa, 2018). While the commercialization of NTFPs has created some cash earning opportunities for local peoples, the income from these products is much higher for the agricultural people than the Baka. In other words, the new economic opportunities did not reduce the gap in cash income between the ethnic groups, but increased it. The

Chapter 4

Table 4.1 Amounts of NTFPs sold by the Baka and Kounabembe (30 August 2012 to 10 June 2013)

Products	Amounts sold by each group		Total (CFA)
	Baka (CFA)	Kounabembe (CFA)	
Agricultural products			
Cacao	106,300	20,977,950	21,084,250
Food crops	0	77,025	77,025
Livestock & Poultry	0	50,500	50500
subtotal	106,300	21,105,475	21,211,775
% of crops to total	10.9	84.2	81.4
NTFPs			
Fruit & nuts	795,850	3,730,600	4,526,450
-peke (Irvingia gabonensis)	(190,900)	(1,837,850)	(2,023,550)
-tondo (Aframomum spp.)	(423,200)	(596,400)	(965,200)
-gobo(Ricinodendron heudelotti)	(86,600)	(966,400)	(1,053,000)
-Other fruit and nuts*	(95,150)	(363,950)	(480,000)
Bushmeat**	37,200	58,000	95,200
Other NTFPs*	40,500	170,400	210,900
Subtotal	873,550	3,959,000	4,832,550
Total	979,850	25,064,475	26,044,325
% of NTFPs	89.1	15.8	18.6

Data derived and calculated from Table 9 in Hirai, 2014. (1 euro ≈ 656 CFA)

*: Other forest products sold during this period include: fruits or nuts of *Afrostyrax lepidophyllus*, *Scorodophloeus zenkeri*, *Pentaclethra macrophylla*, *Piper guineense*, *Monodora myristica*, *Cola* spp, *Beilschmiedia louisii*, *Diospyros crassiflora*, *Baillonella toxisperma*, *Tetrapleura tetraptera*, mushrooms and fresh-water fish.

**: Bushmeat is sold directly among the villagers, without the intermediary of shops and traders.

difference between the two groups was not because the agriculturalists were more intensively engaged in the extraction of forest products, but an effect of the unique transaction system for forest products in the region. In the next section, we will examine the transaction of NTFPs, taking *peke* nuts as an example.

4.5.6. Social problems in the commercialization of NTFPs

The people who collect *peke* and other NTFPs in the project area are mainly Baka hunter-gatherers. The Baka gather *peke* fruit in the forest, crack open the hard shells, extract only the nuts (kernels), and take them back to their camp. They then sell most of the nuts to the Bantu villagers (mainly Kounabembe) waiting in the camp, though they carry a small portion to the village to sell them to the traders. The *pekes* are seldom sold for cash in the forest camp but bartered for food such as *beignets* (fried donuts made from wheat flour) made by the Bantu villagers or for alcoholic beverages. Otherwise, they are used to return the advances received from the villagers in the form of agricultural food and alcoholic beverages (Toda and Yasuoka, 2020). The Bantu villagers bring the nuts obtained from the Baka to the village, dry them thoroughly, and then sell them to traders waiting in the village. Some of the traders are shop keepers who live in Gribe, and others come from Yokadouma and elsewhere in Cameroon, Nigeria, and Gabon. Sometimes the resident traders resell the nuts to visiting traders in large quantities for much higher prices than they purchased from the villagers. Once the nuts are in sufficient quantity, the traders transport the nuts to Yokadouma on a small truck. Some of the nuts are sold there, but most of the nuts are transported to larger towns further away, sometimes even to foreign countries.

At the time of our research, an enameled bowl (about 2 liters) was used as a unit of exchange (called *combo*) in the transaction between the local peoples (Baka and Kounabembe) and traders. The exchange rate in the forest was about 500 CFA (0.76 euros or 95 US cents) for a bowl full of nuts (weighing 1.6 kg on average), but cash is rarely used in this transaction. When *beignets* are used for exchange, 10 *beignets* are exchanged for one combo of *pekes*. The cash price of *beignets* is 50 CFA per piece, or 500 CFA for 10 pieces, in the village. The barter rate is, therefore, equivalent to the cash price. However, the real rate of *peke* is a bit higher because there are cases in which the advance payments received by the Baka is often not fully repaid (Toda and Yasuoka, 2020).

When the Bantu villagers have obtained enough nuts from the Baka, they carry them to their villages and sell to the traders there. The price varies depending on the time of year, but it is usually 1,500–2,000 CFA per *combo* on average in the normal season. In other words, the price of nuts in the village is three times more than at the forest camp, even considering that the nuts shrink a little with drying. The traders transport the nuts to towns and sell them at even higher prices. For example, at the market in Yokadouma, a handful of nuts (42–43 grams on average)

Chapter 4

```
          ┌─────────────────────────────────┐
          │   Baka (Collection of nuts)     │
          └─────────────────────────────────┘
   500 CFA              │        Transaction in forest
                        ▼
          ┌─────────────────────────────────┐
          │   Bantu villagers (Drying)      │
          └─────────────────────────────────┘
 1500–2000 CFA          │        Transaction in village
                        ▼
     ┌──────────────────────────────────────────────┐
     │ Resident & visiting traders (Transportation)  │
     └──────────────────────────────────────────────┘
 Price unknown          │        Transaction in town
                        ▼
          ┌─────────────────────────────────┐
          │      Retailers in town          │
          └─────────────────────────────────┘
 3600–3700 CFA          │        Transaction at town market
                        ▼
          ┌─────────────────────────────────┐
          │     Consumers in town           │
          └─────────────────────────────────┘
```

Fig. 4.3 Price change (CFA/*combo* in dry weight) of *peke* (*Irvingia gabonensis*) in different transactions

was sold for 100 CFA (according to Hirai's personal communication). This means the price was 3600–3700 CFA per *combo* (or 2300–2400 CFA/kg). If the Baka people sold the nuts themselves to the traders in the village, they could get as much as three times the price in the forest. If they took them to the town, they could get 2–3 times more than in the village, or 6–7 times more than in the forest (see, Fig. 4.3).[4]

However, the Baka people have not been engaged much in such transactions to date, instead maintaining their long-standing historical relationship with the Bantu villagers (Kounabembe in this case), who have long mediated the Baka's relationships with outside world. As a result, the Bantu villagers make significant profits by buying large quantities of nuts collected by the Baka and selling them to traders at high prices.

The commodification of NTFPs has certainly brought some cash income to the households of the Baka who had little means of earning

---

4   In a Baka camp surveyed during the 2015 season, 580 kilograms of nuts (in dry weight) were collected, of which three-quarters (427 kg) was bartered with the Konabembe villagers at the camp, with less than a quarter used for their own subsistence. The Baka sold only 14 kg, or 2.4% directly to traders in the village (Hirai, 2015).

cash. However, these new economic opportunities are not being shared equally among the local people, and the commodification of NTFPs has instead widened the economic gap between the Baka and the agricultural villagers. Even more problematic is the fact that unit prices of nuts differ between the Baka and Bantu villagers, when they sell the nuts to the same traders in the village. For example, in the early season of 2012, Kounabembe villagers sold dried *peke* nuts for an average of 1,264 CFA/kg, while the Baka sold similar nuts for an average of 1,061 CFA/kg (Hirai, 2014). As such a difference (15–20%) in the unit price between the different seller groups is seen every year, this is not an exceptional case. Hirai (2014) attributes these price differences to the fact that traders from towns favor the Bantu villagers who sell much larger quantities of nuts at a time, so that they can get the nuts promptly. However, there may be other factors as well. When nuts are sold in their fresh, undried state, in the village, the volume of one transaction is small (usually a few *combos* or less), but even in that case, the price paid to the Bantu (Kounabembe) villagers is 20% higher than the price paid to the Baka (Hirai and Ichikawa, 2018).

The discrepancy in unit prices between the two groups probably arises from the fact that the Baka are not accustomed to "dealing" or "negotiating." Not just for forest products, they are generally not good at negotiating patiently. They also tend to settle for low prices to get immediate income, even when they could get a better price if they waited a little while. The price of nuts sold in the village varies depending on the time of year. At the beginning of the 2012 season when few nuts were available, and few traders visited the village, prices were generally low, 1,000 CFA per *combo* even for dried nuts. The prices rose to 1,500 CFA at high season in late August and reached over 2,500 CFA in October, near the end of the season (Hirai, 2014). Yet the Baka were not prepared to store the nuts and sell them later at higher prices.

Their temperament has often been described as "present oriented" or "immediate-return" oriented (Woodburn, 1982: see also Meillasoux, 1967).[5] It may be a temperament unique to hunter-gatherers and has

---

5 Although hunter-gatherers' "present orientation" or "immediate-return attitude toward life" is typically seen as an obstacle to social development, it has in some cases protected their livelihoods (see Chapter 5).

Chapter 4

Photo 4.10
Drying *peke* (upper right) and *tondo* (below) in village.

Photo 4.11
Peke (center), *tondo* (center-back) and *gobo* (left) sold at Yokadouma market

been described as an obstacle to social development. Social development is said to be achieved through "accumulation" and "investment," but most hunter-gatherers like the Baka do not seem to value future development enough to incur expense in the present, at least until now. However, such a temperament itself may have been reinforced in their historical relationship with others who dominated them. While they maintained a hunter-gatherer lifestyle of "living for the day," their interactions with the outside society did not take place directly, but through the medium of dominant agricultural people. As long as this situation remains unchanged, it will be difficult for the Baka to fully enjoy the new economic opportunities of trading NTFPs. Such unequal (but often interdependent) relationships between hunter-gatherers and agriculturalists have been reported from various parts of the central African forests (Hewlett, 1996, 2014; Grinker, 1994; Guillaume, 2001; Joiris, 1998, 2003; Lewis, 2001; Rupp, 2003). I discuss this matter in the next chapter.

There are also signs that trade in NTFPs is bringing about changes within the Baka society. In recent years, an increasing number of Baka people have been selling *peke* and other forest products to traders, which is creating a disparity of cash income within the egalitarian Baka society. While some Baka earned as much as 40,000 CFA from *peke* sales during the season, most Baka households earned only a few thousand CFA or less (Toda and Yasuoka, 2020). Many households did not sell any nuts at all, either consuming all the nuts they collected or exchanging them for food such as *beignets* or alcoholic drinks at forest camps.

Cash can be used for medical expenses in case of emergency, for children's education, and for purchase of tools, clothes and metal products, lamp oil, soap, and other consumer goods that have now become necessities of their life. It has "general purchasing power" that can be used for a variety of purposes. Cash can also be stored for future use or used for investment to expand production. It can be a driving force for social development. Disparities in cash income among individuals and households are therefore likely to lead to social stratification. As discussed in Chapter 5, some of the Baka living in the border region between Cameroon and the Republic of Congo grow cacao like Bantu agriculturalists[6] when the international market price of cacao rises. There were even a few Baka who used the cash they earn (or the liquor they buy with it) to employ other Baka men to further expand their cacao crops (Oishi, 2016).

To date, however, the society of Baka in our research area (Gribe) has not yet reached that level of social disparity. Although they try to keep their hard-earned cash secret, when they use it to purchase consumer goods, they share with other members of the camp. No individuals have emerged among the Baka in our study area who employ fellow Baka men and women to expand their cultivated lands or to gather forest products. It is necessary to carefully observe how the egalitarian Baka people will deal with the growth in cash income and the widening disparity between individuals in the future.

---

6   Althabe (1965) and Guillaume (2001) noted that there were already some Baka people who cultivated cacao in the 1950s, but it is not known how long their cacao cultivation lasted.

Chapter 4

4.6. Results of the project (2): Sustainable hunting for livelihood

4.6.1. Research on animal population and impacts of commercial hunting

The research on the distribution and ecology of wild animals was mainly conducted by Cameroonian scientists, Dr. Serge Bobo Kadiri and his team from the Agricultural University of Dchang. They had previously conducted a series of studies on the forest mammals and hunting in the Korup National Park and surrounding areas in southwestern Cameroon. Dr. Bobo, accompanied by several graduate students, participated in this project, and did an excellent job. They selected a research area on both sides of the road running through the village of Gribe, north of the two national parks, in a community hunting zone (*zone d'intérêt cynégétique à gestion communautaire*), where hunting by local people was allowed. They set up a total of 126 two-kilometer-long transects in this area and surveyed the animals and their tracks (footprints and feces) found there. A total of 31 species of medium and large-sized mammals were confirmed to inhabit this area. A relatively large number of rare species such as gorillas and forest elephants were also found. At the same time, however, traces of human activities such as hunting were found everywhere, and the increasing demand for bushmeat is having a detrimental impact on the fauna of the region, which, according to Bobo et al (2014), indicates the importance of wildlife conservation in this area.

In addition to Bobo's team, Dr. Hirokazu Yasuoka, who is also a member of our project, has been investigating hunting activities in the study area since the early 2000s, and Kamgaing joined our project in 2013 and has continued his research on animal population and hunting activities until today. They have separately attempted to estimate hunting pressure by the local people (Yasuoka, 2006a; 2014; Bobo et al., 2015; Kamgaing et al., 2018; 2019), and have found that one of the main hunting targets, the blue duikers (*Philantomba monticola*) weighing 4–6 kg, was clearly under pressure from excessive hunting. While its annual growth rate is estimated at 1.28–3.91 head per square kilometer, the number of animals taken reached 12.17 head. Also, for the medium-sized duikers (*Cephalophus* spp., weighing 15–25 kg, and generally called "red duikers"), 2.93 head were taken compared with their average annual growth rate of 0.89–2.85 head per square kilometer (see Chapter 3). This hunting pressure is due to the increased commercial bushmeat trade, as mentioned earlier. In fact, 90% of medium-sized (red) duikers and more than 70% of blue duikers were traded and transported to other places (Kamgaing, et al., 2018).

It is only recently that hunting pressure has increased to such an extent. In the early 2000s, a logging road was built from Yokadouma, through the village of Gribe further into the interior of the forest. The road has been used by outside traders who come to the area in search of bushmeat and other forest products. Traders supplied the Baka hunter-gatherers with large quantities of alcoholic beverages and steel wire for snares as advance payments, tying them up in debt to drive them to hunt. According to Yasuoka (2006), who conducted research before and after the opening of the road, hunting pressure by the Baka people jumped 15–18 times after the logging road was built, compared with before the road was built. If the hunting for bushmeat trade is a short-term phenomenon, the decline in the game population may be compensated by the movement of animals from other places (for example, from the protected area) in the nearby forest. However, if this excessive hunting pressure continues over a long period of time, animal resources will soon be depleted.

4.6.2. Change in the composition of the catch

The most important hunting method routinely practiced by the Baka hunter-gatherers is snare hunting (with spring traps). The main target of trapping is forest antelopes (duikers), which account for 80% of the animals captured (Yasuoka, 2006a). Aka hunters in the northern Republic of Congo and the Mbuti in the Democratic Republic of Congo use nets for collective hunting, where duiker species also comprise the main catch (Ichikawa, 1983; Takeuchi, 1995). While hunter-gatherers in the Congo Basin are generally duiker hunters, the species composition of duikers differs. Among the Mbuti, who hunt in groups with hunting nets, 60% of the animals captured are blue duikers weighing 4–6 kg (Ichikawa, 1983). In contrast, among the Baka in the project area, who mainly hunt with snares (spring traps), medium-sized red duikers (15–20 kg) account for 80% of the total catch, with Peter's duikers making up

Chapter 4

the majority (Yasuoka, 2006a; 2014). In net hunting, larger animals may break through the net and escape.[7] Conversely, in spring trap hunting, smaller animals may not properly trigger the trap. The difference in the main targets between the two methods is due to the difference in hunting methods, but it can also be assumed that the respective hunting methods have been adapted to the relative abundance of target animals. In other words, in the Ituri Forest, where smaller duikers (blue duikers) are more abundant, net hunting is used to capture them, while in the southeastern Cameroon forests, where medium-sized duikers are relatively abundant, snare hunting has become the principal method for capturing them.

However, there are areas in southeastern Cameroon where blue duikers are more abundant than medium-sized duikers. In the forests near the road running west of the Lobéké National Park, on the right bank of the Sanga River, blue duikers are more abundant than medium-sized duikers (red duikers) (see Chapter 3). Baka hunters in this area therefore use a thinner wire for the loops to capture the legs of animals. Normally, a thick bundle of wires sold in local shops is untwisted and then 5–6 thin wires are twisted together again to make a loop, but where smaller animals are common, they use a loop made of only three thin wires twisted together so that even lightweight animals can be caught. Yasuoka (2014) attributes this modification of hunting methods to the decline of medium-sized duikers and the relative abundance of small animals such as blue duikers, due to higher hunting pressure.

As mentioned in Chapter 3, Yasuoka et al. (2015) proposed an indicator to estimate the degree of hunting pressure, the B/M (or B/R) ratio, i.e., the ratio of blue duikers to medium-sized duikers (red duikers). In general, when high hunting pressure persists, smaller species that reproduce faster can better withstand the pressure and will replace larger species.[8] Therefore, the ratio increases as hunting pressure

---

7 The nets used by Aka hunter-gatherers in the Republic of Congo are thicker and stronger than those used by the Mbuti, though they use the same material, the bast of *Manniophyton fulvum* lianas. Therefore, although blue duikers account for 70% of the Aka's net hunting catch by head, medium-sized duikers such as Peters duikers provide the larger proportion of the weight of animals captured (Takeuchi, 1995).

8 In areas of west Africa that have been subject to high hunting pressure for a long time, fast reproducing species, such as porcupines, cane rats and other small rodents have become the main targets of hunting (Davies and Robinson, 2007).

increases (relatively more blue duikers). The advantage of this indicator is that local people can easily understand the impact of hunting pressure from changes in the composition of catch, or the ratio of blue duikers to medium-sized duikers.

Previous studies have indicated that the change in animal species composition affects forest ecosystems through prey-predator relationships (Nasi et al., 2010; 2011; Abernethy, 2013; Wilkie et al., 2011). It has also been reported that hunting has altered the vegetation environment when the number of seed-dispersing mammals, especially primates, declines (Effiom, et al., 2013). Furthermore, continued excessive hunting pressure can lead to the "empty forest syndrome" (Redford, 1992), in which forests remain apparently intact but animals for hunting are nowhere to be seen. Considering that forests are maintained by animals which contribute to seeds dispersal, this will eventually affect the forests themselves. And because these forests serve the function of carbon sequestration, the decline of mammals is not only a loss of biodiversity, but also a serious problem from the perspective of global climate change (Nasi et al., 2010).

The problem, therefore, is how to maintain the local fauna while at the same time ensuring a sustainable source of food (protein source) for the local people. To establish sustainable hunting, accurate information on the animals inhabiting the area is necessary, and at this point the situation is far from satisfactory. This is because it is extremely difficult to estimate the density of animals to be hunted. According to previous surveys, the numbers and densities of animals vary greatly depending on the timing of the survey (season, time of day, etc.) and the survey method (surveys on feces and footprints, by direct observation, or with camera trapping). For example, in a recent survey conducted in this area, the animal density obtained from direct observation at night were 8–18 times higher for blue duikers and 2–3 times higher for medium-sized duikers (red duikers) than those obtained from direct observation and fecal distribution surveys during the daytime (Kamgaing et al., 2018). To obtain more reliable data on the animal densities, long-term surveys using different methods are needed. Currently, a team led by Hirokazu

Chapter 4

Yasuoka in Cameroon is intensively surveying using new methods, including camera traps. Their results are awaited.[9]

4.7. Social system for sustainable use of resources

To ensure the sustainability of forest resource use, social adjustments are necessary to limit competition among the people using the resources. When demand for the resources is small relative to the resource potential, there is little scope for competition. If forest resources can be used by anyone, anywhere, at any time, competition for resources is inevitable. Where unlimited use (open access) is allowed under the current situation of increasing demand for forest resources, people seeking only short-term profit rush in from the outside. As a result, competition among people over the resources intensifies, and resources are depleted. Such examples on excessive hunting pressure are reported from various parts of the world forest areas, especially from south America and Africa, even in the protected areas (Harrison, 2011).

However, there is a customary system of coordination of the resource use that would serve as a basis to prevent excessive competition among the people who have been living there and using the resource for a long time. One of such examples is a "territorial system" which regulates the access to forest spaces among the local people, and excludes outsiders. In central African forests, there have been such a customary system, but the problem there is that there is no exclusive legal right of the local people, and outsiders can easily access the area traditionally used by the locals.

Thus, to establish a sustainable system for using forest resources, it is necessary to first understand the customary systems that have been nurtured and accepted by the people. An example of such a local system that regulates the use of resources is the territorial system, mentioned above. For the Mbuti in the Ituri Forest of the DRC, I found that each Mbuti group of tens of people, related by blood and/or marriage, considered 150–250 km² of forest as their territory, and hunted and

---

9   Recently, camera trap surveys of animal populations have become popular, and the results from such surveys have begun to inform new projects (Hongo et al., 2020).

Toward a Sustainable Use of Non-Timber Forest Products

gathered within that area. Although the boundaries between group territories were not clearly defined, except occasionally by rivers or other clear landmarks, forest paths connecting campsites and hunting and gathering trails extending from the campsites formed the "skeleton" of each group's territory, and the surrounding forest was considered to be the group's forest. When they came across a forest path used by other groups, they turned back toward their own territory. This relatively loose division of territory avoided competition among groups for forest resources. In the research in the Ituri Forest, I used maps made in the colonial period to walk through the forests on a number of occasions, plotting on the maps the main forest paths and campsites used by each group, and thus mapping the distribution of the territories used by nine groups in the study area (Ichikawa, 1978; see the Fig 2.1 in Chapter 2). Recently, however, a more efficient method has become available.

We trialed a method called "participatory mapping" to better understand the use of forest land by local people. This method asks local participants to enter the forest with a GPS device to record location information, identify locations used for resource extraction, and map them using geographic information system (GIS) software to illustrate the overlapping status of forest space used by people. Until recently, participatory mapping had been used, for example, to track and detect illegal logging with the help of local people. Or, it had been used to assert customary rights by establishing which parts of the forest they use daily (Lewis, 2012). We hypothesized that this method could also be used to help local people understand each other's use of resources and forests and minimize conflict. The participatory mapping would reveal how each group's use of the forest overlaps with or avoids neighboring groups. The map can thus be used to coordinate the use of forest space to minimize competition between groups. By controlling competition for resources, the local people may be able to use an area's resources sustainably in the long-term. With that in mind, we attempted participatory mapping of the collection of *peke* and created a tentative map documenting the forest use by each group of the Baka people in Gribe (Hirai, 2015; Hirai and Yasuoka, 2020). Unfortunately, the project ended before it was useful for adjusting the resource use of the Baka people. These attempts are expected to be refined by the successor project which began in 2018 under the leadership of Hirokazu Yasuoka.

Chapter 4

Photo 4.12 Group photo after the workshop in Gribe

In the final year of the project, we compiled the results in a brief pamphlet and held a workshop in February 2016 with the local people. Nearly 100 Bantu villagers and Baka living in Gribe participated in the workshop and had lively discussions. A few demanded direct material benefits such as drinks, clothes and money from the project. Discontent among the Baka toward the Bantu villagers was quite clear; the Baka complained that they were exploited by the villagers.

4.8. Summary of results and implications for forest issues

Tropical rainforests in the Congo Basin are complex ecosystems composed of a diversity of animals and plants. They are also dynamic systems that appear quite different depending on the time and space of the survey. Such diversity and dynamism pose a challenge to those who conduct research in tropical rainforests. Discrepancies frequently arise between the results of surveys conducted in different sites and at different times (seasons and dates) in the same region. Thus, it is dangerous to draw generalizations from surveys conducted over a period of 2–3 years, not to mention those conducted over a period of several months. Yet, such forests of variation and change are the environments that the inhabitants of this region must deal with. With these limitations in mind, let me try to summarize the results of our project and their implications for conservation and sustainable use of forests in this region.

(1) The survey of shifting cultivation practices implied that agricultural land use in the study area seems to be currently sustainable. However, this is on the condition that the current population size and agricultural production levels are maintained. If agricultural production expands due to population growth and/or demand for cash crops, land use will naturally change. Unless new crop varieties and agricultural technologies are introduced to increase land productivity, the fallow period will shorten and larger areas of forest will be converted to crop fields, making sustainable land use more difficult. In this regard, it is necessary to integrate forest conservation with agricultural development, which have traditionally belonged to different sectors.

(2) In the project sites, tree diversity was slightly higher in secondary forests on the abandoned fields than in permanent or mature forests. This challenges the conventional view that agricultural activities inevitably reduce the level of forest diversity. The impact of slash-and-burn agriculture depends on the scale and degree of clearing. A moderate impact may instead lead to increasing forest diversity. This point should be noted from the perspective of biodiversity conservation.

(3) While there are many NTFP species used by the local people, 10 plant species are particularly important. Among them, *peke* (*Irvingia gabonensis*), whose nuts are used as oily condiments, is the most important non-timber forest product (NTFP), providing nearly half of the cash income from NTFPs. As to the habitats of the major NTFPs species, *gimba* (*Afrostyrax lepidophyllus*) and *mbalaka* (*Pentacletha macrophylla*) are more common in secondary forest than in mature forest. The distribution of other species is not significantly different between mature and secondary forests. However, a recent report on the project showed that eight major NTFPs species are more abundant in secondary forests. Since the density of NTFP species varies greatly depending on the surveyed plots and methods, it may be necessary to survey a wider area and with different methods.

Chapter 4

(4) Fruiting of *peke* (*Irvingia gabonensis*) is seasonally uneven and varies as much as 10-fold from year to year, but the factors influencing fruit production are currently unknown. In all years, the amount of *peke* collected by the people is less than several percent of the amount of fruiting in the forests they have traditionally used. *Peke* nuts are under-utilized compared to their ecological abundance. This underutilization is probably due to the tedious process of extracting the nuts. If a more efficient method for extracting nuts is developed, the utilization rate will increase. However, there is a problem of excluding the people from their gathering ground by conservation programs, logging operations and sport hunting. This threatens their subsistence base and cash income opportunities.

(5) *Peke* nuts are gathered in the forest by Baka hunter-gatherers, who barter most of the nuts with Kounabembe (Bantu) villagers. The villagers dry the nuts and sell them to traders. Through this production and trade system, the cash income of the Kounabembe from the nut sold to traders is 10–20 times greater than the income earned by the Baka (Table 4-1). The benefits of new economic opportunities that were expected to bring cash income to the local people are not shared equally among the local peoples but are much more beneficial to the agricultural villagers. The "present orientation" of the hunter-gatherers exacerbates their disadvantaged position.

(6) Regarding fauna, a total of 31 species of medium and large-sized mammals were identified in the study area. Local people hunt the area for subsistence and for sale, but hunting for sale threatens the sustainability of wild animal populations.

(7) The major hunting targets in the region are forest antelopes (duikers). Where hunting pressure is high, the smaller blue duikers are relatively more abundant than the medium-sized red duikers. The ratio of blue duikers to red duikers, or B/R ratio, was proposed as an indicator for local people to quantitatively assess hunting pressure. It is thought that as hunting pressure increases, blue duikers, which are smaller and reproduce faster, become relatively more abundant. It should be noted, however, that animal density estimates vary greatly depending

Toward a Sustainable Use of Non-Timber Forest Products

on the survey method and time of survey. In a current research project, animal surveys are being advanced by new methods such as nighttime surveys, camera traps, etc.

(8) Participatory mapping was attempted as a means of minimizing conflicts among the local peoples over NTFP use. The objective was to visualize the forest space used by different groups of people, and to "segregate" the use of forest space and resources with the mutual understanding of the local people. The establishment of customary rights to specific areas and resources will allow for the management of forest resources from a long-term perspective.

While this research revealed some of the potential of the region's forests, it also highlighted problems such as large variations in the estimation of resource abundance, the social system for establishing sustainable use of the resources, and the unequal share of the benefits derived from NTFPs. It goes without saying that the understanding of the Cameroonian government is necessary to establish sustainable use of forest resources, but at the same time, it is essential that the inhabitants of the concerned area actively participate in the project with a long-term perspective.

The United Nations Intergovernmental Science-Policy Platform on Biodiversity and Ecosystem Services pointed out in its 2019 report (IPBES, 2019; also see, Lewis, 2020) that 80% of the remaining biodiversity on the ground is in lands managed in some form by indigenous or local people. They are doing better than anyone else at maintaining biodiversity on their lands. The same report states that "by recognizing the knowledge, innovations, institutions, and values of indigenous and local peoples and involving them in governance of the environment, their livelihoods and the protection, rehabilitation, and sustainable use of nature are qualitatively enhanced."

A successor project, initiated in 2018 is currently underway with plans to achieve just such an objective. Named "Co-creation of Innovative Forest Resources Management Combining Ecological Methods and Indigenous Knowledge," this project is being building on the close collaboration with local people that has already been established, with young researchers who were core members of the preceding project. The project is developing animal surveys using new methods such as camera

Chapter 4

traps, long-term ecological surveys of tropical forests, and economic surveys including production, exchange, consumption, and market circulation of NTFPs, all with the cooperation of the local people and their indigenous knowledge, skills, and practices. We await the results from these new approaches.

Chapter 5

Hunter-Gatherers Way of Life in Modern Society

Chapter 5

Photo on the previous page: Joyful Mbuti camp

5.1. Present orientation

The main focus of this book is to indigenous hunter-gatherers in central Africa, who have been referred to as Pygmies. As mentioned in the Introduction, they are distributed over 2000 km from east to west across the Congo Basin, and the genetic differentiation between the eastern and western groups is estimated to date back to 20,000 years (Verdu and Destro-Bisol, 2012). Despite such a long distance and separation, there are striking social and cultural similarities among these groups, as we have seen. The most striking social similarities are, among other things, an egalitarian social life characterized by extensive sharing, and interdependent but inequality-laden relationships with neighboring agricultural groups. The egalitarian social relations among themselves and the unequal relations with the agriculturalist others are inextricably linked to their "immediate-return attitude," which was discussed in relation to the trade in forest products in the previous chapter.

In the Ituri Forest of former Zaire (now DRC), where I first visited in the 1970s, measures were being taken to promote changes in Mbuti society (Turnbull, 1983). While they had mainly lived in forest camps, the Zairian government was trying to resettle them along roads. They were being encouraged to cultivate crop fields and to build square-shaped, mud-walled dwellings like the agriculturalists, instead of their traditional dome-shaped huts thatched with leaves. However, at least until 1990, when I was visiting the area, such measures had not been very successful. Even though roadside settlement had progressed, they still spent almost half of the year hunting and gathering from camps in the forest. In the meantime, their small crop fields were covered with weeds or raided by wild animals. The mud-walled houses deteriorated, covered with growing vegetation. After a few years or so, the semi-settled settlements (we called them base camps) were often abandoned, and they moved elsewhere.

A similar situation is found among the Baka in Cameroon and Aka in Congo-Brazaville. Although the measures were introduced to promote settlement and cultivation among the Baka in the 1950s (Althabe, 1965),[1] most Baka households still did not have enough crop fields to

---

1   In the Likouala region of northern Congo and a southern part of Central African Republic, some of the Aka started to settle and cultivate as early as 1930s with

Chapter 5

provide for their needs when we began our research in Cameroon in the 1990s, nearly half a century later. These hunter-gatherer societies appeared to be elastic and resilient; They bend when force is applied, but return to their original state as soon as the force is relaxed. At first glance, this seemed to be a different society from those oriented towards development and progress, in other words, towards cumulative social change.

When I first visited the Mbuti camps in the Ituri Forest, I was deeply impressed that the people were always "sharing." Even for hunter-gatherers who know how to survive in the forest, life in the forest is never easy. Sometimes there are days without any catch, and often there are days when they cannot hunt or gather due to heavy rain. On such occasions, people share the little food they have in order to survive. Here, even children of 10 years old know that they must not satisfy their hunger alone. In the forest camps, everyone was either satisfied or otherwise hungry together. With minimal material possessions, there was little difference between rich and poor in their society. Everyone seemed to have an equal guarantee of life, especially in terms of food intake.

Hunter-gatherer societies have often been characterized as "egalitarian." While some of the indigenous peoples in North America have relatively large organizations with leaders who compete with others for prestige, the hunter-gatherer societies in the tropics have generally not developed complex political systems. There are typically little differences in wealth, status, or class among group members. Although there are individuals who assume a leading role when hunting large animals or performing important rituals – based on their skills, experience, knowledge, and qualities – there are no chiefs or other individuals who generally represent the group or command others with authority (Ichikawa, 1991b; 2005).

These egalitarian societies had an economic system to support them. According to James Woodburn (1982), in an article titled "Egalitarian Societies," equality in these societies "is achieved through direct, individual access to resources and means of coercion and mobility ... and through the procedures that prevent saving and accumulation and impose

the French colonial "taming" and "stabilization" policies, but these remained ephemeral, according to Bahuchet and Guillaume (1979).

sharing." Woodburn called such a social system an "immediate return system." In societies with such a system, people are not caught up in past debt relationships and are less interested in investing for the future. Their main interest is in the present, not in the past or future (Meillassoux, 1967). Such values and "ways of life" probably derive from a hunter-gatherer lifestyle based on "living for the day." However, it must not be forgotten that their hunter-gatherer lifestyle to the present day has long been shaped by interaction with other groups in wider society, including the agricultural groups who have long dominated the hunter-gatherer groups. With this reservation, it is noted that the "immediate-return attitude" still appears to be prominent in contemporary African hunter-gatherer societies. The hunter-gatherers we have been keeping in contact with, such as the Mbuti of the DRC, and the Baka of southeastern Cameroon, also appear to be more interested in the present than in the future, as discussed in Chapter 4. The game they catch in the forest is cooked and eaten as soon as they bring it back to camp. What is left over on the day is eaten within a day or two and is rarely saved for a day when there is no game. The animal meat is preserved only when it is to be exchanged with neighboring agriculturalists or visiting traders.

Their immediate-return attitude is also evident in the cultivation they attempt. They have knowledge of crop cultivation through helping neighboring agriculturalists. Some of the Mbuti (and Baka) had small fields behind the camps they stayed in near the agriculturalists' villages. However, the crops they grew were mainly plantain and cassava, vegetatively reproducing crops of which seedlings are not edible. Seed crops, such as rice and maize are eaten before they are sown. For them, it would be painful to suppress their present desire to eat them, even if those seeds would yield dozens of times more food after several months. As Colin Turnbull (Turnbull, 1983) aptly pointed out, "what is not here and now is meaningless."

The government in Cameroon encouraged the Baka to become settled agriculturalists in the 1950s (Althabe, 1965). While a few Baka had started cacao cultivation by the mid-1960s, still today, few Baka engage in full-scale agriculture like the surrounding agricultural peoples. Agriculture requires systematic input of labor over a period of several months or years, clearing and burning fields, sowing, and planting, weeding, and harvesting at certain times of the year. But Baka cultivation

Chapter 5

remains very much a haphazard process. If they clear a large field, they only plant part of it. Moreover, they move into the forest to hunt and gather, or visit distant relatives for long periods, and are unable to weed or watch for animals (which destroy the fields and crops). Alternatively, the women who work in the fields often prefer to help the agricultural people rather working their own fields. For the women, the clothes, food, and alcoholic drinks that the agriculturalists give them in return for their work seem to be more attractive than future food self-sufficiency. In the end, the main crops grown in Baka fields are plantain and cassava, which are not tied to a specific season or time of year for planting and harvesting and do not require much work after planting (Kitanishi, 2003). More recently, some Baka have tried cacao cultivation, which takes years to harvest, but as discussed below, this too often does not work well because of their attitude which demands "immediate returns."

After all, their societies were not geared to the expansion of production or the accumulation of wealth through the planned input of labor over the long term. Their societies appear to have been oriented towards sharing wealth rather than accumulation and concentration. In other words, they pursue co-existence of the many rather than the success of the few individuals. While economic development is often driven by the success of a few outstanding individuals, they may have been oriented towards social stability rather than economic development. They value coexistence among equals and remain alert to the risk of an individual becoming more prominent. They respond to those who seek to rise above others with jealousy or ridicule (Turnbull, 1965; 1983; Lee, 1989). While this is important to maintaining their egalitarianism, though, it may become an obstacle to the development of their society.

The neighboring agriculturalists looked down on them and their attitude toward life, commenting: "They do not settle down and build durable dwellings, do not cultivate large fields, do not store food for the future, and do not invest in development." This view has been reinforced throughout the historical relationship between the two groups and has supported an unequal relationship.

5.2. Early accounts of relationships between hunter-gatherers and agriculturalists

To develop an understanding of how the hunter-gatherers' "immediate-return attitude" and "present orientation" have been formed and reinforced, and what meaning or problems it might have in the contemporary world, let us look more closely at the relationships between hunter-gatherers, the neighboring peoples, and the outside world, and how these relationships have changed over time.

There is no doubt that their attitude to life is largely shaped by internal factors associated with their lifestyle. Agriculture requires at least several months until harvest, and people need to carry out various tasks in sequence, such as preparing the fields, planting, weeding, watching pest animals, and harvesting. They must consume the harvested food systematically to ensure that it lasts until the next harvest. In contrast, hunting and gathering activities in tropical Africa can be completed in a short time cycle, for several hours or in a few days at the longest. If they fail today, they may succeed tomorrow. When they have no food, other people will share with them, as mentioned.[2] This is probably the basis of their immediate-return attitude toward life. However, this attitude may also have been sustained and reinforced through their relations with others and the outside world over the centuries.

Grinker's (1994) study of the relationship between the Sudanic-speaking Lese agriculturalists and the Efe hunter-gatherers in the northern Ituri forest, concluded that the Lese and Efe formed a social unit, which he termed the "House." "House" was fraught with inequalities. It consisted of Lese (agriculturalists) men, their wives and Efe hunter-gatherers. According to Grinker, the Lese men were all equal among their own clans (patrilineal clans), but within the "House" the members were "different," with wives who married in from other groups and Efe in a subordinate position to the Lese men. Lese and Efe formed personal relationships in which they refer to each other as "*Efe maia* (my Efe) – *Muto maia* (my villagers)," and both sides use kinship idioms such as

---

2   While in the middle latitude regions, seasonal fluctuations in resources facilitate planned consumption through processing and storage, and investment in devices such as fish dams and weirs to capture large seasonal arrivals, hunter-gatherers in the low-latitude tropics seldom undertake such large-scale, long-term work on their natural resources.

Chapter 5

"father – son" (see also Terashima, 1987). Such personal relationships are usually "inherited" from the parents, and have continued to this day. The Lese men say, "we gained independence from Belgium in 1960, but the Efe remain a 'colony' that has not yet become independent from us" (Grinker, 1994).

The Efe provide forest products and labor to the Lese in exchange for crops, clothes and metal products. However, this is by no means an exchange of equivalence. On the one hand, the Efe often get food and other items free from the Lese, and the Efe bring a small amount of forest products, which, according to Grinker, is a sign of loyalty to the Lese. On the other hand, the Lese consider it their duty to give "their Efe" crops and other products. If he does not give them, the Efe is not his Efe. The Lese and Efe are unequal and different, and they move further in different directions rather than trying to be the same. Rather than becoming agriculturalists, the Efe have become even more entrenched as hunter-gatherers. In the process, they have further widened their differences, strengthened their complementarity, and reinforced their inequality (Grinker, 1994).

In Chapter 4 I discussed the similarly unequal relationship between the Baka hunter-gatherers and the Kounabembe agriculturalists. Such relationships are found to varying degrees across central Africa between Pygmy hunter-gatherers such as the Efe, Mbuti, Aka and Baka and the neighboring agriculturalists, as I mentioned in the previous chapter. But were they originally in such a "dominant-subordinate" relationship? I will examine the old literature to understand how such relationships have been maintained and reinforced historically.

As they "explored" the African continent from the 16th century onwards, Europeans began to encounter Pygmy hunter-gatherers. By the time of the earliest European reports, some "Pygmies" had already been involved in exchange relationships with the surrounding peoples, and had (indirect) contacts with extensive trading networks. The accounts of an Englishman named Andrew Battell, who spent 18 years on the Atlantic coast near the equator in late 16th century, describes the following (Battel, 1625; Schlichter, 1892).

> To the north-east of Mani Kesok are a kind of little people called Matimbas...(dotted parts show omission of irrelevant parts. The same applies

hereafter). They pay tribute to Mani Kesock, and bring all their elephants' teeth and tails to him. They will not suffer any to come where they dwell; and if by chance any Maramba, or people of Loango, pass where they dwell, they will forsake that place and go to another.

A 17th century report by Dapper (1686) offers the following description.

> The Negroes assert that there is a Province full of forests, where one finds only these Dwarfs, and that they are the ones who kill the most elephants. These little men are called Bakke-Bakke and Mimos... It is the Lavangos who sell the most ivory to the Europeans, ... they buy it from the Jagos... The Jagos draw the elephant's teeth from ... Mimos and Bakke-Bakke... they have no great difficulty in piercing these animals..., whose flesh they eat and sell their tusks.

The location of the "little people" mentioned by Battell and Dapper corresponds to the area in present-day Gabon where the Babongo Pygmies live. It is evident that they were hunting elephants and involved in the ivory trade through the intermediary of surrounding agricultural groups. However, it appears that they generally avoided daily contact with the agricultural people.

Du Chaillu (1872) explored the region which is now Gabon in the latter half of 19th century. On his second expedition in 1863–65, he met a Pygmy group called Obongo, skilled hunters and fishermen who brought their catch to Ashango in exchange for plantain, iron and earthenware. The Ashango knew well where the Obongo were. When Du Chaillu visited the Obongo camp with an Ashango guide, more than a dozen Ashango women were carrying plantains to exchange for meat. However, Obongo were very wary of other people and had to be approached quietly in small groups. They led a mobile life in Ashango territory and did not stay in one place for long. When asked about their reasons for not settling, they replied "we never like to remain long in the same place, for if we did we should soon starve... We love to move... And if we had villages, the strong and tall people ... might come and make war upon us, kill us, and capture us" (Du Chaillu, 1872).

Ashango, in turn, described the Obongo "as wild as the antelope, and roam in the forest... They feed on the serpents, rats and mice, and

Chapter 5

on the berries and nuts of the forest. They cook on charcoal. They drink with their hands, or with large leaves (Du Chaillu, 1872)." Thus it is clear that in the late 19th century, when Du Chaillu made contact, the Obongo were exchanging forest products (especially animal meat and fish) for agricultural products and iron tools with the surrounding Ashango agriculturalists, and that the Obongo were fearful of the Ashango and other outsiders, and extremely afraid of unexpected visitors. The Ashango, meanwhile, had a low opinion of the Obongo, who moved around the forest and did not use pots and pans or crockery.

The propensity of the Pygmy hunter-gatherers to fear unexpected contacts with outsiders was also apparent during my research in the Ituri Forest in the 1970s, more than a century after these reports. When I was investigating the distribution of Mbuti camps scattered in the forest, our unexpected visit to their camps in the deep forest often sent the Mbuti fleeing into the forest (see Ichikawa, 1982).

In the northern part of the Congo Basin, the German explorer Georg Schweinfurth (1874) travelled up the Nile River in the late 19th century to reach the Welle River (Uele?), a tributary of the Congo River. He encountered Pygmies living in the court of the king of Monbuttoo (Mangbetu). They were called Akka or Bakke-Bakke, and several families were brought to Monbuttoo court to show off the royal authority. The Akka people reportedly lived in a vast forest between one and two degrees north latitude, a three-day journey from the Monbuttoo area. They hunted elephants and traded ivory. The Akka were also used for inter-tribal warfare. Schweinfurth noted that among the soldiers returning from fighting with the southern Mamvu (Momvoo), there was a group composed of Pygmies.

Beginning in the late 19th century, reports of Pygmies became more frequent. According to Stanley (1890), who visited the Ituri Forest on his second journey to the Congo River basin, Pygmies provided meat and pelts to neighboring agriculturalists, in return for bananas, sweet potatoes, tobacco, spear tips, knives and other metal products. He also noted that the Pygmies, with their knowledge of the forest, formed alliances with certain agricultural groups to watch for enemies, and attack them unseen in the forest when necessary (Stanley, 1890). In the

Hunter-Gatherers Way of Life in Modern Society

period of constant inter-"tribal" warfare,[3] it would have been important for the agriculturalists to maintain an alliance with the Pygmies. Similar relationships between Pygmies and surrounding agriculturalists have also been described by others who visited the area in the late 19th century (Casati, 1991; Parke, 1891; Jephson, 1891; Junker, 1891).

When Stanley visited the Ituri Forest, it was a time of many conflicts among different agricultural groups of the Ituri Forest, when Arab traders had reached the area, plundering villagers. Under the circumstances, information provided by hunter-gatherers about approaching "enemies" would have been extremely important for the settled agriculturalists. They played the role of scouts for the agriculturalist in alliance, using their rich knowledge and skills of forest life. The reward was agricultural products and metal products provided by the agriculturalists. Such relations between the two groups continued for some time after the region was pacified by Belgian forces and the inter-"tribal" wars ended.[4]

Schlichter (1892), who in the late 19th century compiled the earlier records on Pygmies, also noted that Pygmies and agriculturalists in many parts of central Africa exchanged forest products, such as meat, for crops and metal products, and that they were elephant hunters, who exchanged ivory with agriculturalists and paid a tribute in ivory to the kings. He also noted that their relations with agriculturalists were generally good, but intermarriages between them were rare.[5]

Burrows (1898) visited the northern part of the Congo Basin in the late 19th century, and described the Pygmies he encountered in similar

---

3   I use "tribal" with quotation marks because, at the time, there was often no such level of social integration beyond the coalition of several villages in the Ituri Forest (see also Grinker, 1994).

4   Turnbull (1965) observed that the Mbuti made good use of agriculturalists to get crops for nothing. While farmers accused Mbuti of stealing crops, they sometimes seemed half-tolerant of what the Mbuti did. This tolerance may be a legacy of a long-term relationship of mutual dependence between the two that was nurtured during the period of turmoil. At least by the 1970s when I started my research, Mbuti's crop theft was condemned but not criminally prosecuted. However, since the economically more rational Nande migrated from the east and formed new economic relations with the Mbuti, the looting of crops by the Mbuti has become unacceptable even to the villagers who had maintained close relationships with the Mbuti.

5   Intermarriage between Pygmy hunter-gatherers and neighboring agriculturalists remains rare. While some cases have been reported between the Efe and Lese

Chapter 5

ways to those outlined above. He, however, emphasized their liberal temperament, writing that "these little people ... are considered as valuable allies ... against an outside foe ... as long as relations between themselves and the chief are friendly. Otherwise, they ... move off at once to the neighborhood of another chief... They are ... quite independent, and preserve their freedom, of which they are intensely jealous, and hold themselves entirely aloof from other natives." This description recalls the free and unrestrained temperament of the Mbuti emphasized by Turnbull (1965) in *Wayward Servants* which was published more than half a century later.

Thus, according to the available literature, at the end of the 19th century Pygmies and agriculturalists had not yet been bound together by the tight relationship of domination and subjugation that Grinker called the "House" (Grinker, 1994), even though the Pygmies were somewhat looked down by the agricultural people. As previously noted, though, the Pygmies preferred the freedom of a mobile life in the forest and feared direct contact with outsiders. Since their first contacts with Europeans in the 17th century, interactions with outside society have been primarily through the intermediary of the surrounding agricultural groups. The absence (and resulting inability) of direct negotiation with the outside world has probably contributed to the enduring hunter-gatherer disposition in contemporary society and their acceptance of unequal relations with neighboring agricultural peoples.

5.3. Incorporation and exploitation of Pygmies during colonial rule

The increasing inequality between the two groups developed through economic change, as agriculturalists increasingly exploited the hunter-gatherers to supply both domestic and international markets. Importantly, in the early colonial period, Pygmies were not incorporated into governance structures and were not obliged to pay taxes or provide

---

in northern Ituri (Terashima, 1987), between the Babongo and Masango in Gabon (Matsuura, 2012), and a few cases between the Baka and agriculturalists in Cameroon (Matsuura, 2012), most of these cases are between agriculturalist men and Pygmy women, except a few cases of Babongo men marrying Masango women.

forced labor. In other words, they were not recognized as full-fledged members of the colonial state. It is therefore necessary to consider how outside economic forces and government policies affected the Pygmy-agriculturalist relationships.

Guillaume (2001), a French ethnologist, examined the development of the relationship between the Aka and surrounding agricultural groups in the former French Equatorial Africa (now Republic of Congo and Central African Republic), using historical documents and various statistical records. Before the arrival of Europeans, the Aka in the region obtained spears, bush knives and other metal goods from neighboring agriculturalists, and in this sense were dependent on them for important hunting and gathering tools. Following the invasion and establishment of colonial rule by French who sought ivory, wild rubber, copal resin, animal skin and other forest products, Aka became important suppliers of these forest products. As the demand for duiker skin increased, the Aka changed their hunting methods to focus primarily on collective hunting with nets, which provided a large and stable catch of medium-sized mammals. The nets belonged to the agriculturalists who made them,[6] and the pelts from the catch belonged to the owners of the nets. Most of the ivory traded at the time was also the product of hunting by the Aka. Importantly, the trade in these forest products was monopolized by the agriculturalists, keeping the Aka isolated from trade with the outside world. As the commercialization of these forest products increased, the influence of the agriculturalists on the production and trade of forest products strengthened, and the Aka became increasingly subordinate to the agriculturalists. The Aka maintained their freedom of movement and could move elsewhere if they did not like their neighbors, but then they would have to forge similar relationships with their new agriculturalist neighbors. After World War II, when cash crops such as cacao and coffee were expanded, the Aka became laborers for the cultivation of these crops in the rainforests where there was plenty of land for cultivation, but a shortage of labor to clear the forests and cultivate the new fields. Thus, through the commercialization of forest products and agricultural development with cultivation of cash crops, the Aka became increas-

---

6   The Aka make their own nets today.

Chapter 5

ingly useful and further subordinate to their agriculturalist neighbors (Guillaume, 2001).

The inhabitants of the Ituri Forest in Congo (DRC) have also been affected by internal and external conditions as Grinker (1994) noted. Following Stanley's expedition down the Congo River (Stanley, 1878), Arab slave traders arrived and began plundering forest products such as ivory. The Lese and Efe fled into the forest, living together in the forest camps. The same was true of the Mbuti and Bira in the southern part of Ituri, where I conducted my research. At the time of my first research in 1974, there were still a few living Bira people who had been born in Mbuti camps during this period.

When the Congo became the private property of King Leopold II of Belgium after the Berlin Conference (1885), mass expropriation of forest products such as ivory and wild rubber began. The demand for wild rubber skyrocketed with the spread of rubber tires, and by 1900, rubber and ivory alone accounted for 95% of all exports (in terms of monetary value) from the Congo, of which rubber accounted for 85% (Jewsiewicki, 1983). Wild rubber was extracted by the local people under harsh quotas,[7] and if they failed to meet the quotas, they were severely punished, with whippings, beatings, and sometimes even slitting their wrists (Hochschild, 1998). The wild rubber turned brown when exposed to air, but it was called "red rubber" in reference to the bloody nature of exploitation. As the rubber-producing trees and vines were thinly distributed across the Ituri Forest, agricultural people such as the Lese and the Bira needed the help of Efe and Mbuti, who knew the forest well, to fulfil their quotas. The first rubber period ended after a decade or so, but the relationship between the Efe and Lese became even closer through rubber collection during this period (Grinker, 1994).

---

7   Powell-Cotton (1907) who travelled in the Ituri, described the situation at the time as follows:

At Makala [on the Lindi river, in the western part of Ituri], each adult man has to bring 5 kilos per month, and this he can collect in 40 working days. Payment is at the rate of 30 centime per kilo, of which about 10 per cent is given to the chief and the balance to the actual gatherer...

It is not hard to imagine that they accompanied the Mbuti, who know the forest well, to meet this demanding quota.

Following international condemnation of the harsh exploitation under Leopold II rule, the Congo Free State ceased to be the private property of the King and became a Belgian colony in 1908. Under the colonial regime, new mines and plantations were opened and roads and other transportation infrastructure was developed. Agricultural production also expanded in the Ituri Forest to supply food to the mines and urban workers, and agricultural labor was imposed on the local people (Grinker, 1994; Mark, 1995). When roads were built through the Ituri Forest from east to west and north to south in the 1930s–50s, the Lese, Bira and other peoples who had previously lived dispersed in the forest were relocated to build and maintain the new roads. The Efe and Mbuti, who had close ties with these agricultural peoples also set up camps near the road. Other people began to move into the Ituri Forest, first as mine and plantations workers, and then as cultivators from the densely populated regions east of the Ituri Forest seeking new land.

In 1910 a new administrative structure was established and the inhabitants of Ituri, who until then had no social or political organization beyond the level of village or several villages linked by kinship, were organized into *chefferies* (or *collecitvités*; equivalent to chiefdoms), under which *localités* (villages) were established, with a *chef de collecitvité*; (*sultani* in Kingwana, a Swahili dialect and the lingua franca of the region) and a village chief (*chef de localité*) appointed to each of them (Grinker, 1994). The colonial government attempted to control the population through these administrative structures. However, the Efe and Mbuti were not incorporated into these governance structures and were exempted from the tax obligations and labor services that were imposed on the agricultural peoples. Their exclusion from the administrative structures of the colonial state was probably a significant factor contributing to the disadvantaged position of the Efe and Mbuti in the post-independence state.

After the trade in wild rubber dropped off, ivory trade continued to flourish, as described in Chapter 3 (see also Ichikawa, 2021). In the Ituri forests, the Efe and Mbuti were major suppliers of ivory. The ivory they harvested was delivered to neighboring village "patrons," who sold it at the concession company's trading posts for large profits. The agricultural villagers who accumulated wealth through the ivory trade further tightened their control over the Efe and Mbuti. The Catholic

Chapter 5

priest and ethnologist Paul Schebesta (1933; 1936b), who investigated the Mbuti and Efe in the Ituri Forest in the 1920s and 1930s, reported cases of Mbuti hunters killed by elephants in the hunts conducted under the pressure from the agriculturalist chief. When Schebesta learnt that most families of that Mbuti group had lost at least one male hunter killed by elephants, he expressed concerns about the greed of Bantu agriculturalists who compelled the Mbuti to hunt elephants, while the Mbuti themselves wanted to hunt smaller animals for food. At this time, a good Mbuti hunter was loaned to other villagers like a possession and, if he was killed by an elephant, the borrower had to pay compensation to the original "owner." The family of the dead hunter would receive only a small portion of the compensation (Schebesta, 1936a). There may have been latent tension between the two sides at the time.

However, as discussed in Chapter 3, elephant hunting by the Mbuti continued to flourish in Ituri forests for decades until it was regulated (prohibited to hunters without license) by wildlife conservation policy. Some Mbuti men in the central and southern part of Ituri emerged as specialist elephant hunters, known as *batuma*, who often moved to the forest near trading posts. Once the Nande people, discussed below, moved in and gained economic power, the Mbuti began to trade ivory directly with the Nande traders at a fixed rate, rather than through the intermediary of their former patrons.

Congo gained independence from Belgium in 1960, but soon entered a political upheaval known as the "Congo Crisis." During the Katanga secession movement, the first prime minister and influential politician, Patrice Lumumba, was ousted by president Kasa-Vubu and Army Chief of Staff Mobutu and assassinated in Katanga in 1961. A few years later, civil war broke out with forces opposed to the new government. This rebellion, known as the "Simba Rebellion" (1963–65), was launched by remnants of the former Lumumba faction. It had an enormous impact even on the remote Ituri Forest. When the rebels reached the area in 1964, Lese and Bira agriculturalists fled into the forests and lived with Efe and Mbuti to escape the raiding and looting Simba soldiers. They managed to survive a difficult time in the forest with the help of Efe and Mbuti. Presumably, this experience strengthened the relationship between these groups.

When the rebellion was effectively quelled in 1965, Mobutu assumed power and the political situation in the Congo stabilized somewhat. Waves of development began to push into the Ituri Forest. The food crops and other goods were commodified alongside the development of population centers in nearby towns. In the south-eastern part of the Ituri Forest, Nande people, whose relatives had arrived in the 1950s to work at the mines and plantations, migrated from the densely populated eastern part of the country to the Ituri Forest in search of new arable land. They cleared the forest and cultivated much larger crop fields than the Bira inhabitants. They needed Mbuti labor to expand their agricultural production. As the Nande did not have traditional ties that Bira had with Mbuti, they introduced a new form of labor, called *parajuru* (daily work, deriving from French *par jour*), to secure the Mbuti labor. They also started direct exchange of crops and clothes for bushmeat hunted by the Mbuti. Some of this meat was then sold in cities in the eastern hills for 5–6 times the price paid in the forest (Hart and Hart, 1986; Ichikawa, 1982; 1991c). Thus both the forest products and Mbuti labor were commodified in this region, which rapidly eroded the traditional "patron-client" relationship between the Bira and the Mbuti, a "House"-like bond like that Grinker (1994) described.

In the northern part of the Ituri Forest, in contrast, there has been little migration of the Nande people, except for a few traders, and the subordinate relationships of the Efe to the Lese were maintained until recently. In the mid-1970s, when I first visited the area, their subordinate relationships were even utilized in a new system of labor mobilization. One of the Lese village chiefs were using Efe labor in the name of *"salongo"* for their personal benefit. *Salongo* derives from the Lingala term for "communal collaboration." The concept was introduced in 1973 by President Mobutu after a visit to China to mobilize local populations for public works such as road maintenance, school building, and bridge repair (Young and Turner, 1985). However, in 1975, I observed a Lese chief using this *salongo* system for expanding his own coffee plantation by mobilizing a lot of Efe people.

Thus, political and economic influences since the 19th century had brought the two sides closer together. Efe and Mbuti were integrated into the political and economic life of agricultural societies of the Lese and Bira, and had more or less exploitative relationships depending on

Chapter 5

the political and economic situation. There were, however, indications of economic independence, at least among the Mbuti in central and southern Ituri, and corresponding weakening of the traditional subordinate relationship with the Bantu agriculturalists, as new arrivals introduced a new system of labor and exchange with the Mbuti.

The so-called "immediate-return attitude" of the Mbuti and Efe hunter-gatherers has at its core a "freedom-loving temperament." But it was precisely this temperament that excluded them from the system of governance and administration of the time. Moreover, the division of labor and interdependence with the neighboring agricultural groups reinforced and perpetuated their exclusion. Once trade in ivory and non-timber forest products began, the agriculturalists monopolized trade with the outside world for large profits. This situation has been found among most groups of hunter-gatherers in the central African forests and continues today. A similar case is found among the Baka and Bantu agriculturalists in southeastern Cameroon. As agricultural production expanded with the introduction of export crops (such as coffee and cacao) and food crops for the urban population, the agriculturalists turned to hunter-gatherers to secure cheap labor to expand production. When new economic opportunities emerged for forest products, the Mbuti, Efe and other hunter-gatherers were excluded from the trade in these products, while their forest products and labor were skillfully exploited. They have been marginalized in the central African forests mainly through this deprivation of political and economic opportunities.

5.4. Infiltration of market economy in the Ituri Forest

The persistence of the Mbuti's (and other central African hunter-gatherers) hunter-gatherer lifestyle is the result of livelihood differentiation and exchange relationship with the agricultural peoples. In return for the hunter-gatherers providing forest products and labor to the agriculturalists, the agriculturalists have given them crops and ironware products. Agriculturalists have also monopolized channels of interaction with outside society in the name of "political patronage." Relations between groups became much closer, especially through trade in forest products such as ivory and wild rubber, which flourished from the end of the 19th century (Jewsiewicki, 1983), and through the demand for labor in the colonial period as agricultural production expanded (see also Guillaume, 2001). Mbuti hunted elephants at the request of the agriculturalists and brought the ivory to the agriculturalists. The agriculturalists sold the ivory at the trading posts for large profits (Schebesta, 1936b; Grinker, 1989; 1994). Through this ivory trade, the Mbuti in Ituri were indirectly linked to the world economy (though ivory trade started much earlier in other areas of central African forests, as previously mentioned). Then, as Belgian colonial management developed and became widespread after World War II, the demand for Mbuti agricultural labor increased as agricultural production expanded. At the same time, the meat of wild animals hunted by the Mbuti became an important source of protein for the emerging urban population and thus an item for trade. In this way, the Mbuti had become involved in the market economy of the wider society (see Ichikawa, 1991c and Chapter 3), although they were until recently excluded from direct contact and transactions with the market economy.

By the 1970s, various industrial products had already entered Mbuti society. In addition to traditional trade items such as salt and tobacco, manufactured items such as clothes, metal pots, bowls and plates had become necessities. Previously, the Mbuti had acquired these industrial products through a sort of "gift exchange" with the agricultural peoples. They were, at the time of my research, acquiring them through direct commodity exchange, either in the form of cash sales or barter at set rates or payment in kind for forest products and labor services (Ichikawa, 1991c). Remuneration for agricultural work was also in the form of *parajuru* with direct compensation, which was paid in cash or in kind for local alcoholic drinks or agricultural food.

Industrial products such as pots and clothes imported from abroad were expensive. For example, one women's loincloth (called *kikuenbe*) was exchanged for five blue-duikers, or one medium-sized duiker (red duiker) and a blue duiker. It took more than a week on average to acquire enough to trade, even if they hunted every day and exchanged all of their catch. And, of course, they could not exchange all of their catch for clothes, as they also needed enough bushmeat to eat themselves or exchange for agricultural food. Traders of bushmeat who visited the Mbuti camps cleverly stimulated the Mbuti's desires. They first ensnare them with brightly colored fabrics and their preferred foods such as

Chapter 5

Photo 5.1 Mbuti boys wearing trendy pants

Photo 5.2 Girls wearing favorite cloths

cassava flour and rice, and then bound them by lending advances. The Mbuti are then forced to either hunt or do agricultural work to repay these advances. Thus, as the Mbuti have gained access to industrial and consumer goods through the market economy, they have had to begin working longer hours than before.

The Baka hunter-gatherers in Cameroon are currently in a similar situation (Toda and Yasuoka, 2020). The commercialization of forest products has provided new opportunities for the Baka people to obtain cash, alcoholic beverages, steel wire, clothes, cooking pots and plates, and other industrial products. But having received these goods in the form of advances, they then had to hunt for bushmeat and gather other non-timber forest products demanded by the farmers and traders. Most profits from these activities were retained by the agriculturalists and traders. As in the case of Ituri (Ichikawa, 1991a), Cameroonian agriculturalists and traders also complain that the Baka do not repay their advances, but it seems unlikely that they would continue to advance loans if they were actually losing on the exchange. The fact that the Baka cannot repay their advances in fact indicates that the exchange rate is so unfavorable to them that they cannot get enough of what they want.

Sahlins (1972) defined the "original affluent society" as one which enjoys "life without the feeling of deprivation." What should we call a life in which the influx of industrial products and consumer goods stimulates new desires, for which the people work hard, and yet their desires are not satisfied? Is there any way to alleviate their sense of deprivation, when it is inevitable that their society becomes ever more embedded in the global economy?

5.5. Stable exchange (barter) in an unstable national economy

The hunter-gatherers' "present orientation" may lead to neglecting to save for the future and to invest for further gains. It appears to run counter to the development and progress demanded by modern society. However, there have been circumstances in which this attitude proved useful for sustaining their livelihoods. In the 1980s, in the former Zaire, when inflation was rapidly rising and the value of money was falling, the Mbuti were able to maintain their way of life because of their "present orientation." Let us look more closely at a case of the exchange of the Mbuti in the Ituri forest, which took place 30–40 years ago.

The cash economy was already quite widespread in the Ituri region in the 1980s. Nevertheless, the Mbuti had little need for cash. They rarely used local shops and markets to obtain food and manufactured goods. Although they depended on agricultural products for 60–80% of their daily food (Ichikawa, 1982; 1986), these were not purchased with cash, but were either bartered for forest products such as bushmeat or through payment in kind for day-based labor (*parajuru*). Industrial products such as ironware, clothes, pots and pans and crockery were obtained similarly.

Chapter 5

Photo 5.3 People selling products at a local market, but there were few Mbuti people

When the Mbuti were near the agriculturalists' villages, they earned their daily food by helping with agricultural work, such as clearing fields, planting crops, weeding, and harvesting, etc. In 1987, the wage for such agricultural work was 30–50 zaires per day (equivalent to USD 0.25–0.40 at the time). However, they rarely received payment in cash, except when needed for specific purposes, such as paying taxes or fines. When Mbuti men were engaged in work such as clearing the fields, they were often paid in local beer (banana beer called *kasikisi*, or rice beer *mandarakpa*). For every six Mbuti men who worked, 25 liters of local beer was provided. The cash price of the beer was about 300 zaires, which means that each man was paid 50 zaires worth of beer, which was roughly equal to the wages paid in cash.

When women were engaged in agricultural work such as planting, weeding, and harvesting crops, each woman was given three cassava plants (with 12–15 kg tubers) per person per day. This amount of cassava was sold at a market for 100–150 zaires, or even higher when bought directly from the farmers' fields, where there was no competition among sellers. In this case, there was a twofold or even greater difference between the Mbuti labor paid in cash and in kind (food): a day's labor (A) would be exchanged for 50 zaires (B) in cash, and for (C) crops worth 100–150 zaires in kind. Logically, if A=B and A=C, then naturally

B=C. According to classical economics, from such a chain of equivalence relations, a consistent value system expressed by money is supposed to be formed. However, in the Mbuti exchange, the third equivalence relation, which follows logically from the two equivalence relations, was not established.

What does such a "double price" mean? To examine this, let us look at the economic situation in Zaire at the time. The discrepancy between cash prices and barter prices, and their meaning will become clearer. Zaire's economy deteriorated year after year, except for a short period immediately after independence in 1960. Despite repeated devaluations of the currency and sudden replacement and abolition of high denomination banknotes, prices soared 60-fold in the 15 years following the independence, while real wages for workers fell by a quarter (Young and Turner, 1985; Obayashi, 1985; see also Figure 5.1). Printing more paper money resulted in further inflation. During the 1970s and 1980s, when I was conducting research, prices continued to rise sharply by as much as 100% per annum, while real wages continued to fall. As reported in Chapter 4, prices continued to rise by 1,000% or more per year in the 1990s, eventually leading to a state of hyperinflation in 1991. Political turmoil further fueled the country's economic downturn. Under these circumstances, many people in town were unable to live on regular wages alone. In large cities such as Kinshasa, the people had to rely on the informal sector to survive. The economy that supported people's livelihoods at the time was what World Bank economist Jean-Marie Cour called the "real economy," which included side jobs, street sales of agricultural and forestry products from their rural homelands, and other activities that were not recorded in statistics and records. It included illegal activities such as the diverted sales of goods or smuggling (MacGaffey, 1991). Depending on well-off relatives was also a means of survival for those who could.

In the Ituri forests, too, the cash prices of food and other products rose from several hundred to more than 1,000 times during the 12 years between my first survey in 1974–75 and 1987: the price of rice rose 1,000 times and plantain bananas soared 1,500 times. The price of cassava tubers, Mbuti's main staple food, also rose 500–800 times. In contrast, wages for agricultural and other work by the Mbuti were only 250 times those of 12 years earlier. In other words, there was considerable change

Chapter 5

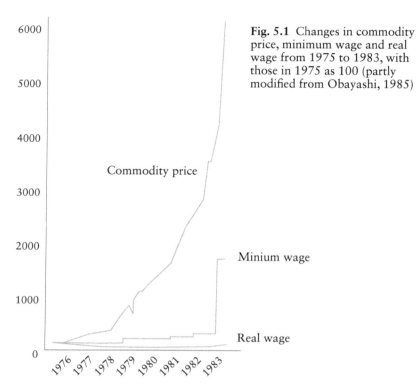

Fig. 5.1 Changes in commodity price, minimum wage and real wage from 1975 to 1983, with those in 1975 as 100 (partly modified from Obayashi, 1985)

in the relative prices of Mbuti's labor wages and food prices during this period (Figure 5.2). In some years, the price of labor wages relative to food prices fell to one fifth.

Although the relative prices of labor wages and food in cash fluctuated wildly, payments in kind to *parajuru* consistently amounted to three cassava plants per day, or 12–15 kg of tubers by weight, during this period. The same was true in the case of trade in bushmeat. The unit of exchange for bushmeat was one hind limb of a medium-sized duiker weighing 15–25 kg (in live weight), or one forelimb and a part of the ribcage attached to it, weighing approximately 1.5–2 kg. Blue duikers weighing 4–5 kg (live weight) were counted as one unit, weighing 2–2.5 kilograms except the head, the tips of the limbs and the internal organs used for self-consumption. At the time of the 1975 survey, there was no difference in exchange rates by type of animal meat, all of which were exchanged for 10 glass cups, or 1800–2000 grams on the average, of cassava flour. In 1987, there was some differentiation in exchange rates;

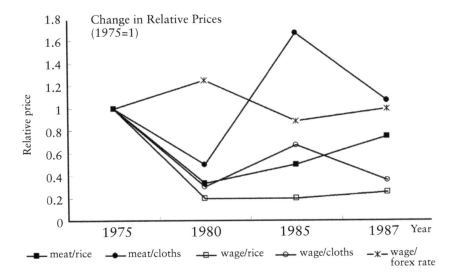

Fig. 5.2 Change in relative prices between products and services, with the rates in 1975 as 1.0. Foreign exchange rates were shown by the actual rates in Kinshasa

a forelimb was exchanged for four small enamel bowls of cassava flour weighing about 1440 grams and the hindlimb for five bowls of cassava flour weighing about 1800 grams, and blue duikers were exchanged for 6 bowls of cassava flour (2160 grams) (Ichikawa, 1991a). Otherwise, there was little change in the exchange rates. This contrasts markedly with the large fluctuations seen in the cash prices for bushmeat and crop foods such as rice and plantain bananas.

Colorfully printed *kikuenbe* clothes (clothes to wrap around the body) are strongly desired by Mbuti women, who are willing to suppress their desire for meat to obtain them. Until the 1980s, the exchange rate of meat for a piece of *kikuenbe* also remained almost constant, despite fluctuations in the cash prices of both. Five units of animal meat (i.e. one medium-sized duiker and one blue duiker or five blue duikers) were exchanged for one piece of *kikuenbe*. Traders brought second-hand clothes, or no clothes at all, when the price of purchasing clothes in the cities rose and the exchange became unfavorable for them. In this way, the exchange rate for bushmeat was maintained. However, when cheaper east African fabrics became available in the late 1980s, the exchange rate changed, as one piece of cloth could be obtained for three

Chapter 5

units of animal meat. Whereas food, a local product, was consistently exchanged at similar rates, exchange rates with imported manufactured products were subject to fluctuate depending on economic factors such as foreign exchange rates and the prices in the foreign country where goods were produced.

5.6. Implications for barter exchange

The reason barter exchange continued in the Ituri Forest is understandable. Barter maintained a stable exchange. As noted above, Zaire's economy had deteriorated rapidly since the 1970s. Moreover, in 1979, the existing high denomination notes were abruptly invalidated with the issue of new notes. The Mbuti were not directly affected by this, because they did not depend much on cash, nor store it for future use. However, one can imagine that they lost trust in cash when the few notes they had were rejected by shops and large quantities of invalidated notes were dumped in the bush. The Mbuti were not alone. Many people in rural Zaire lost trust in paper money and the government that issued it in the face of tremendous inflation and the sudden invalidation of banknotes. Barter exchange was therefore revitalized in many parts of Zaire (Ankei, 1986; Ichikawa, 1991c), a practical response to the unstable economic situation in the country.

In the Ituri Forest, barter and cash transactions had different exchange rates, even though the same goods and services were exchanged. However, the Mbuti did not appear to be concerned about these discrepancies, in large part because they did not consider working for cash and working for food to be the same. Both are exchanges of equivalents, but the systems on which they based their rates of exchange were different. The rate of exchange between labor and food is based on long-standing local balances and value systems, whereas the amount paid in cash is determined by the wage system of the wider society, which in turn is subject to the global capitalist system which seeks cheap labor in Africa. For example, 12–15 kg of cassava from a day's agricultural work can feed a family of four or five people for two or three days. Likewise, when the animal meat obtained from hunting is transported to the village and exchanged for cassava or other agricultural products, one blue duiker or one limb of a medium-sized duiker can provide the same amount of agricultural products as a day's work. This means a Mbuti hunter only needs to catch game every two to three days (Ichikawa, 1983) to satisfy their personal food needs, which is approximately the same workload as engaging in agricultural work. Thus, the exchange rate between food and labor appears to be set at a level at which the Mbuti can sustain themselves. The labor wage of 50 zaire could not buy three days' worth of food, but that is not a problem for the Mbuti who do not buy food with cash. For them, exchanging labor for food and exchanging labor for cash belong to distinct exchange/equivalent system. They recognize this difference, saying *"chakula iko na bei yake mbali"* (food has its different price) in Kingwana, a dialect of Swahili.

In 1980, I saw a Mbuti woman selling cassava tubers at the village market. At the time, it was extremely rare for a Mbuti woman to be a seller at the market, where a total of 800 sellers were observed during the three months research period. This woman was able to sell about 12 kg of cassava, equivalent to a day's work, for 100 zaire. In other words, she earned almost double the amount of cash for a day's labor. It was clear that she had obtained this cassava from an agriculturalist woman, whom she had helped with farm work the previous day. However, the Mbuti woman denied that she had obtained this cassava from the *parajuru*. Instead, she claimed that it was given by the woman who suggested that she sell it at the market. I was struck by her eagerness to deny any connection between these cassava tubers and *parajuru*, which seemed to indicate a strong resistance to acknowledging a connection between *parajuru* and market sales, i.e. barter (payment in kind for food) and cash transactions at the market.

In this light, it is unlikely that the discrepancies in exchange rates, at least during this period, were merely symptoms of the local economy transitioning from bartering to cash transactions, which might be expected to disappear with the spread of the cash economy. The inconsistency of exchange rates as observed here may have been intentionally maintained by the Mbuti, even if the intention was not explicit. It may have involved their peculiar economic practices and values, namely an "immediate return system" (Woodburn, 1982) and a "present orientation" (Meillasoux, 1967). What they expect from trading bushmeat or *parajuru* is not profit or cash itself. What they obtain through these exchanges are mostly consumable goods that

Chapter 5

can be used immediately for daily life, such as food and clothes. When they do want cash, they usually have a specific need for it; to pay for marriage, taxes, fines, child births, and funerals, etc. If a small amount of cash is left over, they immediately spend it on alcohol or tobaccos. For them, cash is, like other goods, a value with a specific use, and in that sense, it is an object of "barter." They do not particularly need cash as long as they can obtain the goods they need for their daily lives by other means. They do not save cash for its general purchasing power in case they want something in the future. Cash can be "saved" to prepare for future life, or "invested" to get richer, but they are not interested in such things. Acting on their "present orientation," they live in an "immediate return system," making exchanges to satisfy immediate needs and wants." This immediate-return attitude may prevent them from pursuing cash-gains and profit. And among themselves, they do not need to store the bare necessities of life for the future because what they cannot get immediately from the forest, they can get through sharing among themselves. In this sense, they invest in social relations through daily sharing for the security of their life.

Barter in the Ituri Forest has also played an ecological role in maintaining a balance between forest resources and the exploitation of them, providing a buffer against the impacts of market economy. That is, in a fully marketized economy, if the cash price of bushmeat declined relatively, the Mbuti would have to catch more animals to secure the same amount of food as before, where as the "double price" system does not increase the demands made upon the forest resources. However, if the money economy penetrates deeper into their society, their lifestyles may change. They might hunt for more game than they need immediately to sell as much meat as possible for cash. Cash can be stored and used for satisfying needs at any time. There would be no such thing as too much cash. Being driven by an "unlimited desire" for cash, though, would be motivation to catch animals as many as possible, which would put excessive hunting pressure on the animals, which in turn would lead to a decline in animal resources and made their lives more difficult. In fact, this sequence of events accurately describes the case in some other areas of Zaire. Because the customary rights of the local people had not been officially established, the forest was exploited by outsiders seeking bushmeat and other forest products for short-term benefits. Open access resources, i.e. where everyone has unrestricted access, can trigger intense competition for the resources in search of short-term profits. This short-term attitude ignores limitations required for proper management of resources for their sustainable use and almost invariably leads to their depletion. This phenomenon is well known as the "tragedy of the commons" (Hardin, 1968).

The principles and practices of the Mbuti's egalitarian social relations provide further disincentives to maximize profits. Individual profit and the social order are often in opposition, and over-zealous pursuit of individual profit can be disruptive to social order. For this reason, as Parry and Bloch (1989) pointed out, many societies have channels which direct individual profits to the maintenance of social order in the form of donations, gratuities and offerings. However, there are no such channels in the Mbuti egalitarian society. Of course, those who are lucky enough to successfully hunt will share their catch with the members of the camp and contribute to the communal welfare, but overly productive hunters are not appreciated. Instead they are jeered at, or conversely, ridiculed. The very fact that they are vigorous and successful undermines equality in society (Turnbull, 1965). After all, their society seems to be geared toward co-existence of the many, rather than the outstanding success of a few individuals. In such an egalitarian social life, stable barter for concrete use value, such as for food and clothes, provides a buffer for the local ecosystem against the demands of the market economy. As a result, at least until the 1980s, almost 30 years after bushmeat trade began in the research area, Mbuti hunting pressure on forest animals remained at no more than 10–15% of the existing stock, which has been well within level of sustainable hunting (Ichikawa, 1986; 1996).

In the Ituri case, the same goods and services were exchanged at different rates for cash transactions and for barter. The exchange rate between bushmeat and agricultural food remained constant despite the tremendous increase in the cash prices and the fluctuations in their relative prices. This double-price system appears to be supported by stable long-term values that are not immediately affected by short-term fluctuations in cash prices. It can be called "traditional value system" which appears to have been fostered through the long-term exchange of

Chapter 5

goods and services between the Mbuti and neighboring agriculturalists and built on a local sense of balance regarding their living standards.

Cash prices, in contrast, can be compared with prices elsewhere because of the universal value measure function of cash. At least in principle, all goods can be arranged according to a single value criterion, represented by "price." Cash prices are therefore strongly influenced by the economy of the wider society. For example, clothes sold in Ituri were either imported from abroad or manufactured in nearby cities from imported cloth and dyes. The volume of cloth in circulation and its price was thus strongly influenced by the country's economic situation. Depending on the exchange rate of the Zairean currency and the quantity of fabric imported, the cash price of clothes in Ituri fluctuated widely. Similar factors apply to Mbuti wages, which are influenced by wages on plantations in other parts of Ituri, with the latter more closely reflecting the wage structure in Zaire at the time. The Zairean wage structure, in turn, was determined within the framework of the international division of labor in the global economy. The relevance of Mbuti wages to such an international economic system is reflected in the fact that changes in the exchange rate between Zairean currency (zaire) and US dollars and Mbuti wages over the 12-year period from 1975 to 1987 show almost similar trends (see Figure 5.2). In other words, wages and the prices of imported industrial products are largely determined by economic mechanisms outside the Ituri Forest.

From this perspective, the significance of the discrepancy in the exchange rates becomes clear, indicating a divergence between the local economy, where concrete use values are exchanged according to the locally nurtured value system, and the capitalist economy, which pursues increased profit on a global scale. The significance of barter for Mbuti extended beyond simply ensuring stable exchange in the unstable Zairean economy. By limiting the purpose of exchange to the acquisition of concrete use value, i.e. remaining free from the desire for unlimited profit maximization (see Matsuda, 1989), Mbuti people were able to maintain the relative autonomy of their society as, in a sense, an economic "enclave" in the pervasive capitalist market economy. This enclave was protected from the full penetration of a state-controlled monetary economy that sought to centralize all value systems. In colonial Congo, barter markets were seen as an obstacle to state control and tax revenue, and were often repressed by the colonial authorities (Ankei, 1984; 1986). I do not mean to suggest that the Mbuti were aware of these implications of barter. Perhaps they simply preferred ready-to-use, tangible goods to cash. But it is precisely such interests that prevented their life from becoming fully entangled in an unstable money economy.

However, over the next few decades, the relentless forces of the market economy appear to have overwhelmed the local values and the associated barter system. The local people were powerless to stop the monetarization of forest products. Despite the extreme instability of being entwined in the national and global economy, they could not remain outside of it. Their customary rights to the forests, which might function as a buffer against the violent effects of the market economy, have not been legally established. The forests remain state property and there is no effective way to stop outsiders from exploiting forest resources,[8] and thus no mechanisms to regulate resource use in the long term. If "development" or "modernization" means integrating local systems of exchange into the national and international economy, or bringing indigenous societies which have long maintained relative autonomy into mainstream society, it would have a significant negative impact on the livelihoods and cultures of the inhabitants and local ecosystem. Given this, it seems that there is still a role to be played by non-market systems of exchange.

5.7. Pitfalls of new economic opportunities

While the "immediate-return attitude" of hunter-gatherers may have played a role in certain economic situations, it was often exploited by more dominant ethnic groups. This ensured their continuing marginalization and widening inequality, enmeshing them into the unequal system that surrounded them. The Mbuti way of life was effective when the Zairean national economy was extremely unstable. In stable economic conditions, though, hunter-gatherers who are satisfied with a small yield or income to meet the needs of the day face an overwhelming disadvantage, easily exploited by others in the modern market economy.

---

8   As mentioned in Chapter 1 (p. 51), the DRC government recently adopted a law which recognized the indigenous peoples' customary rights.

Chapter 5

As discussed in Chapter 4, the commercialization of forest products (NTFPs) provided the Cameroonian Baka people with new means of cash income, but it generated much greater profits for the agriculturalists who play an intermediary role in the trade of forest products. The economic gap and inequality have thus increased between the two groups. This is the dilemma faced by the hunter-gatherer societies today. To solve this problem and build equal ethnic relations, it is necessary to understand the social and historical background that gave rise to such unequal ethnic relations.

Problems with the Baka's cultivated land in the East Region of Cameroon reveal how they have been taken advantage of by the surrounding agriculturalists and traders. As mentioned, the Baka have been cultivating their own fields, though on a small scale, for decades. When the international market price of cacao rose in the late 1990s, some of the Baka started (or re-started) small-scale cacao cultivation (Oishi, 2016). However, cacao cultivation requires much more work and a longer time than hunting and gathering before the harvest, such as clearing the forest, planting seedlings, weeding, spraying pesticides, harvesting the fruit, and drying the cacao beans. When cacao trees have grown large enough to bear fruit, the annual harvest season is still several months away. Baka therefore often receive advance payments from traders for cacao sales to pay for their "immediate needs" such as government taxes, bride wealth, medical expenses, or to buy food, tobacco, and alcoholic drinks. They wanted payment in advance for immediate needs, even though they could expect to earn much more if they waited until the high season of cacao harvest. Alternatively, the Baka, who have little attachment to the land in the first place, often abandoned their cacao fields to visit distant relatives, or moved into the forest for long periods of hunting and gathering. The untended fields were soon covered with weeds or damaged by animals. This led to situations in which agriculturalists and traders rented the Baka's fields for 10–20% of the cacao price expected from the fields (Oishi, 2016; Kitanishi, 2019). Then, after a series of such advance payments and rentals, the Baka's fields were eventually confiscated or sold. The Baka ended up losing the cacao fields they had worked so hard to prepare for a small amount of cash to meet their immediate needs. And in the process they incurred further debts, and found themselves working the fields of their creditors, reproducing the imbalance between the owners of the fields and the Baka, widening the gap between the two groups. Thus, as we can see, new economic opportunities have not always reduced the marginalization of hunter-gatherers, but have often reproduced or even widened existing inequalities.

However, there are also signs of recent change in the social relations between the Baka and the Kounabembe villagers, perhaps related to the commodification of forest products. There were few intermarriages between the Baka and the Kounabembe in Gribe area, at least for the past several decades, because of the latter's discrimination against the former. However, during the ten years from the start of our project in 2011, five intermarriages occurred between the two groups. Even though all these cases are unidirectional (Kounabembe men marrying the Baka women) which may indicate continuing inequality, they clearly represent at least some reduction in discrimination. They may also reflect the increased importance of NTFPs collected by the Baka, as the intermarriage facilitates for the villager partners to procure NTFPs from the Baka family. While the economic interest may have worked for building kinship ties between the two groups, the intermarriages may also work to improve Baka livelihoods through kinship obligations. I would like to see how increasing cases of intermarriage change the relationship between Baka and Kounabembe.

In other parts of Africa, tourism involving indigenous hunter-gatherers (so-called ethno-tourism) has been embraced as an opportunity to earn cash income. In Botswana, for example, a project of San (Bushman) tourism has flourished under the leadership of local white residents, showing tourists from abroad the life of the San people. These new ventures have brought in a small amount of cash income for the San. The San working for the project have been replaced from time to time, which has also limited the widening gap among the San themselves. At first glance, this new economic opportunity appears to be compatible with their traditional life and value system. However, while the business provides the San with a cash income, they have come to face the contradiction of reproducing existing structures in which the white people, or other dominant groups in mainstream society, take control of the business and their own decision-making is restricted (Maruyama,

Chapter 5

2017). To actively engage in the new economic opportunities of tourism, they must negotiate with dominant others.

The UN Declaration on the Rights of Indigenous Peoples (2007) emphasizes the right of indigenous peoples to pursue social and economic development while maintaining their own cultures and institutions. However, this cannot be achieved through their efforts alone. It is to be achieved within the wider society around them, through persistent negotiations with other neighboring peoples, communities, nations, and the international community. It is difficult to predict how their society will be transformed in the future, but we hope that their life and culture will not fall into further hardship because of hasty development projects and market economy.

References

Abernethy, K. H., L. Coad, G. Taylor, M. E. Lee and F. Maisels 2013, Extent and ecological consequences of hunting in Central African rainforests in the twenty-first century. *Phil Trans. R. Soc.* B 368: 20120303. (http://dx.doi.org/10.1098/rstb.2012.0303, accessed 10 July 2019)

ACHPR and IWGIA 2006, Report of the African Commission's Working Group on Indigenous Populations/Communities. Mission to the Republic of Niger, 14–24 February 2006. https://www.iwgia.org/en/resources/publications/305-books/2538-report-from-the-african-commissions-working-group-on-indigenous-populationscommunities-mission-to-the-republic-of-niger-february-2006.html

Althabe, G. 1965, Changements sociaux chez les Pygmées Baka de l'Est-Cameroun. *Cahiers d'études africaines*, 5: 561–592.

Anderson, K. M. 2005, *Tending the Wild: Native American Knowledge and the Management of California's Natural Resources*. University of California Press, Berkeley.

Ankei, Y. 1984, "Genshi kahei" to shiteno sakana: Chūō afurika Songōra zoku no butsubutsu kōkan (Fish as "Primitive money": Barter market among the Songola in central Africa), in J. Itani and T. Yoneyama (eds), *Afurika bunka no kenkyū* (The study of African culture). Academia Shuppankai, Kyoto, pp. 337–421.

Ankei, Y. 1986, Zaīru gawa jouryuubu no butsubutsu koukanichi (Barter markets in upper Zaire River). *Minzokugaku Kenkyu* (Japanese journal of ethnology), 49(2): 169–173.

Attwell, C. A. M. and F. P. D. Cotterill 2000, Postmodernism and African Conservation Science. *Biodiversity and Conservation*, 9: 559–577.

Aubreville, A. 1967, Les etranges mosaiques forêt-savane du sommet de la boucle de l'Ogooué au Gabon. *Adansonia* Série 2, 7(1):13–22.

Awono, A., R. Eba'a Atyi, D. Foundjem-Tita and P. Levang 2016, Vegetal non-timber forest products in Cameroon: Contribution to the national economy. *International Forestry Review*, 18(S1): 66–77.

Bahuchet, S. and H. Guillaume 1979, Relations entre chasseurs-collecteurs Pygmées et agriculteurs de la forêt du nord-ouest du bassin congolais, in S. Bahuchet (ed.), *Les Pygmées de Centrafrique*. SELAF, Paris, pp. 109–139.

Bahuchet, S., D. McKey and I. De Garine 1991, Wild yams revisited: Is independence from agriculture possible for rain forest hunter-gatherers? *Human Ecology*, 19(2): 213–243.

Bailey, R. C. and T. N. Headland 1991, The tropical rain forest: Is it a productive environment for human foragers? *Human Ecology*, 19(2): 261–285.

Bailey, R. C., G. Head, M. Jenike, B. Owen, R. Rechtman and E. Zechenter 1989, Hunting and gathering in tropical forest: Is it possible? *American Anthropologist*, 91(1): 59–82.

Bailey, R., S. Bahuchet and B. Hewlett 1992, Development in the Central African Rainforest: Concern for Forest Peoples, in K. Cleaver, M. Munasinghe, M. Dyson, N. Egli, A. Peukerand and F. Wencélius (eds.), *Conservation of West and Central African Rainforests*. World Bank, Washington D.C., pp. 202–211.

Barume, A. K. 2000, *Heading Towards Extinction? Indigenous Rights in Africa: The Case of the TWA of the Kahuzi-Biega National Park, Democratic Republic of Congo*. International Work Group for Indigenous Affairs (IWGIA), Copenhagen.

Battell, A. 1625, *The Strange Adventures of Andrew Battell of Leigh, in Angola and the Adjoining Region*. The Hakluyt Society, London.

BBC News 2001, *Illegal 'Bushmeat' Traders Jailed*. (http://news.bbc.co.uk/1/hi/uk/1390125.stm, accessed 15 September 2019)

BBC News 2004, *Aids Warning over Bushmeat Trade*. (http://news.bbc.co.uk/go/pr/fr/-/1/hi/programmes/file_on_4/3954963.stm, accessed 31 August 2020)

Beaugrand, P. 1997, *Zaire's Hyperinflation, 1990–96. IMF Working Paper*. (https://www.imf.org/en/Publications/WP/Issues/2016/12/30/Zares-Hyperinflation-1990-96-2174, accessed 31 August 2021)

Beaune, D., L. Bollache, B. Fruth and F. Bretagnolle 2012, Bush pig (*Potamochoerus porcus*) seed predation of bush mango (*Irvingia gabonensis*) and other plant species in Democratic Republic of Congo. *African Journal of Ecology*, 50(4): 509–512.

Benitez-Lopez A., L. Santini, A. M. Schipper, M. Busana and M. A. J. Huijbregts 2019, Intact but empty forests? Patterns of hunting-induced mammal defaunation in the tropics. *PLoS Biol.* 17(5): e3000247. (https://doi.org/10.1371/journal.pbio.3000247)

Bikie, H., J-G. Collomb, L. Djombo, S. Minnemeyer, R. Ngoufo and S. Nguiffo 2000, *An Overview of Logging in Cameroon*. World Resources Institute, Washington, D.C.

Bird-David, N. 1990, The giving environment: Another perspective on the economic system of hunter-gatherers. *Current Anthropology*, 31(2): 183–196.

Bird-David, N. 1992, Beyond "the original affluent society". *Current Anthropology*, 33(1): 25–47.

Bobo K. S., T. O. W. Kamgaing, E. C. Kamdounm, and Z. C. B. Dzefack 2015, Bushmeat hunting in Southeastern Cameroon: Magnitude and impact on duikers (*Cephalophus* spp.). *African Study Monographs*, SI, 51: 119–141.

Bobo K. S., T. O. W. Kamgaing, B. C. Ntumwel, D. Kagalang, P. N. J. Kengne, M. M. Ngo-Badject, and F. F. M. Aghomo 2014, Species richness, spatial distributions and densities of large-and-medium-sized mammals in the northern periphery of Boumba-Bek National Park, Southeastern Cameroon. *African Study Monographs* SI, 49: 91–114.

Bowen-Jones, E. and S. Pendry 2003, The threat to primates and other mammals from the bushmeat trade in Africa, and how this threat could be diminished. *Oryx*, 33(3): 233–246.

References

Brisson, B. and D. Boursier 1979, *Petit Dictionnaire Baka-Français*. Douala.

Burrows, G. 1898, *The Land of the Pigmies*. C. Arthur Pearson, London.

Carrière S. M. 2002, Orphan trees of the forest: Why do Ntumu farmers of Southern Cameroon protect trees in their swidden fields? *Journal of Ethnobiology*, 22(1) :133–162.

Casati, G. 1891, *Ten Years in Equatoria and the Return with Emin Pasha*. Translated by J. R. Clay and I. W. Savage. Fredrick Warne & Co., London.

Chaber, A. L., S. Allebone-Webb, Y. Lignereux, A. A. Cunningham, and J. M. Row-cliffe 2010, The scale of illegal meat importation from Africa to Europe via Paris. *Conservation Letters*, 3: 317–323.

Chase, A. 1987, *Playing God in Yellowstone: The destruction of America's first national park*. Harcourt, Brace and Jovanovich, New York.

Chujo, H. 1992, Nishi afurika Kamerūn toubu ni okeru nettai hanrakuyoujurin no seitai to jizokuteki riyou (Ecology of the tropical semi-deciduous forest and the possibility of its sustainable use in East Cameroon, West Africa), *Ahurika Kenkyu* (Journal of African studies), 41: 23–45 (in Japanese with English summary).

CIFOR 2014, *Ebola and bushmeat in Africa: Q&A with leading researcher*. (https://forestsnews.cifor.org/23924/, accessed 31 July 2021)

Colchester, M. (ed.) 2001, *A Survey of Indigenous Land Tenure*. Food and Agriculture Organisation: Rome (also available on www.forestpeoples.org).

Counsell, S. 2006, *Forest governance in the Democratic Republic of Congo: An NGO Perspective*. (http://www.illegal-logging.info/papers/Forest _Governance_in_ DRC .pdf, accessed 3 August 2006)

Crandell, G. 1993, *Nature Pictorialized: "The View" in Landscape History*. John Hopkins University Press, Baltimore.

Curran, K. B., and R. K. Tshombe 2001, Integrating local communities into the management of protected areas: Lessons from DR Congo and Cameroon, in W. Weber, L. J. T. White, A. Vedder, and L. Naughton-Treves (eds.), *African Rain Forest Ecology and Conservation*. Yale University Press, New Haven, pp. 513–534.

Dapper, D. M. 1686, *Descripiton de l'Afrique*, Wolfgang Waesberg, Boom & van Someren, Amsterdam.

Davenport, T., 1998, *Management of the Proposed Lobeke National Park*. WWF Discussion Paper, WWF-Cameroon.

Davies, G. and J. G. Robinson 2007, Bushmeat: Market and households, in G. Davies and D. Brown (eds.), *Bushmeat and Livelihood: Wildlife Management and Poverty Reduction*. Blackwell, Oxford, pp. 11–14.

Davies, G. and R. Whitten 2007, Regional perspective, in G. Davies and D. Brown (eds.), *Bushmeat and Livelihood: Wildlife Management and Poverty Reduction*, Blackwell, Oxford, pp. 237–240.

Debroux, L., T. Hart, D. Kaimowitz, A. Karsenty and G. Topa (eds.), 2007, *Forests in Post-Conflict Democratic Republic of Congo: Analysis of a Priority Agenda*. A joint report by teams of the World Bank Consultant Group, p. xxii.

Djeukam, R. 2012, *The Wildlife Law as a Tool for Protecting Threatened Species in Cameroon*. Ministry of Forestry and Wildlife (MINFOF), Government of Cameroon.

Dounias, E. 1993, Perception and use of wild yams by the Baka hunter gatherers in south Cameroon, in C. M. Hladik, A. Hladik, O. F. Licares, H. Pagezy, A. Semple and M. Hadley (eds.), *Tropical Forests, People and Food: Biocultural Interactions and Applications to Development*. UNESCO, pp. 621–632.

Dounias, E. 2001, The management of wild yam tubers by the Baka Pygmies in southern Cameroon. *African Study Monograph*, SI, 26: 135–156.

Du Chaillu, P. B. 1872(1892), *The Country of the Dwarfs*. Greenwood Press, London; Facsimile of 1892 edition.

Effiom, E. O., G. Nuñez-Iturri, H. G., Smith, U. Ottosson and O. Olsson 2013, Bushmeat hunting changes regeneration of African rainforests. *Proc R Soc B*, 280:20130246. (http://dx.doi.org/10.1098/rspb.2013.0246, accessed 31 August 2020)

Ernsting, A. and D. Rughani 2007, *Reduced Emissions from Deforestation: Can carbon trading save our ecosystems?* (http://www.biofuelwatch.org.uk, accessed 25 September 2019)

Fa, J. E. 2007, Bushmeat market-white elephant or red herrings? in G. Davies and D. Brown (eds.), *Bushmeat and Livelihood: Wildlife management and poverty reduction*. Blackwell, Oxford , pp. 47–60.

Fairhead, J. and M. Leach 1996, *Misreading the African Landscape: Society and ecology in a forest-savanna mosaic*. Cambridge University Press, Cambridge.

Fairhead, J., M. Leach and I. Scoones 2013, Green Grabbing: A new appropriation of nature? in J. Fairhead, M. Leach and I. Scoones (eds.), *Green Grabbing: A new appropriation of nature*. Routledge, New York, pp. 1–15.

FAO, 2007 (updated) *Global Forest Resources Assessment 2005 Forestry country profiles-legislation*. (http://www.fao.org/forestry/site/30816/en/cod/page.jsp, accessed 25 September 2019)

FAO 2010< *Global Forest Resources Assessment 2010* – Main Report , p. xvi, Fig. 4.

Fongzossie, F. E., T. M. Ngansop, L. Zaphack, V. A. Kemeuze, D. J. Sonwa, G. M.. Nguenang and B. A. Nkongmeneck 2014, Density and natural regeneration potential of selected non-timber forest products in the semi-deciduous rainforest of southeastern Cameroon. *African Study Monographs*, SI, 49: 69–90.

Forbath, P. 1977, *The River Congo: The discovery, exploration and exploitation of the world's most dramatic rivers*. Harper & Row, New York.

Gammage, B. 2011, *The Biggest Estate on Earth: How Aborigines made Australia*. Allen and Unwin, Sydney.

References

Gauthier, M. 2022, *New legislation to protect the rights of the Indigenous Pygmy Peoples in the DRC* (in CEESP NEWS). (https://www.iucn.org/story/202208/new-legislation-protect-rights-indigenous-pygmy-peoples-drc, accessed on 7th August, 2022)

Government of Cameroon 1994, *Law No. 94-01* of 20 January 1994.

Government of Cameroon 1995, *Decree 95-466 PM* of 20 July 1995.

Government of Cameroon 2006, *Ordinance No. 0648* of 18 December 2006.

Government of DRC 2002, *Loi N°011/2002 du 29 Aout 2002 Portant Code Forestier.*

Grinker, R. R. 1989, *Ambivalent Exchange: The Lese farmers of central Africa and their relations with the Efe Pygmies.* Ph.D. diss., Harvard University.

Grinker, R. R. 1994, *Houses in the Rain Forest.* University of California Press, Berkeley.

Guillaume, H. 2001, *Du Miel au Café, de l'Ivoire a l'Acajou.* Peeters, Louvain.

Hanawa, R. and K. Komatsu 1993, A brief account of the Bondongo in the Motaba river, Lokouala Region. *Rapport Annuel 1992–1993.* Centre des Etudes Africaines, Université de Kyoto, pp. 9–12.

Harako, R. 1976, The Mbuti as Hunters: A study of ecological anthropology of the Mbuti Pygmies (I). *Kyoto University African Studies,* 10: 37–99.

Hardin, G. J. 1968, The tragedy of the commons. *Science,* 162: 1243–1248.

Harrison, R. D. 2011, Emptying the forest: Hunting and the extirpation of wildlife from tropical nature reserves. *BioScience,* 61(11): 919–924.

Hart, J. 1978, From subsistence to market: A case study of the Mbuti net hunters. *Human Ecology,* 3: 325–353.

Hart, J. 2000, The impact and sustainability of indigenous hunting in the Ituri Forest, Congo-Zaire: A comparison of unhunted and hunted duiker populations, in J. G. Robinson and E. L. Bennett (eds.), *Hunting for Sustainability in Tropical Forests.* Columbia University Press, New York, pp. 106–153.

Hart, T. B. 2001, Forest dynamics in the Ituri Basin (DR Congo), in W. Weber, A. White, L. J. T. Vedder and L. Naughton-Treves (eds.), *African Rain Forest Ecology and Conservation.* Yale University Press, New Haven, pp. 155–164.

Hart, T. B. and J. A. Hart 1986, The ecological bases of hunter-gatherer subsistence in African rain forests: The Mbuti of eastern Zaire. *Human Ecology,* 14(1): 29–55.

Hart, T. B., J. A. Hart and P. G. Murphy 1989, Mono-dominant and species-rich forests of the humid tropics: Causes for their co-occurrence. *The American Naturalist,* 133(5): 613–633.

Hart, T. B., J. A. Hart, R. Dechamp, M. Fournier and M. Ataholo 1996, Change in forest composition over the last 4000 years in the Ituri Basin, Zaire, in L. J. G. Van der Maesen, X. M. van der Burgt and J. M. van Medenbach de Rooy (eds.), *The Biodiversity of African Plants.* Kluwer Academic Publishers, Dordrecht, pp. 545–563.

Hattori, S. 2006, Utilization of Marantaceae plants by the Baka hunter gatherers in Southeastern Cameroon. *African Study Monographs*, SI, 33: 29–48.

Hattori, S. 2012, *Mori to hito no kyouzon eno chousen: Kamerūn no nettaiurin hogo to shuryousaishumin no seikatsu bunka no ryouritsu ni kansuru kenkyu* (Challenges for the Coexistence of Forests and People: Conservation of tropical rainforests and the culture of hunter-gatherers in Cameroon). Shoukado-shoten, Kyoto (in Japanese with English abstract).

Headland, T. N. 1987, The wild yam question: How well could independent hunter-gatherers live in a tropical rain forest ecosystem? *Human Ecology* 15(4): 463–491.

Headland, T. N. 1997, Revisionism in ecological anthropology. *Current Anthropology* 38(4): 605–630.

Hewlett, B. S. 1996, Cultural diversity among African Pygmies. in S. Kent (ed.), *Cultural Diversity among Twentieth Century Foragers: An African perspective.* Cambridge University Press, Cambridge: 215-244.

Hewlett, B. S. and J. M. Fancier 2014, Central African research traditions, in V. Cummings, P. Jordan and Zvelebil (eds.), *The Oxford Handbook of the Archaeology and Anthropology of Hunter-gatherers.* Oxford University Press, Oxford, pp. 936-957.

Hirai, M. 2014, Agricultural land use, collection and sales of non-timber forest products in the agroforest zone in southeastern Cameroon. *African Study Monographs,* SI, 49: 169–202.

Hirai, M. 2015, *Potentials, Livelihood and Social Relationship of Non-timber Forest Product Use: A Case of* Irvingia gabonensis. Paper presented at FOSAS International Symposium. Yaounde, 11 and 12 November 2015.

Hirai, M. and M. Ichikawa 2018, *Social problems in the Commercialisation of NTFPs in Southeastern Cameroon.* Paper presented at International Conference of Ethnobiology, 7–10 Aug., Belem, Brazil.

Hirai, M. and H. Yasuoka 2020, It's not the availability, but the accessibility that matters: Ecological and economic potential of non-timber forest products in southeast Cameroon. *African Study Monographs,* SI, 60: 59–83.

Hladik, A., S. Bahuchet, C. Ducatillion and C. M. Hladik 1984, Les plantes à tubercules de la forêt dense d'Afrique centrale. *Revue d'Ecologie* (Terre et Vie) 39: 249–290.

Hladik, A. and E. Dounias 1993, Wild yams of the African forest as potential food resources, in C. M. Hladik, A. Hladik, O. F. Licares, H. Pagezy, A. Semple and M. Hadley (eds.), *Tropical Forests, People and Food: Biocultural Interactions and Applications to Development*, UNESCO: 163–176.

Hochschild, A. 1998, *King Leopold's Ghost: A Story of Greed, Terror, and Heroism in Colonial Africa.* A Mariner Book, Boston.

Hogenboom, M. 2014, *Ebola: Is bushmeat behind the outbreak?* BBC News, October 18 (https://www.bbc.com/news/health-29604204, accessed 2 September 2020).

References

Hongo, S., Z. C. B. Dzefack, L. N. Vernyuy, S. Minami, A. Nakashima, C. Djietolordon and H. Yasuoka 2020, Use of multi-layer camera trapping to inventory mammals in rainforests in southeast Cameroon. *African Study Monographs, SI,* 60: 21–37.

Hulstaert, G., 1986, La Langue des Jofe. *Annales Aequatoria,* 7: 227–228.

Ichikawa, M. 1978, The residential groups of the Mbuti Pygmies. *Senri Ethnological Studies,* 1: 131–188.

Ichikawa, M. 1981, Ecological and sociological importance of honey to the Mbuti net hunters, eastern Zaire. *African Study Monographs,* 1: 55–68.

Ichikawa, M. 1982, *Mori no shuryoumin; Mbuti Pigumī no seikatsu* (Hunters of the Forest: The life of the Mbuti Pygmies). Jinbun-shoin, Kyoto (in Japanese).

Ichikawa, M. 1983, An examination of hunting-dependent life of the Mbuti Pygmies. *African Study Monographs,* 4: 55–76.

Ichikawa, M. 1986, Ecological bases of symbiosis, territoriality and intraband cooperation among the Mbuti Pygmies. *SUGIA (Sprache und Geschichte in Afrika),* 7(1): 161–188.

Ichikawa, M. 1987, Food restrictions of the Mbuti Pygmies, Eastern Zaire. *African Study Monographs, SI,* 6: 97–121.

Ichikawa, M. 1991a, The impact of commoditisation on the Mbuti of Zaire. *Senri Ethnological Studies,* 30: 135–62.

Ichikawa, M. 1991b, Byoudoushugi no sinkasiteki kousatsu (Egalitarianism from an evolutionary perspective), in J. Tanaka and M. Kakeya (ed.), *Hito no shizenshi* (Natural History of Man). Heibonsha, Tokyo, pp. 11–34 (in Japanese).

Ichikawa, M. 1991c, Zaīru Ituri chihou ni okeru butsubutsu koukan to genkin torihiki: koukan taikei no huseigou wo megutte (Barter and cash transactions in the Ituri Forest of Zaire: Inconsistency of the exchange rates), in Y. Tani (ed.), *Bunka wo Yomu: firudo to tekisuto no aida* (Understanding culture: between field and text). Jinbun-shoin, Kyoto, pp. 48–77 (in Japanese).

Ichikawa, M. 1992, Afurika shuryou saishuumin no shinrin riyou ni okeru tayousei to tajuusei (Diversity and multiplicity in forest use by African hunter-gatherers). *Nettaiseitai (Nihon nettai seitai gakkai shi)* (Tropics (Journal of Japanese society of tropical ecology)), 2(2): 107–121 (in Japanese with English summary).

Ichikawa, M., 1996, The co-existence of man and nature in Central African rainforest, in K. Fukui and R. Ellen (eds.), *Redefining Nature.* Berg, Oxford, pp. 467–492.

Ichikawa, M. 1998, Mori no tami no seitai to shizenkan (Ecology and a view of nature of the Mbuti Pygmies in the African forests). *Nettaiseitai (Nihon nettai seitai gakkai shi)* (Tropics (Journal of Japanese society of tropical ecology)), 8(1–2): 119–129.

Ichikawa, M., 2001, The forest world as circulation system: The impact of Mbuti habitation and subsistence activities on the forest environment. *African Study Monographs, SI,* 26: 157–168.

Ichikawa, M. 2005, Food sharing and ownership among the central African hunter-gatherers: An evolutionary perspective, in T. Widlok and W. Tadasse (eds.), *Property and Equality*. Berghahn, Oxford, pp. 151–164.

Ichikawa, M. 2006, Problems in the conservation of rainforests in Cameroon. *African Study Monographs*, SI, 33: 3–20.

Ichikawa, M. 2007, Animal food avoidance among central African hunter-gatherers, in E. Dounias, E. Motte-Florac and M. Mesnil (eds.), *Le symbolisme des animaux – L'animal "clé de voûte" dans la tradition orale et les interactions homme-nature*. Colloques et Séminaires-IRD, Paris (CD-ROM).

Ichikawa, M. 2008, Busshumīto mondai: Afurika nettaiurin no aratana kiki (Bushmeat problem: A new crisis of the African rainforests), in Y. Hayashi and K. Ikeya (eds.), *Yasei to kankyou* (Wildness and environment). Iwanami-shoten, Tokyo, pp. 163–184. (in Japanese).

Ichikawa, M. 2020, Toward sustainable livelihood and use of non-timber forest in Southeastern Cameroon: Overview of the results from Forest Savanna Sustainability Project (FOSAS). *African Study Monographs,* SI, 60: 5–20.

Ichikawa, M. 2021, Elephant hunting by the Mbuti hunter-gatherers in eastern Congo, in G. Konidaris, R. Barkai, V. Tourloukis and K. Harvati (eds.), *Human-Elephant Interactions: from Past to Present*. University of Tubingen Press, Tubingen, pp. 451–463.

Ichikawa, M., S. Hattori and H. Yasuoka 2016, Bushmeat crisis, forestry reforms and contemporary hunting among central African forest hunters, in V. Reyes-García and A. Pyhälä (eds.), *Hunter-gatherers in a Changing World*. Springer, Cham, pp. 59–75.

Ingram, V., O. Ndoye, D. M. Iponga, J. C. Tieguhong and R. Nasi 2010, Non-timber forest products: Contribution to national economy and strategies for sustainable management, in C. De Wasseige, D. Devers, P. De Marcken, R. Eba`A Atyi, R. Nasi and P. Mayaux (eds.), *The forests of the Congo Basin: State of the forest 2010*. Publications Office of the European Union, Luxembourg, pp. 137–154.

Ingram, D. J., L. Coad, B. Collen, N. F. Kumpel, T. Breuer, J. E. Fa, D. J. C. Gill, F. Maisels, J. Schleicher, E. J. Stokes, G. Taylor and J. P. W. Scharlemann 2015, Indicators for wild animal offtake: Methods and case study for African mammals and birds. *Ecology and Society*, 20(3): 40. (http://dx.doi.org/10.5751/ES-07823-200340)

Intergovernmental Science-Policy Platform on Biodiversity and Ecosystem Services (IPBES) 2019, *The Global Assessment Report on Biodiversity and Ecosystem Services*. (ISBN No: 978-3-947851-13-3)

Itani, J. 1974, Ituri no mori no monogatari (A story of the Ituri Forest). *Seibutu Kagaku* (Biological science), 26(4):184–193 (in Japanese).

IUCN 2006, *IUCN Red List of Threatened Animals*, IUCN, Gland.

James, J. 2007, *A Pygmy Conference in the Rainforest*. (http://news.bbc.co.uk/2/hi/programmes/from_our_own_correspondent/6646115.stm, accessed 15 September 2019)

References

Jewsiewicki, B. 1983, Rural society and Belgian colonial economy, in D. Birmingham and P. M. Martin (eds.), *History of Central Africa*. Longman, London, pp. 95–125.

Joiris, D. V. 1998, *La Chasse, la Chance, le Chant: Aspects du système rituel des Baka du Cameroun*. Université Libre de Bruxelles, Bruxelles.

Joiris, D. V. 2003, The framework of central African hunter-gatherers and neighboring societies. *African Study Monographs*, SI, 28: 57-79.

Kamgaing, T. O. W., K. S. Bobo, D. Djekda, K. V. B. Azobou, R. H, Bobo, M. Y. Balangounde, K. J. Simo and H. Yasuoka 2018, Population density estimates of forest duikers (*Philantomba monticola* & *Cephalophus* spp.) differ greatly between survey methods. *African Journal of Ecology*, 1–9. DOI: 10.1111/aje.12518

Kamgaing, T. O. W., Z. C. B. Dzefack and H. Yasuoka 2019, Declining ungulate populations in an African rainforest: Evidence from local knowledge, ecological surveys and bushmeat records. *Frontiers in Ecology and Evolution, 7*: 249. DOI: 10.3389/fevo.2019.00249

Kimura, D. 2017, *Kongo minshu kyouwaku ni okeru choukyori toho koueki* (Long distance trade on foot in the Democratic Republic of Congo). (https://blogos.com/article/216004/?p=2, accessed 17 September 2019)

Kirby, A. 2002, *The Cost of Bushmeat*. (http://news.bbc.co.uk/1/hi/sci/tech/ 2019193. stm, accessed 31August 2020)

Kitanishi, K. 2001, Bunpaisha to siteno shoyuusha (Owner as distributor), in M. Ichikawa and H. Sato (eds.), *Mori to hito no kyouzon sekai* (Coexistence between human and forest). Kyoto University Press, Kyoto, pp. 61–91 (in Japanese).

Kitanishi, K. 2003, Cultivation by the Baka hunter-gatherers in the tropical rain forest of central Africa. *African Study Monographs*, SI, 28: 143–157.

Kitanishi, K. 2011, Pigumī to iu kotoba no rekishi: kodai girisha kara kinsei yōroppa made (History of the "Pygmy": From ancient Greece to early modern Europe). *Yamaguchi daigaku kyouiku gakubu kenkyuu ronsou* (Bulletin of the Faculty of Education, Yamaguchi University), 60(1): 39–56 (in Japanese).

Kitanishi, K. 2012, Pigumī to yōroppa jin no deai: 1860–1870 nendai wo chuusin ni (European encounters with "Pygmies": Focusing on the period from 1860s to the 1870s). *Yamaguchi daigaku kyouiku gakubu kenkyuu ronsou* (Bulletin of the Faculty of Education, Yamaguchi University), 61(1): 51–74 (in Japanese).

Kitanishi, K. 2013, 1880–1890 nendai ni okeru yōroppa jin ni yoru Pigumī kenkyuu no shiten (Advances of field research for the Pygmies by Europeans in 1880s–1890s). *Yakmaguchi daigaku kyouiku gakubu kenkyuu ronsou* (Bulletin of the Faculty of Education, Yamaguchi University), 62(1): 57–80 (in Japanese).

Kitanishi, K. 2014a, Herkhuf no kobito to Pigumī: Ejiputo gaku ni okeru kenkyuu no gaiyou (The dwarf of Herkhuf and the Pygmies: Review of the research in Egyptology). *Yamaguchi daigaku kyouiku gakubu kenkyuu ronsou* (Bulletin of the Faculty of Education, Yamaguchi University), 63(1): 83–94 (in Japanese).

Kitanishi, K. 2014b, Kodai Ejiputo to Pigumī no kankei: Pigumī kenkyuusha no shiten wo chuusinn to site (The relationship between ancient Egypt and the Pygmies: From the viewpoint of Pygmy researchers). *Yamaguchi daigaku kyouiku gakubu kenkyuu ronsou* (Bulletin of the Faculty of Education, Yamaguchi University), 63(1): 69–82 (in Japanese).

Kitanishi, K. 2019, Kamerūn tounanbu no nettaiurin chiiki ni kyojuu suru Baka no 2000 nendai ni okeru tochi riyou no henka: Kakao saibai to ijuusha no eikyou (Change in land use of the Baka living in the tropical rainforest area of southeastern Cameroon in the 2000s: Influence of cacao cultivation and migrants). *Yamaguchi daigaku kyouiku gakubu kenkyuu ronsou* (Bulletin of the Faculty of Education, Yamaguchi University), 68: 249–261 (in Japanese).

Klieman, K. A., 2003, *"The Pygmies were our compass": Bantu and Batwa in the history of west central Africa, early times to c.1900*. C. E. Heinemann, Portsmouth.

Koster, S. M. and J. A. Hart 1988, Methods of estimating ungulate populations in tropical forests. *African Journal of Ecology,* 26: 117–126.

Laws, M., R. Ntakirutimana and B. Collins 2019, "One Rwanda For All Rwandans": (Un)covering the Twa in post-genocide Rwanda, in N. Hitchcott and H Grayson (eds.), *Rwanda Since 1994*. Liverpool University Press, Liverpool, pp. 125-144.

Lee, R. B. 1989, *The Kung San: Men, women and work in a foraging society*. Cambridge University Press, Cambridge.

Letouzey, R. 1968, *Etude Phytogeographique du Cameroun*. Editions Paul Lechevalier, Paris.

Letouzey, R. 1984, *Notice de la Carte Phytogéographique du Cameroun au 1:500000*. Institute de la Recherché Agronomique (Herbier National), Paris.

Lewis, J. 2000, *The Batwa Pygmies of the Great Lakes Region*. Minority Rights Group International Report, London. (https://minorityrights.org/wp-content/uploads/old-site-downloads/download-150-Batwa-Pygmies-of-the-Great-Lakes-Region.pdf., accessed 20 September, 2020)

Lewis, J. 2002, *Forest Hunter-gatherers and Their World*. PhD thesis: University of London, London.

Lewis, J. 2008, Ekila: Blood, bodies and egalitarian societies. *Journal of the Royal Anthropological Institute*, 14(2): 297–315.

Lewis, J. 2012, Technological leap-frogging in the Congo Basin, Pygmies and global positioning systems in central Africa: What has happened and where is it going? *African Study Monographs,* SI. 43: 15–44.

Lewis, J. 2020, Living with the forest: Pygmies thrived in the Congo. *Scientific American*, May: 56–63.

Lewis, J. and J. Knight 1995, *The Twa of Rwanda*. World Rainforest Movement and International Work Group for Indigenous Affaires.

MacGaffey, J. 1991, Issues and methods in the study of African economies, in J. Macgaffey (ed.), *The Real Economy of Zaire: The contribution of smuggling and other unofficial activities to national wealth*. James Currey, London.

References

Mark, J. T. 1995, *The King of the World in the Land of the Pygmies*. University of Nebraska Press, Lincoln.

Mandjumba, M. M. 1985, *Chronologie generale de l'histoire du Zaire*. Centre de Recherches pédagogiques, Kinshasa.

Maruyama, J. 2017, Botsuwana chuuseibu ni okeru "Bushuman kanko" no seiritu to tenkai: Kanko to chiiki no shakaikankei no dainamizumu (Establishment and development of "Bushman Tourism" in Ghanzi area, Botswana: Dynamism of tourism and social relationship in local communities). *Ahurika Kenkyu* (Journal of African studies), 92: 55–68 (in Japanese with English summary).

Maruyama, J. 2018, Senjuusei to idousei no kattou: Botsuwana no shuryou saishuumin San no yuudou seikatsu to tochiken undou (Conflict between indigeneity and mobility: Nomadism and land rights movement among the San hunter-gatherers in Botswana), in N. Miyama, J. Maruyama and M. Kimura (eds.), *Senjuumin kara miru gendai sekai* (The modern world as seen by indigenous peoples). Shouwado, Kyoto, pp. 245–264 (in Japanese).

Matsui, T. 1989, *Semi-domesuthikēshon: noukou bokuchiku no kigen saikou* (Semi-domestication: Rethinking the origins of agriculture and pastoralism). Kaimeisha, Tokyo (in Japanese).

Matsuda, M. 1989, Hitsuzen kata bengi e (From necessity to expediency), in H. Torigoe (ed.), *Kankyou mondai no shakai riron* (Social theory of environmental problems). Ochanomizu shobou, Tokyo (in Japanese).

Matsuura, N. 2012, *Gendai no "mori no tami": Chuuou hBabongo Pigumī no minzokushi* (The modern "forest people": Ethnography of Babongo Pygmies in central Africa). Shouwado, Kyoto (in Japanese).

Meillasoux, C. 1967, Recherche d'un niveau de détermination dans la société cynégétique. *L'Homme et la Société*, 6: 95–106.

Mercader, J. 2002, Forest people: The role of African rainforests in human evolution and dispersal. *Evolutionary Anthropology*, 11(3): 117–124.

Mercader J., F. Runge, L. Vrydaghs, H. Doutrelepont, C. E. N. Ewango and J. Juan-Tresseras 2000, Phytoliths from archaeological sites in the tropical forest of Ituri, Democratic Republic of Congo. *Quaternary Res,* 54: 102–112.

Mercader, J. and A. S. Brooks 2001, Across forests and savannas: Later stone age assemblages from Ituri and Semliki, Democratic Republic of Congo, *Journal of Anthropological Research*, 57(2): 197–217.

Milius, S. 2005, Bushmeat on the menu: Untangling the influences of hunger, wealth and international commerce. *Science News Online*, 167(9).

Ministry of Foreign Affairs, Japan 2020, *Midori no kikou kikin* (Green climate fund). (https://www.mofa.go.jp/mofaj/ic/ch/page1w_000123.html (accessed 31 August 2020)

Mita, S. 1996, Kankyou no shakaigaku no tobira ni (Door to the sociology of environment). *Gendai shakaigaku 25: Kankyou to seitaikei no shakaigaku* (Sociology of environment and ecosystem). Iwanami-shoten, Tokyo, pp. 1–12 (in Japanese).

Murota, T., M. Tabeta and A. Tsuchida 1995, *Junkan no keizaigaku: Jizokukanou na shakai no jyouken* (Economics of circulation: Conditions for a sustainable society). Gakuyou-shobo, Tokyo.

Nakamura, O. 1996, *Naze keizaigaku wa shizen wo mugen to toraetaka* (Why economics saw nature as infinite). Nihon Keizai Hyouronsha, Tokyo (in Japanese).

Nasi, R., D. Brown, D. Wilkie, E. Bennett, C. Tutin, G. van Tol and T. Christopherson 2008, *Conservation and Use of Wildlife-based Resources: Bushmeat Crisis.* Secretariat of the Convention on Biological Diversity, Montreal, and Center for International Forestry Research (CIFOR), Bogor, Technical Series no. 33.

Nasi, R., T. Christophersen and C. Belair 2010, Ending empty forest. *Tropical Forest, Update,* 20(1): 19–21.

Nasi, R., A. Taber and N. Van Vliet 2011, Empty forests, empty stomachs? Bushmeat and livelihoods in the Congo and Amazon Basins. *International Forestry Review,* 13(3): 355–368.

Nasi, R. and J. Fa 2020, *COVID-19 wild meat ban deprives forest dwellers.* (https://www.scidev.net/asia-pacific/indigenous/opinion/covid-19-wild-meat-ban-deprives-forest-dwellers.html, accessed 20 April 2020)

Nelson, S. 1994, *Colonialism in the Congo Basin 1880–1940.* Ohio University Center for International Studies, Athens.

Neumann, R. P. 1998, *Imposing Wilderness: Struggles over livelihood and nature preservation in Africa.* University of California Press, Berkeley.

Ngansop, T. M., H. Elvire, E. H. Biye, E. Fongnzossie, P. F. Forbi and D. C. Chimi 2019, Using transect sampling to determine the distribution of some key non-timber forest products across habitat types near Boumba-Bek National Park, South-east Cameroon. *BMC Ecol,* 19:3. (https://doi.org/10.1186/s12898-019-0219-y, accessed on 31 August 2020)

Ngegues, P. R. and R. C. Fotso 1996, *Chasse Villageoise et Consequences pour la Conservation de la Biodiversite dans la Reserve de Biosphere du Dja.* ECOFAC, Yaounde.

Nishida, M. 1997, Saibai to noukou: Shutsugen katei no seitaigaku (Origins of cultivation from ecological standpoints). *Reichourui kenkyu* (Primate research). 13: 173–181 (in Japanese with English summary).

Noss, A. 1998, The impacts of BaAka net hunting on rainforest wildlife. *Biological Conservation,* 86(2): 161–167.

Obayashi, M. 1985, *Zaīru no nougyou* (Agriculture in Zaire). Nihon noringyou kyouryoku kyoukai (Association for International Collaboration of Agriculture and Forestry (AICAF)), Tokyo (in Japanese).

Oishi, T. 2016, *Minzoku kyoukai no rekishi seitaigaku: Kamerūn ni ikiru noukoumin to shuryousaishuumin* (Historical ecology of the ethnic boundary: Agriculturalists and hunter-gatherers in Cameroon). Kyoto University Press, Kyoto (in Japanese).

Oliver, R. 2008, All about forests and carbon trading story highlight. CNN. 11 February. (http://www.cnn.com/2008/TECH/02/10/eco.carbon/#cnnSTCTextMon, accessed 25 September 2019)

References

Parke, T. H. 1891, *My Personl Experience in Equatorial Africa, as Medical Officer of the Emin Pasha Relief expedition*. C. Scribner's sons, New York.

Parry, J. and M. Bloch 1989, *Money and the Morality of Exchange*. Cambridge University Press, Cambridge.

Posey, D. A. 1992, Indigenous Peoples and Conservation: Missing links and forgotten knowledge, in N. Itoigawa, Y. Sugiyama, G. P. Sackett and R. K. R. Thompson (eds.), *Topics in Primatology: Behavior, Ecology and Conservation*. University of Tokyo Press, Tokyo, pp. 329–341.

Powell-Cotton, P. H. G. 1907, Notes on a journey through the great Ituri Forest. *Journal of the Royal African Society*, 7(25): 1–12.

Putnam, P. 1948, The Pygmies of the Ituri Forest, in C. S. Coon (ed.), *A Reader in General Anthropology*. Henry Holt, New York, pp. 322–342.

Redford, K. H. 1992, The empty forests. *Bioscience*, 42(6): 412–422.

Richards, P. W. 1996 (1952), *The Tropical Rain Forest: An ecological study*. Cambridge University Press, Cambridge.

Roberts, P. 2019, *Tropical Forests in Prehistory, History, and Modernity*. Oxford University Press, Oxford.

Robinson, J. G. and E. L. Bennett 2000, Carrying capacity limits to sustainable hunting in tropical forests, in J. G. Robinson and E. L. Bennett (eds.), *Hunting for Sustainability in Tropical Forests*. Columbia University Press, New York, pp. 13–30.

Rupp, S. 2003, Interethnic relations in southeastern Cameroon: Challenging the 'hunter-gatherer' – 'farmer' dichotomy. *African Study Monographs*, SI, 26: 123-134.

Sahlins, M. 1972, *Stone Age Economics*. Aldine-Atherton, Chicago.

Sato, H., 2001a, The potential of edible wild yams and yam-like plants as a staple food resource in the African tropical rain forest. *African Study Monographs*, SI, 26: 123–134.

Sato, H. 2001b, Mori to yamai (Forest and diseases), in M. Ichikawa and H. Sato (eds.), *Mori to hito no kyouzon sekai* (Coexistence between human and forests). Kyoto University Press, Kyoto, pp. 187–222 (in Japanese).

Sawada, M. 1998, Encounters with the dead among the Efe and the Balese in the Ituri Forest: Mores and identity shown by the dead. *African Study Monographs*, SI, 25: 85–104.

Schebesta, P. 1933, *Among Congo Pigmies*. Hutchinson, London.

Schebesta, P. 1936a, *My Pygmy and Negro Hosts*. Hutchinson, London.

Schebesta, P. 1936b, *Revisiting My Pygmy Host*. Hutchinson, London.

Schebesta, P. 1938–1950, *Die Bambuti Pygmean vom Ituri*. Librairie Falk FIls, Bruxelles.

Schlichter, H. 1892, The Pygmy tribes of Africa. *The Scottish Geographical Magazine*. 8: 289–301.

Schweinfurth, G. 1874, *The Heart of Africa: Three years' travels and adventures in the unexplored regions of Central Africa from 1868 to 1871*. Sampson Low, London; Harper, New York.

Shikata, K. 2006, Mori wa nani wo katarunoka? Kamerūn tounanbu no nettaiurin ni kurasu yakihata noukoumin no seikatsu to shinrin syokusei no kakawari (What does the forest tell us: Relationships of shifting cultivators with forest vegetation in southeatern Cameroon). *Nettai seitai* (Newsletter of the Japanese society of tropical ecology), 62: 1–7 (in Japanese).

Stanley, H. M. 1878, *Through the Dark Continent*. Sampson Low, Marston, Searle, & Rivington, London.

Stanley, H. M. 1890, *In darkest Africa*. Charles Scribner and Sons, New York.

Stern, N. 2006, *The Economics of Climate Change: The Stern Review*. Cambridge University Press, Cambridge.

Steward, J. 1955, *Theory of Cultural Change: Methodology of multilinear evolution*. University of Illinois Press, Urbana.

Sunderlin, W. D., O. Ndoye, H. Bikie, N. Laporte, B. Mertens and J. Pokam 2000, Economic crisis, small-scale agriculture, and forest cover change in southern Cameroon. *Environmental Conservation*, 27(3): 284–290.

Swaine, M. D. 1992, Characteristics of dry forest in west Africa and the influence of fire. *Journal of Vegetation Science*, 3: 365–374.

Swing, W. 2007, The United Nations Mission in the Democratic Republic of Congo (MONUC): Experiences and Lessons. *Situation Report,* Institute for Security Studies, 23 November 2007 Issue. Remarks made at the Brookings Institution. 18 December. Washington, D.C.

Tajeukem, V. C., F. E. Fongzossie, V. A. Kemeuze and B. A. Nkongmeneck 2014, Vegetation structure and species composition at the northern periphery of the Boumba-Bek national park, Southeastern Cameroon. *African Study Monographs*, SI, 49: 13–46.

Takeuchi, K. 1995, Shuryou katsudou ni okeru gireisei to tanoshisa: Kongo hokutoubu no shuryousaishuumin Aka no netto hanthingu ni okeru kyoudou to bunpai (Ritual aspects and pleasure in hunting activity: Cooperation and distribution in the net-hunting activity of Aka hunter-gatherers in northeastern Congo). *Ahurika kenkyu* (Journal of African studies), 46: 57–76 (in Japanese with English summary).

Tanno, T. 1981, Plant utilization of the Mbuti Pygmies: With special reference to their material culture and use of wild vegetable food. *African Study Monographs* 1: 1–53.

Terashima, H. 1987, Why Efe girls marry farmers? Socio-ecological backgrounds of inter-ethnic marriage in the Ituri Forest of Central Africa. *African Study Monographs*, SI. 6: 65–83.

Terashima, H. 2001, The relationships among plants, animals and man in the African tropical rain forest. *African Study Monographs*, SI, 27: 43–60.

Terashima, H. and M. Ichikawa 2003, Comparative ethnobotany of the Mbuti and Efe hunter-gatherers in the Ituri Forest, Democratic Republic of Congo. *African Study Monographs*, 24 (1, 2): 1–168.

Theuerkauf, J., W. E. Waitkuwait, Y. Guiro, H. Ellenberg and S. Porembski 2000, Diet of forest elephants and their role in seed dispersal in the Bossematie Forest Reserve, Ivory Coast. *Mammalia,* 64: 447–459.

References

Toda, M. 2014, People and social organizations in Gribe, Southeastern Cameroon. *African Study Monographs*, SI, 49: 139–168.

Toda, M. and H. Yasuoka 2020, Unreflective promotion of the non-timber forest product trade undermines the quality of life of the Baka: Implications of the *Irvingia gabonensis* kernel trade in Southeast Cameroon. *African Study Monographs*, SI, 60: 85–98.

Trilles, H. R. P. 1932, *Les Pygmées de la Forêt équatoriale*. Bloud et Gay, Paris.

Turnbull, C. 1961, *The Forest People*. Simon and Schuster, New York.

Turnbull, C. 1965, *Wayward Servants: The two worlds of the African Pygmies*. The Natural History Press, New York.

Turnbull, C. 1983, *The Mbuti Pygmies: Change and adaptation*. Holt Rinehart & Winston, Chicago.

UK Parliament Office 2005, *The Bushmeat trade. Postnote*. Parliamenatry Office of Science and Technology, No.236. (https://post.parliament.uk/research-briefings/post-pn-236/, accessed 31 August 2020)

United Nations Security Council 2003, *Resolution 1457*. Adopted by the Security Council at its 4691st meeting. 24 January.

United Nations 2007, United Nations Declaration on the Rights of Indigenous Peoples. (https://www.un.org/development/desa/indigenouspeoples/wp-content/uploads/sites/19/2018/11/UNDRIP_E_web.pdf, accessed 1 September 2020)

Vansina, J. 1990, *Paths in the Rainforests: Toward a history in Equatorial Africa*. University of Wisconsin Press, Madison.

Verdu, P. and G. Destro-Bisol.2012, African Pygmies, What's behind a name? *Human Biology*, 84(1): 1–10. (https://www.jstor.org/stable/41466783, accessed 31 August 2020)

White, L. J. T. 2001, Forest-savanna dynamics and the origins of Marantaceae forest in central Gabon, in W. Weber, L. J. T. White, A. Vedder and L. Naughton-Treves (eds.), *African Rain Forest Ecology and Conservation*. Yale University Press, New Haven, pp. 165–182.

Wilkie, D. S. and J. F. Carpenter 1999, Bushmeat hunting in the Congo Basin: An assessment of impacts and options for mitigation. *Biodiversity and Conservation*, 8: 927–955.

Wilkie, D. S. and J. T. Finn 1990, Slash-burn cultivation and mammal abundance in the Ituri forest (Zaire). *Biotropica*, 22: 90–99.

Wilkie, D. S., E. L. Bennett, C. A. Peres and A. A. Cunningham 2011, The empty forest revisited. *Annals of the New York Academy of Sciences*, 1223: 120–128.

Williams, R. 1973, *The Country and the City*. Chatto and Windus, London.

Wilmsen, E. 1986, Historic Processes in the Political Economy of San. *Sprache und Geschicht in Afrika*, 7(2): 413–423.

Wilmsen, E. 1989, *Land Filled with Flies: A political economy of the Kalahari*. University of Chicago Press, Chicago.

Indigenous Peoples and Forests

Wilson, M. /Survival 2006, *Minorities Under Siege: Pygmies today in Africa*. IRIN in Depth. (https://www.yumpu.com/en/document/read/23510308/minorities-under-siege-pygmies-today-in-africa-irin, accessed on 25 September 2020)

Woin, N., B. Foahom, S. Araki and Y. Sugiyama 2012, *Progress Report 2011: Forest-Savanna Sustainability Project in Cameroon*. Center for African Area Studies, Kyoto University, Kyoto.

Wolfe, N., W. Switzer, T. Folks, D. Burke and W. Heneine 2004, Simian retroviral infections in human beings. *The Lancet*, 364(9429): 139–140.

Woodburn, J., 1982, Egalitarian Societies. *Man* (New Series), 17(3): 431–451.

World Bank 1991, OD 4.20 on Indigenous peoples (later modified as OP4.10 in 2005).

World Bank 2002, *Forest Strategy and Operational Policy*.

World Bank 2006a, *Bank Management Response to Request for Inspection Panel Review of the Democratic Republic of Congo: Transitional Support for Economic and Social Recovery Operation and Emergency Economic and Social Reunification Support Project.* (https://www.inspectionpanel.org/sites/www.inspectionpanel.org/files/ip/PanelCases/37-Management%20Response%20%28English%29.pdf accessed 25 May 2020)

World Bank 2006b, *Report and Recommendation on Request for Inspection Democratic Republic of Congo: Transitional Support for Economic Recovery Credit Operation (TSERO) and Emergency Economic and Social Reunification Support Project (EESRSP)*. World Bank. (http://siteresources.worldbank.org/EXTINSPECTIONPANEL/Resources/EligibilityReportFinal.pdf, accessed 25 May 2020)

World Bank 2007a, *Investigation Report on DRC: Transitional Support for Economic Recovery Grant (TSERO) and Emergency Economic and Social Reunification Support Project (EESRSP)*. World Bank.

World Bank 2007b, *Management Report and Recommendation in Response to the Inspection Panel Investigation Report*. (https://www.inspectionpanel.org/sites/www.inspectionpanel.org/files/ip/PanelCases/37-%20Management%20Report%20and%20Recommendations%20%28English%29.pdf, accessed 31 August 2020)

World Bank 2009, *Progress Report to the Board of Executive Directors on the Implementation of the Management's Action Plan: In Response to the Democratic Republic of Congo Inspection Panel*. (https://www.inspectionpanel.org/sites/www.inspectionpanel.org/files/ip/PanelCases/36First%20Management%20Progress%20Report%20%28English%29.pdf, accessed 31 August 2020)

World Bank 2011, *Second Progress Report to the Board of Executive Directors On the Implementation of Management's Action Plan In Response to the Democratic Republic of Congo Inspection Panel Investigation Report.* (https://www.inspectionpanel.org/sites/www.inspectionpanel.org/files/ip/PanelCases/37-Second%20Management%20Progress%20Report%20%28English%29.pdf, accessed 22 September 2020)

References

World Bank 2012, *Third Progress Report to the Board of Executive Directors on the Implementation of Management's Action Plan In Response to the Democratic Republic of Congo Inspection Panel Investigation Report.* (https://www.inspectionpanel.org/sites/www.inspectionpanel.org/files/ip/PanelCases/37-Third%20Management%20Progress%20Report%20%28English%29.pdf, accessed 22 September 2020)

World Bank 2013, Operational Policy 4.10- Indigenous Peoples. (https://policies.worldbank.org/sites/ppf3/PPFDocuments/090224b0822f89d5.pdf, accessed 22 September 2020)

WWF n.d. *Congo Basin-FACTS.* (https://www.worldwildlife.org/places/congo-basin, accessed 20 September 2021)

WWF-Cameroon 2001, *Jengi: l'Esprit de la Foret.*

Yasuda, H. 2015, *Manuel de Construction de la Maison Economique en Terre.* Center for African Area Studies, Kyoto University, Kyoto.

Yasuoka, H. 2006a, The sustainability of duiker (*Caphalophus* spp.) hunting for the Baka hunter-gatherers in southeastern Cameroon. *African Study Monographs,* SI, 33: 95–120.

Yasuoka, H. 2006b, Long-term foraging expedition (*molongo*) among the Baka hunter-gatherers in the northwestern Congo Basin, with special reference to the "Wild Yam Question." *Human Ecology,* 34(2): 275–296.

Yasuoka, H. 2009a, The variety of forest vegetations in southeastern Cameroon, with special reference to the availability of wild yams for the forest hunter-gatherers. *African Study Monographs,* 30(2): 89–119.

Yasuoka, H. 2009b, Concentrated distribution of wild yam patches: Historical ecology and the subsistence of African rainforest hunter-gatherers. *Human Ecology,* 37: 577–587.

Yasuoka, H. 2014. Snare hunting among Baka Hunter-gatherers: Implications for sustainable wildlife management. *African Study Monographs,* SI, 49: 115–136.

Yasuoka, H., M. Hirai, T. O. W. Kamgaing, Z. C. B. Dzefack, E. C. Kamdoum and K. S. Bobo 2015, Changes in the composition of hunting catches in southeastern Cameroon: A promising approach for collaborative wildlife management between ecologists and local hunters. *Ecology and Society,* 20(4): 25. (http://dx.doi.org/10.5751/ES-08041-200425, accessed 25 September 2019)

Yatsuka, H. 2018. Seigyou henyou to tochi wo meguru kenri: Tanzania no shuryou-saishuumin Hatza to Sandawe (Change in subsistence mode and land rights: The cases of Hatza and Sandawe), in N. Miyama, J. Maruyama and M. Kimura (eds.), *Senjuumin kara miru gendai sekai* (The modern world as seen by indigenous peoples). Shouwado, Kyoto, pp. 240–244 (in Japanese).

Young, G. and T. Turner 1985, *The Rise and Decline of the Zairian State.* University of Wisconsin Press, Madison.

Index

Subjects

Aboriginal peoples, 62
access to forests, 48, 153
adaptive management, 137
advance payment, 116, 157, 163, 204
Aframomum, 68, 74, 155
African Commission of Human and
    People's Rights, 53
agroforest zone, 146–148
Aka, 6, 87–88, 104, 108, 131–133,
    163–164, 175, 180, 185
Akka, 6, 182
alternatives (to logging), 38, 43
animals, class A, B, C, 121–122
annual yams, 81–83
Apakumandura (master of the forest),
    61, 71, 106
arrow poison, 70
Australia (Aboriginal peoples), 62
avoidance (of animals), 105, 107

B/M (B/R) ratio, 126, 164, 170
Babongo, 181, 184
Baka, 2–4, 6, 39, 64, 80–84, 86, 103–
    104, 108, 116, 120–121, 132–133,
    140–141, 145–146, 152–161,
    163–164, 167–168, 170, 175,
    177–178, 180, 184, 190, 192–193,
    204–205
bamiki na ndura (children of the forest),
    93
Bantu agriculturalists, 37, 120–121,
    131, 145, 152, 161, 188, 190
barter, 80, 113, 157–158, 170, 191,
    193, 195, 198–203
Batswa, 6, 20–21, 23–26, 37–38
Batua (Batswa), 6, 20
batuma, 113, 188
Batwa, 6, 92
Belgian colony, 187

Berlin Conference, 64, 110, 186
bi (forest gap), 81–82
biodiversity conservation, 13, 49, 169
Bira, 186–189
blue duiker, 114, 122, 126–127,
    162–165, 170, 191, 196–197,
    see also duiker
Boumba-Bek National Park, 136,
    141, 147
bushmeat
    hunting, 49, 99, 119, 115
    problem, 13, 102–103, 109–110,
        115–116
    trade (in Africa), 110, 113, 115,
        135, 163
    trade (in Europe), 99–100

cacao cultivation, 145, 161, 177–178, 204
Caesalpinioideae, 77, 86, 149
cahier des charges, 21, 37, 39
capacity development, 19, 43, 141
carbon (sequestration), 8, 44, 48–49, 165
cash income
    from hunting, 123
    from NTFPs, 154–155
charcoal (in the soil), 88
children of the forest, 93–94
CIFOR, 103
Code Forêstier, 28–32, 35–36
co-existence (of the many), 178, 201
Cola acuminata, 72
collective hunting, 163, 185
coltan, 64
combo, unit of exchange, 157–159
commercial hunting, 117, 135, 162
commercialization (of forest products),
    14, 32, 34, 74, 110, 185, 192, 204
commodity exchange, 191

225

Indigenous Peoples and Forests

community
 forest, 39, 119–120
 hunting zone (ZICGC), 120, 143, 162
Congo Crisis, 188
consultation, free, prior and informed, 30, 35, 44
cornucopia, 67–68
COVAREF, 120
cultural ecology, 10–12, 66
customary rights, 31–32, 35–36, 38, 44, 50–51, 54–55, 95, 142, 167, 171, 200, 203

Dchang Agricultural University, 138, 140, 162
deforestation, 4, 11–12, 42, 45–46, 49, 61, 134–137
democratization, 132
devaluation (of CFA), 133, 195
Dioscorea praehensilis, safa, 68, 81
Dioscorea semperflorens, esuma, 81
discrimination, 7, 51, 53, 55, 205
distribution
 of meat, 104–105
 of wild yams, 81
diversity (of tree species), 148, 169
double price, 195, 200–201
dualistic view of humans and nature, 90
duiker hunters, 163, see also blue duiker, red duiker, Peter's duiker

ecological potential, 13, 139
economic
 crisis (Cameroon), 115–116
 gap between Baka and kounabembe, 14, 159, 204
 value of NTFPs, 36, 40, 124
ecosystem services, 43, 171
EESRSP, 28–29
Efe, 6, 67–68, 76, 107, 110–111, 179–180, 183, 186–190
egalitarian, 38, 161, 175–176, 178, 201
eke, 108

ekila, 108
eko, Julbernardia seretii, 86–89
elephant hunting, 111–113, 181, 188
empty forest, 95, 117, 137, 165
Entandrophragma, 26, 35
environmental revisionism, 10, 89
environmental services, 8, 31, 44, 48
esuma, 81
ethnobotanical knowledge, 67
exchange relationships, 54, 180
exclusion, 92, 137–138, 187, 190

FCPF, 42, 46
fluctuations (in cash prices), 197, 201
fluctuations (in fruit production), 151
food plants, 68, 74, 84, 149
forest
 gap, 74–75, 81–82, 85
 island, 61–62, 85
 law
  Cameroon, 118–119, 121, 146
  DRC, 18–19, 30, 36, 44, 50
 reform, 12, 17, 39, 43–44
 zoning
  Cameroon, 118, 119
  DRC, 29, 30
forestry reform, 53
fruit production, 151, 153, 170

GCF, 47
GEF, 42
genetic studies, 6, 133
gift exchange, 191
Gilbertiodendron dewevrei (mbau), 66, 86–87, 89
GIS, 44, 167
global warming, 8, 12, 45–46, 136
gobo, 84, 149, 151, 155, 160
gold (mining), 64, 66, 113
GPS, 145, 167
green grabbing, 49, 142
greenhouse gas, 45–46, 118

Index

Hatza, 51
historical ecology, 10–12, 83, 85
hunger
    energy hunger (*nja*), 103
    meat hunger (*kpelu*), 103
hunting
    methods, 120, 164, 185
    net, 106, 113, 164
    pressure, 13, 49, 50, 61, 64, 116,
        117, 119, 125, 126, 162–166,
        170, 200, 201
    regulations, 13, 119–121
    zone (*ZIC*), 120

immediate return, 14, 159, 175,
    177–179, 190, 199, 200, 203
indigenous peoples
    definition, 51–53
    safeguard, 41–42, 44, 53
    UN declaration, 12, 51, 53–54, 206
infinite nature, 59, 60
informal sector, 39, 48, 195
inspection panel (role), 17–19
intermarriage (between Baka and
    Kounabembe), 205
Investigation Report (Inspection Panel),
    41
IPDP, 41–42, 44
IRAD (Cameroon), 138, 143
Irvingia gabonensis (peke), 68, 79, 84,
    149–152, 154–155, 158, 169–170
IUCN, 117
ivory, 14, 64, 73, 110–111, 113,
    181–183, 185–188, 190–191

JICA, 138
JST, 138
Julbernardia seretii (eko), 87, 89

Kayapo, 61
kola nut (*Cola acuminata*), 72
Kounabembe, 84, 140–141, 146, 152,
    155–170, 180, 205

kpala, 38
kpelu, 103
kuweri, 72, 106–108

land
    burning, 62
    right, 37, 51
landscape
    polarization, 63
    misreading, 62
Lese, 179–180, 183, 186–189
Lobeke national park, 137
logging
    in Cameroon, 133, 134
    zone, 40, 143, 148

manja (closed forest), 81
Marantaceae plants, 66, 85
marginalization, 14, 53, 203, 205
market economy, 60, 73, 190–192,
    200–203, 206
master of the forest, 61, 71, 106
material culture, 6, 61, 66, 69, 71, 133
mbau, 66, 86–89
Mbuti
    distribution, 6
    plant food, 68–69
    territory, 76, 78
    hunting, 113, 201
meat trade, 13, 99, 100, 115–116, 124,
    163, 201
medicinal uses (of plants), 69
MINFOF, 2, 121
mixed forest, 87–88
molongo, 80–82
mtuma, 113

Nande, 183, 188–189
net hunting, 106, 113, 164
nja, 103–104
Nki National Park, 82, 136
nkolo, 38

227

non-permanent forest, 118–120, 141, 146–147, 149

NTFPs
    for cash, 155
    for subsistence, 154

Obongo, 5, 181–182
operational policy (OP), 17, 30, 41, 44, 52
Organisations Autochtones Pygmées, 29
over-exploitation, 14, 32, 50, 139

parajuru (par jour), 189, 191, 193, 196, 199
participatory mapping, 44, 167, 171
patron (-client relationship), 37–38, 50, 54, 111–112, 187–190
peace agreement, 17, 27–28
peke, 79, 84, 149–161, 167, 169, 170
permanent forest, 118–120, 135, 141, 147–149
Peter's duiker, 121, 163, *see also* duiker
poachers, 2, 35, 40, 50, 137
political ecology, 10, 11, 93
polyphony, 133
poverty reduction, 38, 41
present orientation, 14, 159, 170, 175, 179, 193, 199–200
principle of indigeneity, 50
protectionism, 136
protein deficiency, 101, 122
protein source, 3, 101, 103–104, 135, 165
Pygmy (Pygmies), 5–7, 9

real economy, 195
red duiker (medium-sized duikers), 121–122, 126, 163–165, 170, 191, *see also* duiker
REDD⁺, 12, 42
representation (political), 37–38, 54
revisionism, 10, 79, 89
Ricinodendron heudelotti (gobo), 84, 149, 151, 155

ritual performances, 93, 113

safa, 81
safeguards (World Bank), 41–42, 44, 53
salongo, 189
San (Bushmen), 60, 79, 205
satellite image, 65, 77
SATREPS, 13, 138, 142
sharing, 39, 105, 175–178, 200
Simba Rebellion, 188
single-species-dominant forests, 87
slash-and-burn cultivation, 145
snare hunting, 163–164
social disparity, 59, 161
soil nutrients, 76, 93–94, 139
sport hunting, 40, 119–120, 122, 141–143, 153–154, 170
spring trap, 163–164
Stern Review, 45
structural adjustment, 115–116, 134
sun trees, 74–75, 86, 149
sustainability of hunting, 13, 119, 125

territorial system, 76, 166
tondo, 155, 160
tragedy of the commons, 95, 201
transaction of NTFPs, 156
transect, 147–148, 162
tri-national conservation area, 136
TSERO, 28–29

UN
    Declaration (2007), 12, 51, 53, 206
    Resolution 1457, 28
under-utilized, 13, 153, 170
unequal relationships, 14, 38
University of Yaounde, 138, 140, 147

wage (Mbuti), 195, 196
war (in DRC), 17, 27–29, 34, 43, 65, 115, 188
WCS, 2, 136

Western view of nature, 90
wild rubber (red rubber), 64, 110–111, 185–187, 190
wild yam (distribution), 81–83
wild yam question, 79, 81, 83
wildlife sanctuary, 90, 118
WWF, 2, 8, 48, 136–137

Yellowstone, 91

ZIC (zone d'intérêt cynégétique, hunting zone), 120
ZICGC (zone d'intérêt cynégétique à gestion communautaire, community hunting zone), 120
zoonoses (zoonosis), 100

Personal Names

Araki, Shigeru, 138
Bobo Kadiri, Serge, 140, 162
Crandell, Gina, 90
Du Chaillu, P. B., 5, 181–182
Grinker, R. R., 179–180, 184, 189
Guillaume, Henri, 185
Hart, Terese B., 77, 88
Hirai, Masaaki, 140, 145, 149, 151–154
Kitanishi, Koichi, 5, 131–133
Leopold II, 64, 110, 113, 186–187
Mobutu, Sese Seko, 131, 188–189
Nasi, Robert, 103

Neumann, Roderick, 90
Nkongmeneck, Bernard Aloy, 139, 147
Sato, Hiroaki, 80
Schweinfurth, Georg, 6, 182
Schebesta, Paul, 188
Stanley, Henry Morton, 63, 111, 183, 186
Terashima, Hideaki, 131–132, 180
Turnbull, Colin, 93, 177, 183
Woodburn, James, 176, 177
Yasuoka, Hirokazu, 80–82, 122, 126–127, 140, 153, 162–163

Printed in the USA
CPSIA information can be obtained
at www.ICGtesting.com
LVHW071454291124
797957LV00009B/270